THE MAN
WHO MASTERED
GRAVITY

A TWISTED TALE OF SPACE, TIME
AND THE MYSTERIES IN BETWEEN

by
PAUL SCHATZKIN

The Man Who Mastered Gravity

Incorrigible Arts / Embassy Books & Laundry

Incorrigiblearts.com / ttbrown.com

Credits:

Author / Publisher:	Paul Schatzkin
Editor:	Mike Williams
Proofreader:	David Rosignoli
Cover Design:	MST Shema (fiverr.com/create_shema)
Design and Formatting:	Muzammil Faarooq (fiverr.com/muzammilfaarooq)

All Rights Reserved

Catalog / Publication Data

Schatzkin, Paul

The Man Who Mastered Gravity : A Twisted Tale of Space, Time and the Mysteries in Between / Paul Schatzkin

Paperback:	ISBN: 978-0-9762000-2-4
Hard Cover	ISBN: 978-0-9762000-3-1
eBook	ISBN: 978-0-9762000-4-8
Audiobook	ISBN: 978-0-9762000-5-5

For
Josephine
and
Ellen

Contents

PART 2. Black

The Universe is filled with Magical Things,
patiently waiting for our wits to grow sharper.

——Eden Phillpotts

There is a supreme intelligence in the universe,
which wishes for communion with us.

– Elizabeth Gilbert

Introduction to the 2023 Edition

The mystery of Life isn't a problem to be solved.
It is a reality to experienced.

- Frank Herbert, Dune

From 2003 to 2008, I researched and wrote a biography of a man named Thomas Townsend Brown. Or just Townsend Brown. Or 'Dr. Brown' to those who knew him.

This was going to be the follow-up to my first published book, a biography of Philo T. Farnsworth. When *The Boy Who Invented Television* was published in 2002, I felt like I had found my new calling as a 'biographer of obscure 20th century scientists.' The Townsend Brown bio was going to be the first sequel.

Until I was visited by the dreaded 'sophomore curse.'

In 2009, I abandoned the Townsend Brown project – because after 6 years of research and writing, I still had no idea what I was writing about.

Countless times over the ensuing years, I have had conversations that go like this:

Listener: "You were writing a book. What happened to that? What was it about?"

Me: "Have you ever heard of the Ionic Breeze Air Purifier?"

Listener: "You mean the thing that was advertised in the Sharper Image catalogs?"

Me: "Yes. The one that circulates air without any moving parts...."

The listener nods in recognition. And then I start:

"The Ionic Breeze is based on an anomalous electrical effect that was discovered by Thomas Townsend Brown when he was a teenager in the 1920s..."

In my research I encountered what I can only describe as loosely knit network of people who believe that Townsend Brown's discovery, when applied in a slightly different manner and with different materials, produces what might be described as an 'anti-gravity' effect (though Brown himself decried the term).

Let's just say for argument's sake that he did just that.

*

In his career-crowning work, *The General Theory of Relativity*, Albert Einstein postulated that gravity is induced by a curvature in the space-time continuum

– meaning that massive objects like planets and stars physically warp the space around them.

In the last years of his life, Einstein tried to formulate a 'Unified Field Theory' – 'The Theory of Everything' – which could make the mathematical connection between electricity, magnetism, and gravity.

Some who are familiar with his work believe that Townsend Brown discovered the physical manifestation of what Einstein could only calculate mathematically: a way of creating synthetic gravitational fields with electricity. If – as Einstein asserts – gravity is a warp in the fabric of the spacetime continuum, then by manipulating gravity, Brown unlocked the door to intergalactic communication, interstellar navigation – and, yes... time travel.

I wanted to believe that, too.

Over the course of six years, I dug into the life of Townsend Brown, drawing on the small archive of papers he left with his family, extensive contact with his daughter Linda, some Freedom of Information inquiries, and an extensive correspondence with at least two individuals who professed to have intimate, first-hand knowledge of Brown's activities. These sources alluded to deep connections to America's military intelligence and national security apparatus – and made frequent allusions to unseen forces beyond that.

Eventually I succeed in amassing a manuscript of more than five-hundred-and-seventy pages.

I was operating on the Michelangelo Principal: when asked how he made his masterpiece sculpture of David, Michelangelo replied, "I just got a block of marble and removed all the parts that were not David." As I saw it, my first draft was my block of marble, and as I got into a second draft, all I had to do was remove the bits that did not drive the narrative. About halfway into a rewrite, I hit a wall: I had no idea what my 'David' looked like.

All I could safely say about Townsend Brown was that "he spent half of his life engaged in some kind of classified military research, and the other half of his life engaged in covert intelligence operations – much of it intended to cover up the classified military research."

In other words, I had written 'the biography of a man whose story cannot be told.'

*

At this point in my conversations, I typically turn to my listener and say,

"OK, now it's your turn. I want you to ask me: 'So, Paul, what's that book about?'"

With some prodding, I can finally get them to ask me, "OK, Paul. So... what's that book about?"

"It's about five-hundred-and-seventy fucking pages."

*

I started the Townsend Brown project in the spring of 2003.

The first draft manuscript was written over three years from 2005 to 2008. As they were written, the chapters were posted on a website and open to discussion.

I reached my wits end and closed the book in the first weeks of 2009[1]

There was a fair amount of fallout from that abrupt abandonment, and while I didn't reconsider my decision at the time, I was reluctant to bury the material entirely. Then it dawned on me that given the new media at my disposal – which I had already been using to build a nascent audience for the story – there was no reason I couldn't 'publish' the material myself.

You never really know what the future might hold – so I released the raw manuscript under the masthead of 'Embassy Books and Laundry' – a deliberate nod to a period in the 1950s when Townsend Brown said that he was "done with science.[2]" I suspected I might return to the story at some point, just as Brown never really turned his back on science.

I didn't think it would be thirteen years. Maybe that's how long it takes to dry off when you've been drenched by a cosmic firehose.

*

One copy of the manuscript fell into the hands of one of my oldest friends, Mike Williams, who I have known since I moved to Nashville in 1994. Mike and his wife Kathy hosted the weekly '6-Chair Pickin' Parties' that supplied some of the inspiration for the Internet music business[3] I started in 1995. When I was fishing for a title for my first book, which I said was about "the boy who invented television," it was Mike who said, "That's your title!"

So, it seems fitting Mike would a have role in this undertaking, as well.

Mike had told me many times that he was intrigued by the story, that he was drawn to the mystery and the challenges of the telling. He asked for a digital copy of the manuscript and in 2018 presented me with an extensively edited revision. Mike even went so far as to paginate his edit and present it to me bound as an actual book – the first time I had ever seen my own work in such a physical form.

What Mike's edit showed me was how horribly *over*-written my first draft was. Like I was trying to conceal the fact that I didn't really know what story I was telling by just piling an overabundance of words on it.

But even though it appeared I had abandoned the project, certain essential themes kept nagging at me until they could no longer be ignored.

In 2022 a change in personal circumstances – a clearing of the decks, if you will – propelled this project to the front burner again.

*

This story lives at the center or the Venn diagram where science, science fiction and pseudo-science, conspiracy and reality all intersect. It is often hard to tell one from the other.

An expression I heard often during the course of this endeavor inferred that the life of T. Townsend Brown represented one phase of a 'multi-generational project' unfolding alongside the thread of mankind's evolution.

Twenty years after I first started, it seems my contribution to that story has now entered its second generation.

Paul Schatzkin

February 5, 2023

Regarding Endnotes, Bibliography And Appendices:
Readers can find links to online resources cited in the endnotes at
https:ttbrown.com/footnotes
The bibliography is found only online at
https://ttbrown.com/biblio
Appendices will be accessible from
https://ttbrown.com/apxs

Preface
Down the Rabbit Hole

In another moment, down went Alice after the rabbit – never
once considering how in the world she would get out again.
> – *Lewis Carroll, Alice's Adventures in Wonderland*

This is not a fairy tale, but perhaps it should begin:

Once upon a time, there really was a T. Townsend Brown.

Somehow, all the Big Mysteries of the century past – nuclear physics,
relativity, quantum mechanics, UFOs and alien contact cover-up conspiracies,
the clandestine operations of the military industrial complex – all converge in the
life of this one mercurial man.

We know where he was born and where he was raised. We know who his
parents were, his wife, his children and even his grandchildren. We know most
of the dozens of places where he lived. We know where he died, and where he
is buried.

Beyond that, Townsend Brown is a ghost. A zephyr. A myth.

*

In the summer of 2002, I was putting the finishing touches on *The Boy Who
Invented Television* – a biography of Philo T. Farnsworth, who, truly, invented
television. Every one of the billions of video screens on the planet – including
the tiny displays we carry in our pockets today – can trace its origins to a sketch
that Farnsworth drew for his high-school science teacher in 1922, when he was
just 14 years old. That his name is not more familiar is one of the confounding
curiosities of our time[4].

I first heard of Philo Farnsworth in the summer of 1973, as I was graduating
from Antioch College in Maryland and heading to the west coast to seek my
fortune in the TeeVee business. A profile in a publication called Radical Software[5]
piqued my curiosity, but the harpoon didn't sink in until I started hearing about
his unfinished work in fusion energy – the *still unanswered* riddle of 'how do you
bottle a star?'

That riddle was first posed to me later that same summer, on a bluff overlooking
the Pacific Ocean in Santa Cruz, California, when an acquaintance introduced
me to the concept[6] of nuclear fusion and the promising work toward clean, safe,
cheap and abundant energy that Farnsworth allegedly scuttled in the 1960s. *Thirty
years later* that conversation led me to Townsend Brown.

As I wrapped up my Farnsworth biography, I felt like I'd found a new calling: researching and writing 'biographies of obscure 20th century scientists.' I wondered what I could do for an encore.

The universe must have been reading my mind when an email showed up in my inbox on July 9, 2002:

> **T. Townsend Brown was another inventor who is forgotten and swept under the rug. He died on Catalina Island in 1985.**
>
> **Science in the late 50s said what he did was against physical law, yet the government classified his work. A bunch of government contractors both American and foreign have been working on it ever since.**
>
> **So where did all the R&D go? If you go out in the desert about 125 miles southwest of Las Vegas at night you will see an object flying around in the distance with a bluish haze around it. That's where it went. Also Sharper Image is selling an air purifier on cable TV for $60. He never collected the royalties for that either.**

That message was signed simply 'Janoshek' and the 'from' address was untraceable.

I Googled up a website[7] dedicated to the life and work of this T. Townsend Brown. From the opening paragraphs I learned that:

> **Thomas Townsend Brown, an American physicist, was a leader in developing theories concerning the link between electromagnetic and gravitational fields theorized by Dr. Albert Einstein. He advanced from theory to application with the development of solid and disc-shaped apparatuses, which are believed to have created and utilized temporary, localized gravitational fields.**
>
> **Brown's work became very controversial due to the similarity between his work and what is believed to be the propulsion method of some observed UFO's. His name is also often mentioned in the same breath as the so-called "Philadelphia Experiment," as a possible candidate along with Nikola Tesla, A.L. Kitselman and Dr. Einstein.**

Gravitational fields? Einstein's Unified Field Theory? That all sounded reasonable. But "disc-shaped apparatus and UFOs"? Hey, I write serious science biographies, not pseudo-science. And I am not easily drawn into conspiracy theories – UFO or otherwise.

I found the email address of the website's creator and sent him a message. Not wanting to sound too eager, I asked benign questions about how he started the website, and how and why he cared about Townsend Brown.

Then I pretty much forgot all about it.

A month later, somebody named Andrew Bolland replied. He had developed a relationship with the Brown family during the mid 1980s. What he told me got my attention. It sounded similar in some respects to the just-published Farnsworth story, and also entirely different. I proposed writing a biography of T. Townsend Brown.

Another month went by with no answer. Then Andrew wrote:

> **I spoke with Brown's daughter, and she thinks it would be fun to get involved. She was his primary research assistant – building prototypes and whatnot. Let me know if you want to pursue it.**

And that, Alice, is how rabbit holes are opened.

Part 1:
White

Imagine if you lost your child, and the technology existed to go back to the day before and prevent that. You would do anything to make that happen. So it would have to be a top-secret program that almost nobody knew about.

−Emily St. John Mandel

Prologue
Every Cabbie In Catalina
(1985)

Linda and Townsend on Catalina Island in the 1980s.

"Daddy, you can't do this! You'll kill yourself! Mother and I will have to go to San Antonio to bring back your body!"

Townsend Brown packed his overnight bag, a travel-worn satchel, the kind that doctors once took on house calls. He shuffled papers into an equally battered attaché.

"I have to do this," Townsend said. "I have to take these papers to San Antonio."

"Daddy, who the hell is in San Antonio? Why can't they come here? Why can't you just mail these papers?"

Linda Brown was nearly forty years old. Her father was eighty and in failing health. His left lung had been removed a decade earlier – damaged, physicians suspected, by the ozone and radiation his body absorbed during decades of experimenting with high voltages and intense electrical fields. Now his right lung was showing similar symptoms.

Townsend and Josephine – his wife of more than 50 years – lived with Linda, her husband George, and their daughter, the five of them sharing a weather-beaten, World War II-vintage Quonset hut on the island of Santa Catalina, off the southern California coast. Father and daughter argued in a tiny bedroom cluttered with electronic instruments and sensors, the last vestiges of his life's work, investigating the mysterious, cosmic force he called 'sidereal radiation.'

"You can't come with me," Townsend said.

The words stung. For nearly two decades, Linda had been at her father's side in his lab, moving equipment, twisting the wires in his inventions – whatever he needed, whatever he asked of her. Now she was afraid she'd never see him alive again.

Townsend had arranged for a helicopter to fly him to Long Beach, where he would board a private jet. He needed a cab to take him to the chopper. He reached for the phone.

"Go ahead Daddy," Linda cried. "But remember, I know every cabbie on this island and not one of them is going to take you anywhere if I tell them not to."

When the cab arrived, Townsend folded his fragile frame into the rear seat. He leaned out the window and took his daughter's hand. "Don't worry, Sweetie," he said with the calming tone that had reassured her before so many similar departures. "Everything is going to be all right."

Linda let go of her father's hand and watched the cab disappear.

The helicopter touched down in Long Beach, where a limousine waited to ferry Townsend to the charter. Peering through the windshield, he was pleased to see a muscular man of military bearing behind the wheel – the protégé he had recruited twenty years earlier: Morgan.

1

The Boy With The Chestnut Hair
(1963)

Ashlawn, on the Philadelphia 'Main Line' – The Brown family home from 1963-64.

Great Valley High School in the 'Main Line' Philadelphia suburb of Malvern opened in the fall of 1963. Its soaring glass-and-steel architecture, long wide corridors, bright fluorescent lighting, and shiny vinyl floors were a space-age departure from its Georgian and Colonial pre-war predecessors. The new school drew on the heritage of the area. Its varsity teams were called 'The Patriots' – their mascot a jut-jawed, musket-toting Minute Man, replete with bayonet and tri-corn cap.

Tall and powerfully built, Morgan had transferred into Great Valley for the school's foreign language program, which offered classes in Russian. Morgan wanted to learn Russian so that he could serve his country in the Cold War. He read a lot of espionage thrillers and amused himself with romantic notions of becoming a spy.

Great Valley High School greeted its first students with the smell of fresh paint and empty spaces along the hallways where the lockers had yet to be bolted in. "We had to carry all our books," Morgan recalled, "so nobody ever went to the library to get more." Except for Morgan, who encountered among the stacks a classmate with wavy, chin length brown hair and inquisitive eyes. Morgan watched as Linda Brown ran her fingertips along the spine of the books like they were old friends. Linda thumbed the pages of a James Joyce novel; The incomprehensible Irish master was one of Morgan's favorites.

Their eyes met, Linda nodded toward Morgan with a wistful half-smile and returned to the book.

"Hmmm," Morgan thought, "this one is different."

Checking into a political science class an hour later, Morgan found himself a seat beside this girl. "Good thing the chair was empty," he recalls, "because I would have made it so if it had been occupied."

"He was a good-looking guy, with chestnut hair that he wore in a 'Princeton cut,' Linda recalled. "He was very 'Main Line' but he was also very different. He was a member of the Chess club but was also a champion wrestler. I found him fascinating." In the weeks that followed, Linda watched how the other girls at Great Valley nearly fell all over themselves to get his attention.

"I was a bit of a jerk," Morgan recalled, "but I had an interesting thing going. There was a whole assortment of girls who wanted to sleep with me, and I was carried away with the idea of how much fun sex was. I had no scruples, and that oddly seemed to make me more of an attraction."

Linda had a steady boyfriend named Howie, but that didn't stop her from engaging in intellectual food fights with her new classmate. In poly-sci, they debated national security, with Linda asserting privacy rights while Morgan defended the security needs of the state.

"She fought me when no one else would," Morgan recalled, "and ignored me when I needed to be ignored. I teased her like a brother teases a sister, but neither of us was very good at that kind of thing. I really didn't know how to do it, and she didn't really know how to respond, so we just sort of squared off. It took a while before we realized there was chemistry brewing."

Linda sensed the chemistry too but had a different reaction: "I would kick myself for being so outspoken. I was absolutely positive that I had broken all the rules on how to attract a man!"

Morgan wondered about Linda's family. "The buzz at school was that her dad, a gentle scientist, was actually a member of the mob. The kids at Great Valley would say, 'He seems a gentleman, but his sidekick has got to be a hired killer.'"

The sidekick was a lean, dour, chap named Charles Miller, who drove the limousine in which Linda, Howie and their friends often went on dates. Linda's girlfriends thought having a limo at their disposal was "just the coolest thing ever," but Charles was a mystery. One night after a movie, Charles picked the kids up at the theater and dropped them all off – without ever asking any of them where they lived.

When the limo pulled up to his house at the end of a remote country road, Howie wondered aloud, "How did he know where I live? I certainly didn't tell him how to get out here. In fact, none of us told him where we live, he just drove right up to everybody's house!"

Linda looked up and caught Charles looking back in the rear-view mirror, with his cap pulled down tightly over his eyes as if to say, "Oh crap, I screwed up." She covered for him, explaining that Charles had gotten directions when they first started dating. "After all," Linda said, "that's his job." Howie was satisfied and never mentioned it again, but after that Linda realized that Charles knew more about whoever she dated than she did.

Such intrigue only piqued Morgan's interest in his confrontational classmate. He started shadowing Linda's movements. When she went on a date with Howie, Morgan would bump into them; when she went walking with her girlfriends, their paths would cross, a tactic that often backfired. When the other girls started flirting with Morgan, Linda just lowered her eyes and slipped away.

The Brown family lived in a stately fieldstone Colonial called Ashlawn, just a cornfield away from Great Valley High. As fall frosted into winter, Linda hosted skating parties on the pond behind the house. One cold afternoon she saw two girlfriends coming through the field; between them was the tall boy with the chestnut hair.

Morgan wasn't all that interested in ice-skating. When the rest of the party headed outside to the pond, Morgan wandered through the big house. He looked through the door of one wood-paneled room and found Linda's father tinkering with something on his desk. Morgan watched from the doorway.

Townsend looked up, and in a tone that suggested that he had been expecting this particular visitor, said simply, "Hello there."

2
No Moving Parts
(1963)

As he entered the study, Morgan found Townsend Brown working on an invention that could move air without any moving parts. Looking much like an oversized window fan, the three-foot-square wooden frame stood perched on a triangular base. Dozens of parallel metal strips and wires stretched like Venetian blinds across the front of the box. There were no whirling blades and no electric motor, yet air poured silently and steadily through the baffles.

Morgan peered through the front panel. He felt the air on his face. He walked around the back, looking for the magician's secret. How could air be moving through if there was no fan?

Townsend explained that an electrically induced force field squeezed the air, "the way your fingers would squirt a watermelon seed."

"How cool," Morgan thought, trying to reckon with something totally foreign to his experience.

Townsend flipped a switch, and suddenly the fan became a loudspeaker. Clear, bright sound poured out, without any cone or magnetic coil to produce the vibrations. "He turned up the volume," Morgan recalled, "and some kind of bomb went off inside my head."

Townsend explained that since the machine had no moving parts, there was no distortion, so the frequency could go well beyond the range of any kind of conventional loudspeaker. And if you had a matching pair, one could transmit and the other could receive.

"So, if there's no limit to the frequency, you could use this as a communications device. You could send a signal with this, and nobody else would be able to hear it, huh?"

Townsend smiled, "Nope." He put his glasses on and went back to work.

Linda appeared at the door. "Unlike my other friends who had seen the fan in operation, Morgan was asking insightful, intelligent questions," she recalled. "I could tell that Daddy was pleased. Nobody else I knew had ever come even close to understanding the possibilities."

"Are you coming skating with us?" Linda asked.

Instead, Morgan "made up some excuse and beat it out of there after a hurried goodbye and a sincere 'thank you' to Linda's father. I just needed to be out in the cold air, to hide in the dark a bit. I was a half-mile down the road when I realized I'd just passed a turning point in my life."

*

Morgan was accustomed to sizing people up, ferreting out their strengths and weaknesses before he made any moves. But none of his usual seduction techniques worked with Linda Brown.

"I found myself doing strange and stupid things. I'd drive by her house in my brother's old car, and just sit in the dark, listening to the classical music that poured forth from her father's study and smelling the wood smoke rising out of the chimney. One time, I even stomped my initials in the snow that covered their lawn."

Linda didn't notice.

"I had my classes in order," Morgan recalled. I was making solid A's, ruled the roost in most of my classes. I worked hard. I was prepared and in control. I did my homework. But Linda fought with me in class and won. That's when I decided I was determined to seduce her. I devised a plan that started with calling, just to ask for a date. But rather than Linda, I found myself talking with a stiff, curt man named Charles, who assured me that 'Miss Brown will be unavailable that evening.' I was not easily intimidated, but this Charles character scared the crap out of me."

When Morgan finally managed to talk to Linda long enough to ask her for a date, she declined his invitation, informing him she was going steady with Howie.

Morgan had heard scuttlebutt around school that Howie would be leaving in the spring for basic training with the National Guard.

"Yes, Linda said, "he'll be leaving in May."

"I'll be around," Morgan offered, certain that he caught an expression of relief in Linda's slight smile.

Winter melted into spring. Howie shipped out in early May, and word got back to Morgan that Linda had given Howie back his ring. Morgan made every possible effort to make his path cross Linda's. But as much as he was thinking about Linda, he found himself thinking as well about the curious device he had seen in her father's study.

3

A Bitter Pill
(Notes from The Rabbit Hole #1)

"Have you guessed the riddle yet? The Hatter said, turning to Alice again.

"No, I give up," Alice replied. "What's the answer?"

"I haven't the slightest idea," said the Hatter.

"Nor I," said the March Hare.

Alice sighed wearily. "I think you might do something better with the time," she said," than wasting it asking riddles that have no answers."

– Lewis Carroll, Alice's Adventures in Wonderland

My correspondence with Townsend Brown's only surviving child started in the late fall of 2002, five months after I'd first contacted Andrew Bolland through his Townsend Brown website.

Andrew explained Linda's reluctance to tear the lid off difficult memories:

Being part of the Townsend Brown family has made Linda pretty much a recluse. The public believes that she was killed some years ago, and she prefers that actually. Her father began NICAP[8] and became associated with UFOs through his research into gravitational fields. I'm sure you can get an idea of what type of people might want to look her up.

Through Andrew, I sent Linda a copy of my now-published Farnsworth biography, *The Boy Who Invented Television*. A few weeks later, our correspondence began with a warning that I might have been well to heed:

My inclination is to keep things as they are. Pulling myself into the past I know will be difficult and sometimes painful for me. I hope you understand I have reservations about how much help I will be to you. I was only involved in Dad's development of what he called the "electrohydrodynamic fan/speaker." Our family was glued to our involvement in development of 'The Fan' throughout my teenage years and into my early twenties. The fact that we suffered so much for what seemed later to be nothing has been a bitter pill.

A variation of the device that blew Morgan's mind earned some notoriety in the 1990s as an informercial staple, The Sharper Image *Ionic Breeze* air purifier. Linda's remarks seemed to affirm what that first anonymous email had said, that her father's work had become profitable, but not to the family's benefit.

My memories are from a twenty-year-old's perspective. The fact that none of our expectations were realized formed that great bitter pill. How that dead end developed, has always raised more questions than answers.

I wrote back,

I'm attracted to the mysteries buried in the life of T. Townsend Brown in the same way that I have been compelled to explore the mysteries in the life of Philo T. Farnsworth. Somewhere at the heart of those mysteries are important insights into what sort of Universe we *really* live in.

Therein lie the first steps on a quest I was cautioned early on is part of 'a multi-generational' project.

4
The Second Edison
(1915)

The future boy electrician with his parents Mary Townsend and L.K. Brown ca. 1915 (age 10).

In the spring of 1915, a visitor to the home of Mr. and Mrs. Lewis K. Brown in the posh Terrace section of Zanesville, Ohio, observed a lad of about ten years walking along the wrought-iron fence that ringed the estate, casually picking earthworms off the surface of the manicured lawn and dropping them into a bucket.

"What are you doing?" the visitor asked.

"I'm collecting worms," the boy replied.

"But you're not digging for them. They're just wiggling along on the surface!"

"That's because I've electrified the fence," the boy said, pointing to a battery he had connected to the metalwork. "The electricity in the soil excites the worms and brings them to the surface."

"So what will you do with all these worms?"

"I'm going fishing."

*

Thomas Townsend Brown was born to one of Zanesville's most prominent families on March 18, 1905 – the same year an obscure Swiss patent clerk named Albert Einstein published a scientific paper on the subject of 'Special Relativity.'

As the only male of his generation, Thomas was expected to take the reins of a family fortune that began with the boy's maternal grandfather. Thomas Burgess 'T.B.' Townsend was a second generation American. His own parents William Townsend and Harriet Burgess, met somewhere on the North Atlantic, aboard the ship that brought them both to the New World from their native Gloucestershire in England in 1834 or 1835. The couple was married in Pittsburgh, and T.B. was the first of their thirteen children. A hagiographic family history says T.B. Townsend "did not have a dollar when he started out in life." His formal schooling ended when he was nine years old, "his total attendance at school covering just six months."

As a teenager, T.B. apprenticed to his father's brick and stone mason's trade in Beverly, Ohio. At the age of nineteen he "started out for the distant west." Traveling by steamboat up the Mississippi River to Burlington, Iowa, he found work cutting and laying stone for the state's new Governor's Mansion.

Some years later, T.B. returned to Beverly and took over his father's contracting business, "...carrying on the business with constantly growing success...his patronage constantly increasing in volume and importance." He expanded his interests to include marble and granite quarries, and when those business flourished, he moved his operations to Zanesville, which was at the time "the center of operations of wholesale dealers in marble and granite."

In the final decades of the 19th century, T.B. Townsend supplied the building stone for much of Zanesville and surrounding Muskingum County, including the classically ornate Tuscarawas County courthouse, which stands today as a testament to the extravagance of the Gilded Age.

With the arrival of the new century, T.B. created much of the infrastructure of the area, starting with Zanesville's first streetcar system. After selling his interest in that enterprise, he began to pave "the greater part of the streets of Zanesville and built most of the sewers." Furnishing stone from his own quarries, he constructed foundations for more than a dozen bridges across the Muskingum River.

Among his "other important investments," Mr. Townsend was most proud of his "extensive and valuable ranch of thirty-six hundred acres in Marion County, Kansas" which raised, among other things "cattle, hogs, horses, corn, alfalfa and sorghum hay." With a perimeter fence stretching more than 50 miles, Mr. Townsend could count among his assets some 16,500 fence posts strung with more than 200 miles of barbed wire.

T.B. Townsend's wife, Sybil Nulton Townsend, bore five children, three of whom survived into adulthood: eldest son Orville served as vice-president and general manager of the Townsend Brick and Contracting Company; daughter Hattie married Rufus Burton, who served as the secretary and treasurer; daughter

Mary and her husband L.K. Brown bore the next generation's sole male heir, Thomas Townsend Brown.

In the expressive language of the day, T.B. Townsend's 1905 biography extols "...the extent and importance of the business interests which have claimed his attention and the success which has attended his efforts makes his history a notable one... he is a man of distinct and forceful personality, broad mentality and mature judgment and in his ready recognition and utilization of opportunity is found the secret of his prosperity."

Such were the shoes that the boy who electrified earthworms was expected to fill.

*

In deference to his mother, Thomas chose to be called by his middle name. His experiments with electricity led him to build his first wireless set in 1917, when radio was still only useful for transmitting Morse code. His efforts drew the attention of one of the local papers with the headline, "Townsend Brown Has A Complete Wireless Set."

Calling him "Zanesville's second Edison," the story noted that that he could barely understand the coded messages he was receiving: "Master Brown has paid most of his attention to the mechanical side of wireless telegraphy and is not yet able to read messages with proficiency. He is practicing hard, however." Another of his gadgets was described as "...a wireless telephone. When he is at play away from home, he wears a wireless telephone over his ear. Members of the family are able to call him wherever they want to, merely speaking into the wireless transmitter in the house, and he can hear them perfectly."

The young prodigy's experiments also caught the attention of the federal government. With The Great War unfolding in Europe, an officer from the Post Office showed up at the Brown's home to request that he dismantle the antenna he had mounted on the roof. A rumor was circulating that the boy could pick up radio signals from Germany; the authorities were afraid that somebody could also use the apparatus to send messages to the enemy.

That was Townsend Brown's first brush with national security.

*

Few records survive of the boy's schooling, with scant evidence of any merit or distinction.

In 1922 and 1923 Townsend attended Doane Academy in Granville, midway between Columbus and Zanesville in central Ohio, a tree-lined village with a church at each corner of the main intersection. Looming from a hill above the town is the campus of Denison University, founded in 1831 by the Ohio Baptist Education Society and named for William S. Denison – also of Zanesville – in gratitude for his generous contribution to the school's endowment.

At the edge of the campus stood Denison University's most distinctive structure, the Swasey Observatory – a rectangular concrete building with a white, rotating, dome-topped turret. Considered one of the finest academic observatories in the country, from 1911 until 1934 the observatory was administered by school's Professor of Astronomy, Dr. Paul Alfred Biefeld.

Townsend spent two years at Doane, preparing to enroll at Denison after graduation in 1923, earning mostly B's and C's in courses like Latin, Algebra, and English. His only A's were in Physics and History.

He was more proud of the school's first radio station, which he built around a DeForest Audion tube that had been personally supplied by Lee DeForest after Brown tracked the inventor down during a trip to New York with his mother. With a mere ten-watt signal, Denison Station 8YM could be heard as far away as California. On Saturday nights the station broadcast a performance by a local band, The Green Imps. When the school tried to shut off power to the radio station in order to impose a 10:00 PM curfew, Townsend built his own Delco generating station and kept the music going well into the night

In a personal memoir composed years later, Brown sums up his academic career by recalling, "I slept in the Physics room."

5

A Different Well
(Notes from the Rabbit Hole #2)

"How queer everything is to-day! And yesterday things went
on just as usual. I wonder if I've been changed in the night? Let
me think: *was* I the same when I got up this morning?"

– *Lewis Carroll, Alice's Adventures in Wonderland*

The history of science and invention is replete with stories of study and
forethought rushing headlong into accidents and inspiration.

My personal interest in such things traces back to a warm day in the spring
of 1960 in Rumson, New Jersey. I was only in the third grade, but my mother
was concerned that I wasn't reading enough, so she hauled me off to the Oceanic
Public Library on the Avenue of Two Rivers and told me to pick a book. I pulled
a 'Signature Series' biography of Thomas Edison,[9] and devoured it as quickly
as a nine-year-old could. The following year, I portrayed Edison in the fourth-
grade class play and delighted my classmates by inventing the lightbulb from the
auditorium stage at Forrestdale School.

A dozen-some years later – at another library, in Santa Monica, California – I
stumbled on to the story of Philo T. Farnsworth[10] – the fourteen-year-old Idaho
farm boy who drew a sketch for his high school science teacher in 1922, telling
him, "This is my idea for electronic television." The technology has evolved in the
decades since, but every video screen on the planet today can trace its origins to
that sketch (which the teacher saved and introduced into patent litigation a decade
later). I was fascinated to see photos from television's pre-history in the 1920's and
30's and learn of the inspiration that replaced spinning wheels and mirrors with
electrons bouncing around in a vacuum tube.

By then I was already a devotee to the writings of Marshall McLuhan, who
wrote that "the medium is the message" – meaning that "Societies have always
been shaped more by the nature of the media by which men communicate than
by the content of the communication."

This was during the late 1960's, a time of great turmoil, much of it generated
by new technologies like television and satellite communications. In McLuhan's
parlance, we were living in a 'global village.' McLuhan seemed to be saying that
the path to mankind's destiny would be paved with new gadgets and gizmos. By

that reckoning, I figured that the people who came up with those new technologies were the ones who really changed things.

That was the beginning of my pursuit of 'biographies of obscure 20th century scientists,' which came to its first fruition when I wrote and published a biography of Philo Farnsworth[11] in 2002.

Embodied in the Farnsworth story and others like it is the notion that inventors and scientists – as well as artists, musicians, and writers – arrive on Earth with certain ideas and information uniquely pre-coded into their brains. It seems these seminal geniuses are visited by a singular ability to draw from a different well of knowledge than the rest of us. At some point in their lives, typically while they are still teenagers, these uniquely inspired minds tap into this well, and then draw forth the inventions and technologies that alter life on our planet forever.

They have special access to the 'Universe of Magical Things' and arrive pre-programmed to deliver what the modern vernacular often refers to as a 'technology transfer.'

We know where the technology is being transferred *to*. Of greater interest, perhaps, is where that knowledge is being transferred *from*.

6

On The Shoulders of Giants
(1687-1923)

A pantheon of giant shoulders. (l-r) Benjamin Franklin, Heinrich Hertz, Isaac Newton, James Clerk Maxwell, Albert Einstein, Hans Christian Oersted, Michael Faraday, Max Planck.

Modern science finds its origins in the 17th century – the Age of Enlightenment.

In 1687 Sir Isaac Newton published the *Principia Mathematica*[12], his epic articulation of a fixed and stable universe where time was absolute and unbending, ticking away at the same rate for everyone, everywhere. *Principia* provided the foundation for an explosion of scientific knowledge in the 18th and 19th centuries.

Every discovery rests on those that preceded it. As Newton himself said, "If I have seen farther than others it is because I have stood on the shoulders of giants."

By the dawn of the 20th century, the firm foundations of Newton's universe began to tremble with the investigation of a phenomenon unknown to Newton: electricity. Electricity was not really new; it has always been present in one form or another, in the static discharge from a cold piece of metal, or the violent, radiant outburst of a lightning strike. But it was not until the 18th century that science began to master this mysterious force. Given the extent to which electricity propels the modern world, it's curious to think this now-indispensable force has only been at our command for roughly 200 years - not even the blink of an eye in human history.

In the 18th century, new giants climbed on to Newton's shoulders.

In 1752, Benjamin Franklin flew a kite into an electrical storm to capture the discharge from a bolt of lightning. In 1820, the Danish scientist Hans Christian Oersted noticed that an electrified wire could deflect a compass needle – the first recorded observation of the linkage between electricity and magnetism. Another decade passed before the English scientist Michael Faraday inverted Oersted's discovery, demonstrating that a magnet could induce an electrical current in a metal wire.

In the 1860s, Faraday's protege, the Scotsman James Clerk Maxwell, compiled the equations that proved that electricity and magnetism are a single fundamental force, electromagnetism.

Maxwell further observed that waves of electromagnetic energy could travel through space at the speed of light – a concept later verified by his own protégé, Heinrich Hertz, for whom radio frequencies are named. Maxwell also proposed that light itself was a form of this electromagnetic radiation – an idea that would ultimately challenge the very principals that had led him there in the first place.

At the dawn of the 20th Century, the German physicist Max Planck postulated that matter absorbs heat energy and emits light energy discontinuously in 'lumps.' Planck's lumps, which he called "quanta," sparked the new scientific field of quantum mechanics.

The breakthrough that separated the 20th Century from all those that preceded it arrived with the 'Annus Mirabilis' – the year of wonders, 1905 – when Albert Einstein published not one, not two, but four papers that changed the world.

Einstein's first 1905 paper analyzed the photo-electric effect, by which certain metals emit electrons when their surface is struck by light[13]. For defining the relationship between light and electrical energy, Einstein was awarded the Nobel Prize in Physics in 1921. Einstein's second paper discussed the behavior of atoms in circumstances called 'Brownian movements,' proving the existence of atoms – a concept that was still hotly contested at the time.

It was Einstein's third paper, *On the Electrodynamics of Moving Bodies*, that rearranged the paradigms of physics into an entirely new cosmology. Here was the Special Theory of Relativity that knocked Newton's immutable universe off its foundations.

Einstein' fourth paper, *Does the Inertia of a Body Depend Upon Its Energy Content?* defined the relationship between mass and energy in history's most famous equation: $E=mc^2$.

Newton's enduring calculations on gravity got humans to the moon and back in the 1960s. But the 'why' of gravity – where it comes from and how it works – remained unexplained for another decade, when Einstein published his grandest theory of all.

In 1916's *General Theory of Relativity*, Einstein defined gravity as a curvature in space, a distortion caused by the presence of a massive object like a planet or a star. Standing on the shoulders of all who had gone before him, Einstein synthesized everything from Newton to Planck, casting mankind adrift in a universe where space could be bent and time was elastic.

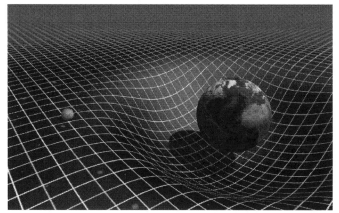

Einstein's explanation of gravity is often illustrated as a massive object like the Earth stretching the fabric of space – like a ball suspended on a membrane, the moon orbiting in the resulting curvature.

*

In the fall of 1923, eighteen-year-old Townsend Brown enrolled at the California Institute of Technology and began setting up a private laboratory at the family's California residence in Pasadena.

Meanwhile, Albert Einstein was not done twisting the fabric of the universe. Earlier that year, he produced the first of several dissertations that dominated the remainder of his life's work – his quest for the Unified Field Theory. Having redefined gravity, Einstein peered over the edge of the space-time continuum in search of an equation that would connect gravity with the other fundamental force of nature known at the time – electromagnetism.

Einstein had no way of knowing that on the other side or the world, a Cal Tech freshman had found the physical proof of what Einstein could only express as a theory.

7

A Brute and Awkward Force
(1923)

There is no record of a precise moment of inspiration – no apple falling on Townsend Brown's head, no lightning striking a sky-bound key, no parallel furrows in a sugar beet field – only Brown's insistence that whatever he knew, "he knew it all at once." Something of the experience was described in a short memoir that Brown dictated to his wife decades later:

> **During the summer or fall of 1923, I not only made considerable progress in chemistry, but in physics. I devised an X-Ray spectrometer for astronomical measurements – specifically the sun – and began to cultivate the thesis that a radiation other than light prevailed in the Universe, independent of our Solar system. I felt that this radiation could be gravitation. That it exerted a pressure (however small) on all forms of matter. This gave rise, in my view, to what could be considered as a new theory of gravitation. Such a theory called for gravitation being a "push" and not a "pull." This seemed logical in that Nature abhors a vacuum. A mechanism for the transmission of gravitation theoretically was needed.**

The thesis that shines through this statement – indeed, the central concept that engaged Brown's imagination for the rest of his life – is *a radiation other than light prevails in the Universe…"*

*

Another biographical sketch of Townsend Brown comes to us from the pen of A. L. Kitselman, known as 'Beau' to his friends and a colleague of Brown's on classified defense projects during the 1940s and 50s. Beau and his wife Betsy were as close friends as the constantly relocating Browns ever had. Kitselman published a scathing critique of the credentialed scientists who had dismissed Townsend Brown, in a pamphlet he called *Hello, Stupid*[14]. Variations of the stories contained in that pamphlet have supplied the foundation of subsequent accounts of Brown's early years.

According to Kitselman, young Thomas Brown looked to the heavens, dreamed of traveling among the stars – and pondered the means of propulsion by which that might be accomplished. He dismissed rocket power as "a brute and awkward force," and wondered if electricity could shrink the distance between the stars more efficiently than the controlled explosion of combustible gasses.

Such thoughts simmered as his Cal Tech physics class conducted experiments with an X-Ray tube. While the rest of the class was focused on the tube itself, "Tom" observed that when a high-voltage current was applied, the cables connecting the tube to the power supply appeared to jump with snake-like convulsions. And here, Kitselman says, is where the hopeful space traveler believed he'd found his means of transport through the cosmos.

Unfortunately, Cal Tech was the kind of institution that encouraged its freshman to conform rather than experiment. It wasn't long before the enthusiastic student with the big ideas was failing in both chemistry and physics. "As soon as I'd get an experiment set up," he recalled, "the bell would ring and I would have to dis-assemble everything. I could never finish an experiment!"

To compensate for that institutional limitation, the young man's father installed a private laboratory on the second floor in the family home that was the equal of Cal Tech's, so that his son could experiment freely.

8

Impossible, And Not To Be Considered
(1923)

During Townsend Brown's freshman year at Cal Tech in 1923, his physics professor, Dr. Robert Andrews Millikan, was awarded the Nobel Prize in physics – making him the first member of Cal Tech's faculty to be so honored, and an accolade that linked Millikan to the most renowned scientist of the 20th century. Millikan was recognized for measuring the negative charge of a single electron, and for confirming the calculations on the photoelectric effect for which Albert Einstein had been awarded his own Nobel two years earlier.

Millikan came reluctantly to physics. As an undergraduate at Oberlin College, Millikan favored mathematics and classic languages. Not until his professor of Greek asked him to teach an elementary physics class – telling him that "Anyone who can do well in Greek can teach physics" – did his interests begin to shift. With his 1891 Bachelor's degree in Classical Studies behind him, Millikan pursued physics at Columbia University, where he earned that institution's first Ph.D in the field in 1895. Doctorate in hand, he followed a professor's advice and spent a year at the heart of the world of theoretical physics in Germany.

After his year abroad, Millikan accepted an invitation to join the faculty at the University of Chicago as an assistant to Albert A. Michelson – the co-author of the most famous failed experiment in the history of science[15].

In 1887, Michelson and his colleague Edward Morley conducted a series of experiments intended to measure the medium through which light and radio waves travel. Borrowing from an idea as old as Aristotle, James Clerk Maxwell had proposed that electromagnetic waves are conveyed through the 'luminiferous ether' in the same way that sound waves travel through the air; the Michelson-Morley Experiment attempted to measure the Earth's movement through that cosmic firmament. Instead, their elaborate and expensive apparatus failed to detect even a whiff of ether, raising still more questions about the nature of light and energy but assuring both Michelson and Morley an asterisk in the annals of theoretical physics.

Robert Millikan joined Michelson in Chicago despite the modest salary offered, on the promise that Millikan would have ample time to spend on his own research. Instead of blazing his own trail, Millikan found himself preoccupied with academics, authoring several textbooks while Max Planck, Albert Einstein and others transformed the world with their revolutionary ideas about particles and waves. At the age of thirty-eight, Millikan was still an associate professor among a faculty where thirty-two was the average age to become a full professor.

Einstein's Annus Mirabilis refocused Millikan, who wrote in his autobiography[16], "...by 1906 I knew that I had not yet published results of outstanding importance, and certainly had not attained a position of much distinction as a research physicist." Motivated less by divine inspiration than ego, Millikan set about to make a name for himself. He decided it would be useful to determine the precise electrical charge of an electron, the sub-atomic particle that the English scientist J.J. Thompson had discovered in 1887. Millikan correctly surmised that finding that value would offer valuable insights into the nature of both matter and electricity.

For four years Millikan sprayed droplets of oil out of a perfume atomizer. By finding the precise charge that could suspend the oil particles against gravity, he could calculate the charge in the droplets[17]. He published the results of these experiments in 1910, calculating the charge of a single electron down to a constant value (about $1.602 \times 10\text{-}19$ Coulomb if you're counting...). That same year, he was finally awarded a full professorship at the University of Chicago.

*

In 1917 Millikan left the University of Chicago for a position at Cal Tech, where he played a key roll in making that institution one of the preeminent schools of science in the world. In 1921, Millikan was named the director of Cal Tech's Norman Bridge Laboratory of Physics.

Two years later, in the fall of 1923, young Townsend Brown showed up at that very same laboratory – expressing frustration with the lab's protocols and procedures. By the following spring, Townsend had endured as much he could of the laboratory's restrictions. What he needed now was a mentor who would listen to his ideas without passing judgment. He hoped to find such a willing ear in Robert Millikan – Cal Tech's recently anointed Nobel Laureate.

Townsend set up his experiments in his home laboratory and invited the students and faculty to see a demonstration. When the appointed hour arrived, there were no knocks on the door at the big Pasadena house. Nobody came to see Townsend Brown's inventions. Back at school, his classmates derided him and made jokes behind his back.

Among those who ignored his invitation was Dr. Millikan. Townsend set aside his wounded pride and tracked Millikan down in his office on the Cal Tech campus. Button-holed, Millikan reluctantly listened as his student explained the link he had found between electricity and gravity. When Townsend was done,

Millikan dismissed him brusquely, saying that what he'd just heard was "utterly impossible and not to be considered."

"He admonished me to continue my education before I gave any thought to such things," Townsend wrote later in his brief autobiography.

He did not have long to dwell on his disappointment. Despite the rejection of Cal Tech faculty and classmates, Townsend Brown's discoveries were about to be revealed to the world.

9

A "Push," Not A "Pull"

(1924)

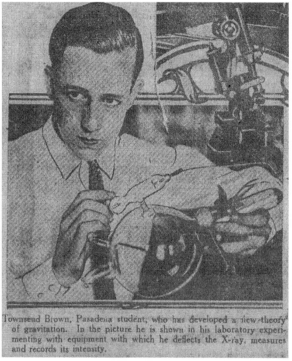

Townsend Brown, Pasadena student, who has developed a new theory of gravitation. In the picture he is shown in his laboratory experimenting with equipment with which he deflects the X-ray, measures and records its intensity.

Photo from the Los Angeles Evening Express May 26, 1924

One invitee who did show up at Townsend Brown's show-and-tell was a reporter for the *Los Angeles Evening Express*. Readers opening their paper on Monday, May 26, 1924, found a headline that read "Claims Gravity Is A Push, Not A Pull:"

Experiments now going on in a private laboratory at Pasadena by a youth of 18 may revolutionize the whole theory of gravitation as first deduced by Sir Isaac Newton.

Townsend Brown, a student of 706 Arden Road, has conducted experiments since last September which have convinced him that while there is a law of gravitation, the force is caused by a 'push' and not by a 'pull,' and development of this theory by practical inventions will revolutionize industry.

Young Brown has his laboratory at home filled with expensive equipment to pursue his investigations. He is a normal, serious-minded young man with no false illusions about his mission in life, but with a desire to become a pioneer along the line of scientific research that will open the way for startling discoveries and inventions.

STATEMENT OF THEORY

In plain words, his theory is this: That ether waves from outside space push from all directions against the earth, and against other objects and planets in space, forcing objects the way the wave extends, instead of drawing them, according to the old Newton theory of gravitation.

By means of his equipment he conducts experiments with the X-ray, which is of the same family as light and the ether wave, and by means of which it is possible to test the theory. By means of this machine, he says, that since the X-ray is deflected, the gravity wave, being of the same family, also can be deflected.

REVOLUTIONARY

If this theory is proved so thoroughly that it displaces the Newton theory, inventions of the future will revolutionize human industry, according to the young scientist. By deflecting ether waves that are pushing against objects, man can control weight to such an extent that his deflecting machinery would enable him to lift a battleship out of the sea and set it on dry land.

After hitting the wire services, the story ran in the Zanesville, Ohio, *Times Recorder,* reminding local readers that...

Friends of the Brown family will remember that almost from infancy, Townsend has been interested in science and that he was the first person in Zanesville to have a radio, which he installed himself.

The story even made it into the pages of the *New York Times*, with a photograph of the "Pasadena student experimenting with equipment with which he deflects the X-ray" and showing Brown holding a Coolidge tube, at the time the most advanced – and expensive – device of its kind, which Townsend's father purchased for his son. But it was not the 'X-ray beams' that Brown was curious about detecting. It was the tube itself – and how it behaved under high voltages.

The Coolidge tube was asymmetrical, built with a big difference in the size of the positive and negative electrodes. As Beau Kitselman wrote later,[18] this difference inspired Brown's experiments:

Brown mounted the Coolidge tube in a careful balance, as if it were an astronomical telescope. His idea was to point the tube in different directions and somehow find a variation in the power used by the tube, the strength of the X-Rays generated, or something. He didn't find what he was looking for, no matter where he aimed his apparatus, no tell-tale differences appeared. *But he did find something he wasn't looking for; he found that the X-ray tube generated a thrust, as if it wanted to move.*

He soon learned that the new force was not produced by the X-Rays, but by the high voltages which they required. Many experiments were necessary to make certain that the force was not one of the known effects of high voltage, and that it is a *mass* force, like gravity, rather than an *area* force, like most known electrical forces.

Kitselman said that these experiments with the Coolidge tube were the first indication that Townsend Brown had found a physical link between two elemental forces, electromagnetism and gravity – just as Einstein had predicted in theory.

The story in the *Evening Express* went so far as to speculate that "...control of gravitation might pave the way for a visit to Mars in a few years." Though his ideas were being picked up on the wire services and printed as far away as New York, Brown still felt the sting of rejection from classmates and faculty at Cal Tech. At the end of his freshman year, he packed up all his gear and returned to Ohio. The following fall, he resumed his studies at Denison University in Granville, where he sought the counsel of the Professor of Astronomy, Dr. Paul Alfred Biefeld.

10

The Biefeld-Brown Effect
(1924)

*Swasey Chapel and Observatory – Denison
University, Granville Ohio, ca. 1924*

When Denison University opened its new Swasey Observatory in 1911, Professor of Astronomy Dr. Paul Alfred Biefeld was named its Director.

Biefeld earned his B.S. in electrical engineering at the University of Wisconsin in 1894, after which – like Robert Millikan – he pursued graduate studies in Europe. He earned his Ph.D. from the Zurich Polytechnic Institute in 1900. When Biefeld's name finds its way into publication, he is often dubiously described as a colleague or classmate of Albert Einstein, though it is unlikely that the two had anything more than the passing acquaintance of students attending a large university at roughly the same time. The only thing that Einstein and Biefeld really had in common was music. They both played the violin.

Einstein failed his first entrance examination for the Zurich Polytechnic Institute in 1894, was finally admitted in 1896, and graduated as a secondary school teacher of mathematics and physics in 1900 – the year that Biefeld earned his doctorate. Biefeld remained at Zurich Polytechnic for six years, while Einstein left academia and found work as a clerk at the patent office in Berne, Switzerland. Despite scant evidence that the two actually knew each other, 74-year-old Dr. Biefeld told a newspaper in 1941 that "When Einstein would forget to go to a class, he would come and borrow my notes to get caught up on what he had missed. He was rather careless in his appearance and made no show of himself. Yet he had strong ideas and wasn't afraid to speak them out."

In 1924, Cal Tech dropout Townsend Brown showed up at Denison University chastened by his experience in Pasadena and determined to devise the sort of practical invention that would demonstrate a link between electricity and gravity. He found a sympathetic ear in Dr. Paul Biefeld:

> **Dr. Biefeld had been interested in the subject of gravitation for many years. This interest probably coincided with Einstein's interest in the Unified Field Theory and in the new concept of Relativity which was gaining recognition at that time. Biefeld believed in the possibility of some connection with gravitation. As he expressed it, "I am constantly on the look-out for something that might represent an 'electrodynamic-gravitational' coupling."**

A pivotal exchange took place when Brown asked Biefeld, "If a coupling did exist, what instrument might it resemble?" Biefeld thought for a few minutes and then answered without equivocation, "The capacitor."

A capacitor stores and discharges electrical energy. It typically consists of two charged metal plates – the electrodes – that are separated by an insulating substance called a dielectric, which cause the electrodes to absorb their charge without conducting it between them. A typical electrical circuit has anywhere from one to hundreds of capacitors, each capable of storing a different level of charge and discharging that charge according to the requirements of the circuit.

In this telling of the tale, Brown suggests that it was Biefeld who first suggested that the mechanism for the transmission of gravitation might resemble the common capacitor. But Brown had already observed the effect in his Coolidge X-Ray tube, which, with its asymmetrical electrodes, acted as precisely the kind of capacitor Biefeld was supposedly proposing.

In 1977 Townsend Brown wrote in his brief memoir,

> **The basic Biefeld-Brown effect is quite simple. It is manifested as a departure from the Coulomb Law of electrostatic attraction, in that the opposite forces are not equal. The negative electrode appears to chase the positive electrode so that there is a net force of the system... in the negative-to-positive direction.** [19]

By "departure from Coulomb Law," Brown is referring to the electrical theory that opposite charges attract and like charges repel, as first articulated in 1785 by the French physicist Charles Augustin de Coulomb.[20] Under normal circumstances, oppositely charged particles or surfaces of equal mass would attract each other equally. But the behavior Brown observed in his Coolidge tube – where the negative charge is slightly greater than the positive charge – the negatively charged surface is drawn toward the positive. Or as Brown put it, "the negative electrode appears to chase the positive electrode."

There is not much more in the record about the relationship between Paul Biefeld and Townsend Brown, or how the Biefeld-Brown effect came to be so named. What seems likely is that after his unpleasant experience at Cal Tech, Townsend Brown sought cover for his ideas – by attaching a credentialed elder's name to a discovery that could just as easily have been named wholly for himself. Calling his own discovery 'Biefeld-Brown' may be the first example of a practice that would recur throughout his life: hiding in plain sight.

11

"He Made Things Up"
(Notes from the Rabbit Hole #3)

> "Imagination is the only weapon in the war with reality."
> *– Lewis Carroll - Alice's Adventures in Wonderland*

When I called the campus of Denison University in the fall of 2004 and spoke to archivist Heather Lyle, I was hardly the first to inquire about Townsend Brown. Ms. Lyle did not hesitate to cast aspersions into the vacuum where the details of his life should be found.

"He made things up," Ms. Lyle told me.

"How's that?"

"We have files on him. These queries come up frequently, because apparently he was not very truthful in things that he said about himself, and gave the impression of a lot contact here at Denison. He even claimed to have been faculty or staff here when he really wasn't even a student, and claimed to have worked with Professor Paul Biefeld, who hardly even knew him. I mean, he just made a lot of claims that were false. People are constantly contacting us, so we have a whole file ready to refute these claims."

I asked if she would make me a copy of that file.

"Oh no," Heather said. "It's pretty extensive, so I'm not willing to do that" – at which point I started making plans to visit Granville to inspect the file myself. Before hanging up I pressed a little further.

"The effect that Brown discovered, he named it the Biefeld-Brown Effect. But you're telling me he had little contact with Biefeld?"

"He made up a lot of things," Heather giggled as though she was revealing a secret. "That's the impression that we all have. There is a kind of a detailed history of the various scams that he pulled based on various letters and people that were ripped off by him and that sort of thing."

"If that's all in your file, I can hardly wait to see it...."

In the final week of October – as the Boston Red Sox were winning their first World Series in 86 years – I descended on Denison University with Townsend Brown's daughter Linda, who maintained her anonymity by masquerading as my research assistant 'Elizabeth Helen Drake.' In a conference room at the university library, Heather Lyle let us examine her file on Thomas Townsend Brown.

The file opens with a print-out of an email from former archivist Cara Gilgenback that circulated around the campus in 1999:

> **Those of you who have been here for some time may have already run into reference questions involving:**
>
> **-T. Townsend Brown (purportedly a student at DU in the 1920s).**
>
> **- Dr. Paul A. Biefeld (physics faculty member at DU, 1911-1934, resident astronomer during that period).**
>
> **- "The Biefeld-Brown effect" (supposedly a joint research project between the two men conducted at DU, which resulted in a significant discovery about anti-gravity).**
>
> **This year I've received three requests for information on this topic, two of them in the past week. I asked the Physics Dept. for help since the archives yield little on Biefeld, nothing at all on T. Townsend Brown, and nothing at all on this so-called Biefeld-Brown effect.**
>
> **I want to let you all know that the Physics Dept. feels that Brown's credentials as a physicist are suspect. They cannot find any documentation linking Biefeld and Brown either at Denison or outside of Denison. There are no known published papers or monographs within the scholarly arena on the Biefeld-Brown effect. I am compiling the few popular/alternate press accounts I can locate.**
>
> **Also, I was unable to find any evidence that Brown ever attended Denison. I found lots of information on him on the Internet (mostly on UFO sites), including a biography I believe to be bogus.**
>
> **The reason I'm telling you all this is so that you can deal with researchers who come asking about the topic. According to Mike Mickelson, the Physics Dept. has received hundreds of requests for info on this over the years, and interest does not appear to be flagging. You could spend a lot of time searching indices and other reference tools on this topic and would find next to nothing useful.**
>
> **I would suggest that you refer interested persons to me. I'm compiling a file of relevant info that might be useful to these people. I'm also planning to write to the Naval Research Lab (where Brown reportedly worked) to see if they have any records.**

Another email in the file from a "former DU faculty member" from August 2001 attests to the scams Heather Lyle alluded to:

> **[Townsend Brown arrived in Meadville, PA] in 1962 or 1963 to start a company making ozone generators and an electronic levitation**

system. Supposedly for use by satellites (and purported to be one of the possible systems used by UFOs). He arrived in a shiny black Cadillac equipped with a radio telephone system (very uncommon in those days). He visited a number of Meadville's wealthy citizens, concentrating on the elderly, especially widows. A number of these individuals invested in his "new venture." He established charge accounts all over town.

This email describes two devices Townsend demonstrated in his sales pitch, an "ozone generator" and a "levitation device" (". . . like a large pizza dish . . ."). The email concludes:

A short time after this presentation, Brown vanished, leaving bills at all the places he had established charge accounts, including over $500 at a small grocery store. I don't know how hard the stockholders tried to find him, but they were unsuccessful.

Also in the file are two letters from another, still earlier Denison University archivist Florence Hoffman, who says Townsend Brown was...

...a student at Doane Academy in 1922 and 1923. Brown is listed as a graduate of Doane Academy in June 1923. The Denison University Catalog lists him as a member of the Freshman Class in 1924/25. He did not return the following year and I do not know where he may have completed his education.

We have never been able to find any evidence of a collaboration by Biefeld and Brown on any project, and Biefeld's son (now deceased) told us that his father knew Brown only slightly during the latter's student days but never worked with him at any time.

Other correspondence in the Denison file suggests that Biefeld's family in the 1940s knew nothing about Townsend Brown or the effect that bore the two men's names. In November 1956, UFO investigator Leon Davidson – apparently interested in NICAP (about which more later[21]), wrote to Biefeld's son Dr. L. P. Biefeld asking about his father's relationship to Townsend Brown. L. P. Biefeld replied:

My father never did collaborate with Mr. Brown in a scientific sense. Since Mr. Brown was extremely interested in experimentation in the field of physics and astronomy, he hung around the Physics Department and the Observatory quite a bit and talked to father often. My father was not too impressed with his ideas.

L.P. Biefeld also corresponded with science journalist Gaston Burridge[22], who speculated in the 1950s about anti-gravity propulsion systems, telling Burridge:

Your mention of the 'Biefeld-Brown effect' is news to me. I never heard my father speak of this effect. I am very surprised to hear of this and would be very interested to know where you obtained information regarding this so-called effect.

*

During the time in 2004 when I was digging into Denison University's unflattering file on Townsend Brown, Linda Brown and I had been trying unsuccessfully to obtain military records for her father's Navy service that began with his voluntary enlistment in 1930[23]. That quest delivered its first results just after our visit to Granville, when a thick manilla envelope arrived in my mail. Inside were Townsend Brown's naval records – or, at least those records that were not entirely classified, nor referenced anything that was classified[24].

Among the Naval records was an affidavit from someone who had visited Townsend's home laboratory in Zanesville in August 1930. The visitor had traveled "at the request of Mr. Thomas Townsend Brown… to personally conduct tests and examine certain apparatus and setups thereof and act as witness therefore with respect to the operativeness of said apparatus."

The visitor then describes equipment that consisted of "two principal or essential parts, a stator and a rotor – a generator-and-motor system based on what is now known as "The Biefeld-Brown effect." The visitor testifies:

It is apparent that systematic variations occur in the output of the apparatus which are not to be accounted for and not localized within the system itself. Though the phenomenon is not understood at the present time, it is quite certain that the above-named variations are caused by forces external to the system.

The visitor is describing the effect Brown had first noticed in his X-ray spectrometer, the effect which led him to conclude that "a radiation (other than light) prevailed in the Universe, independent of our Solar system" – the observation triggered his conclusion that "gravity is a push, not a pull."

The visitor concludes that what he has observed in the young man's laboratory...

...is novel and valuable; leading to probable identification and measurement of forces hitherto not recognized in physical science or astronomy.

The visitor signed the affidavit: Paul Alfred Biefeld.

12

Can We Talk?

(1964)

Linda returned Howie's ring when he joined the National Guard in May. "He is such a good guy," she wrote in her journal, "and I love his family, but if I stay with him, how long will it be before I get bored? He will want to get married, I know." The girl who had lived in forty-some different places before graduating high school added, "I just can't imagine staying in the same town for the rest of my life."

True to his word, Morgan was "around." He'd drop by for a visit at Ashlawn, occasionally taking Linda for a ride on his motorcycle. Most of what Linda knew about him, she learned from gossipy girlfriends.

Like the last Friday in August, when Morgan attended the Philadelphia Folk Festival and invited some friends to spend the night on his family's farm. Next morning, Morgan's father found several couples in various stages of undress nestled in the hayloft. "I won't have this sort of activity here," he bellowed. "You have a reputation to think about and this is never going to happen again!"

Later that same Saturday, the phone at Ashlawn rang. Linda was surprised to hear Morgan's voice on the other end.

"Can I come over?" he asked – "so sweetly," she wrote in her journal, "I am sure that I am just an afterthought to him, but he has made me very happy." Half an hour later, Morgan's father's car pulled into the driveway at Ashlawn. Morgan emerged with a guitar, a towel, a toothbrush, and a comb.

"I'm moving in for the day," he announced to a bemused Linda.

Later that afternoon, Morgan told her about the party in the barn. "I guess my Dad figures that you are a better influence on me!"

Linda studied Morgan as he turned and walked toward the pool, noticing how much fun he was to watch, how tall and handsome he was. "Not if I can help it," she thought to herself.

As they lounged around the pool, Morgan struggled with the guitar he'd bought the night before – a Gibson J200 jumbo flattop, just like the one Elvis played. They raided a nearby strawberry patch and in her journal, Linda confessed, "I flirted outrageously with him, but I was so shy I don't think he even noticed."

Back at the pool, Morgan swept Linda into his arms. "He was going to throw me into the pool," she wrote in her journal, "But I hung on so hard he couldn't pull himself away from me, and I pulled him into the water with me."

Morgan sputtered to the surface. "Damn," he laughed, "you are one strong girl!"

Before the sun set, Morgan was gone.

"Damn Amazon!" Linda moped, "that's what he's probably thinking! That was the only move he made on me the entire day! Here he is a champion wrestler, and he can't even rip me loose long enough to keep me from pulling him in the pool with me. He loves to dance, and I can barely do a waltz. His favorite song is *Dancing in the Streets* and I just can't seem to keep up with him. He loves that big guitar and I can't begin to strum it. He can sing, and I am just too shy to even try. I just know that I am so drawn to him that I can barely breathe when he stands next to me. And he hasn't even kissed me!"

Linda's journals from the summer of '64 also reflect on the socio-political climate of the time. Race riots in Philadelphia that summer prompted a curious observation from her father: "Daddy commented that he felt it was humankind's response to an outside force that is affecting all of us. He says it's the same type of force that has probably encouraged revolutions and wars… It makes us all feel like fighting. I dunno…. Those are not exactly the kinds of emotions that I have been entertaining lately."

Sunday morning Linda wrote, "I guess that Morgan has made things even worse. Word from the grapevine is that last evening he took a girl skinny dipping in the farm pond, and then made the mistake of using his Dad's car to drive back to the main house to get some towels. His Father stormed out of the house to 'pull the keys,' only to discover a naked girl dripping wet in the front seat." All Linda could think of was how jealous she was. "I wondered if I had to stand in line – or didn't he think of me at all in a sexual way? Morgan and I," she wrote with sad resignation "live in an entirely different reality."

Linda expected the last Sunday in August was going to be "a quiet day." Hattie, the Ashlawn housekeeper and her husband Taft, the butler, had the house "looking wonderful" prior to their departure for a vacation. Taft and Charles – taking a break from his driving duties – were working in the garden; Mother was reading and "Daddy was working at his desk in the study."

And as for herself, Linda wrote, "I was purely agitated."

As Sunday evening settled in, the big house was quiet. Linda, still feeling restless, had retired to the rec room to watch an old movie on the TV when she heard an unexpected knock at the door. When she opened it, there was Morgan, whispering, "I know it's late, but can we talk for a while?"

"A while" drifted on until four the following morning. Lying at the edge of the pool, their legs dangling in the cool water under the hazy summer's night sky, they stared up at the moon and stars, they spun into an expansive dialog about the planets, the stars, the vastness of space and even the possibility of time travel.

Morgan talked about his family. His parents had drifted apart when his younger sister drowned in a swimming pool accident. His mother never recovered from her grief and blamed his father; Now his older brother was also trapped in an unhappy marriage.

"I just don't think marriage is in the cards for me," Morgan said. "I'm never going to take my father's place in society. I just don't want the big house and mortgage. I don't want to have to stay in one place except for two weeks every year."

Linda could tell that the very thought made him restless and uncomfortable. She smiled at Morgan and looked away.

"What do you want, Morgan," Linda asked quietly, looking skyward.

Startled at the question, Morgan's answer came out in a rush. "I'll go to college," Morgan said, "and then I want travel and adventure. It's weird, but I have this very clear vision of myself, I don't know where, or when, but I'm in someplace that's mountainous, and really rocky. No trees anywhere. I can see small pebbles on the trail tumble away from my boots. It's strange because I don't know of any place like that around here. I don't even think it's in this country, and the vision gives me this overwhelming sense of danger and excitement. I don't know where that picture comes from, but somehow, that's the answer to your question. That's what I imagine for myself, sometime in the near future."

Absorbing the curious majesty of Morgan's vision, Linda warmed herself with the thought that these were not the sort of things that he shared with those other girls. She offered a vision of her own.

"You just have to listen to your own soul about these things," she said, "and somehow, you'll just know what to do. I have my own peculiar premonitions. Sometimes I can just clearly see myself riding horse-back over golden hills, past strange, gnarled trees. I've even drawn the trees in art class, but the teacher says I should stick to reality, that trees like that don't exist anywhere in nature. I don't know where that picture comes from any better than you know where yours comes from. But I know my trees are real, and I'm sure your pebbles are real, too."

"Amazing..." was all Morgan could manage to say.

The spell was broken by the sudden ringing of a telephone. Linda sprang to answer it before the entire household was awakened. On the other end of the line, Linda's older brother Joseph was calling from Oregon, and he wanted to speak with his mother. Linda set the phone down and whispered to Morgan, "wait, *please* wait…" Morgan just wiggled his fingers at her, gesturing a silent "goodbye…"

Linda tip-toed into the house to awaken her mother, who took the call on the phone by her bed. By the time she got back to the pool, Morgan had slipped away. In the distance, she heard the trailing rumble of his motorcycle.

Returning to the house, Linda noticed Morgan's big Gibson, still leaning near the door where he'd left it earlier.

13

A Rare Force of Nature

(1964)

When Linda answered the phone in the greenhouse at 4 AM, there was no friendly "hello" or a polite "sorry to bother you..." The voice on the other end just asked, "Hi, can I speak to Mom?" which left Linda wondering, "who is this??" It had been so long since she'd even heard from Joseph Brown, much less actually talked to him, that she'd almost forgotten that she had an older brother.

Joseph Townsend Brown was twelve years older than Linda, who was a toddler when the family lived in the tropical wilderness of the Hawaiian island of Kauai in the late 1940s. When the family returned to the mainland in the early 1950s, Joseph went off to college and served a stint in the Air Force. Simmering tension between Joseph and his father left Joseph out of touch with the family. As she returned to the main house, Linda figured it had been at least two years since she had heard the sound of Joseph's voice.

Linda found Josephine hanging up the phone, sitting up among the overstuffed pillows and covers of a four-poster bed that practically filled the room. Josephine patted her hand on the mattress beside her, and Linda climbed onto the big bed and snuggled in with her mother.

"What did Joseph want," Linda asked her mother. "And why was it so important that he was calling in the middle of the night?"

"He says he's found the girl he wants to marry", Josephine said. "He wants to give her the diamond ring I promised him years ago." Realizing how long it had been since she, too, had spoken to her son, Josephine laughed self-consciously, "It took a diamond to get him to call." Linda detected the sadness beneath her mother's good nature. She also knew that even if Joseph's call had bothered her, she would never have mentioned it.

The ring that Joseph was asking about was a family heirloom that Josephine had hung onto even through the most threadbare of times. It broke Linda's heart knowing that her mother was being asked to part with a treasure that Joseph would slip on the finger of a woman Josephine had never even met.

"What's the girl's name," Linda asked.

"I don't know, Sweetie. He didn't tell me that. He just asked me to send him the ring."

Linda's thoughts drifted through the hours she'd just spent by the pool with Morgan.

"Momma," Linda blurted, "How did you know that Daddy was going to be the one true love in your life?"

As the pale predawn light filtered into the bedroom, Linda's mother put her arm around her daughter and told her of the day in 1926 when young Thomas Townsend Brown took young Josephine Beale sailing on Ohio's Buckeye Lake.

"I thought that he would be talkative and egotistical, but he was quiet and very shy – completely different from what I expected him to be! And he had those crystal blue eyes that were just wonderful! All of my friends had painted this picture of a womanizing playboy, but all those preconceptions just dissolved that afternoon."

Linda giggled at the thought of anyone calling her father a playboy. Mother and daughter hushed themselves like a couple of teenagers at a slumber party. "Mom fluffed up her big pillow and I snuggled in beside her," Linda recalled. "We continued in a whisper, and I remember the sun was just beginning to break."

"Was that glimpse of Daddy really all you needed?"

"Sweetie, I guess that it's different with every person. I pushed away from that dock believing that I was in the company of a spoiled cad. By the time we sailed back to the dock I was thoroughly convinced that he was a rare force of nature and already the love of my life.

14

We Will Just Sail Away

(1927)

Josephine Beale ca. 1928

Josephine Beale was a pretty, slender girl with soft, dark blonde hair, an enthusiastic smile and blue-grey eyes, a junior at Lash High School in Zanesville. She had seen Townsend Brown around town, heard people refer to him as "the second coming of Einstein," and knew that he was the heir to one of the town's more prominent families.

Josephine caught Townsend's eye while performing in a school play. She didn't know what to make of it when her gossipy girlfriends mentioned that Townsend Brown had been asking about her.

Josephine heard all kinds of stories: That he owned his own cruiser out on Buckeye Lake – a refitted pilot boat called the *Viking*. His devilishly handsome friend Paul Grey had a reputation with the girls. Josephine's girlfriends giggled whenever they mentioned Paul Grey and Townsend Brown. Now the gossip mill was starting to grind on Josephine Beale, who did all she could to feign disinterest.

As the Beale family gathered for dinner one night, Josephine's father Clifford Beale – a prosperous businessman with an avocation in woodcraft – mentioned an inquiry he'd had that day about a carpentry project.

"I had an interesting visitor today," Dr. Beale started. "That young man Townsend Brown came to ask what I would charge to build a curio cabinet for his mother's birthday."

Dr. Beale watched his daughter hold her breath.

"He asked about you," Dr. Beale said. "Well, more precisely, he asked my permission to call on you."

"Poppa, are you serious? He came here? Oh Poppa! You don't know what everyone is saying about him! I can't believe that he would have the nerve to come straight to you like this!"

Dr. Beale delighted in his daughter's reaction. "Don't be so quick to believe what others say," he said. "This fellow made quite an effort to ask my permission in the most proper way. He stressed that you could select a chaperone if you wanted to. But I don't think that will be necessary."

Townsend's gaff-rigged sailboat, the TomCat, on Buckeye Lake in Ohio.

Josephine and Townsend's first date was a picnic on the shore of Buckeye Lake in the spring of 1927. In a fitting prelude to their future together, Townsend showed up late, having found it difficult to pull himself away from his laboratory. Josephine acted indifferent when he finally arrived in the Brown family's chauffeur-driven Packard.

Their second date was more memorable. It began with Townsend showing Josephine around his private laboratory, which she found impressive even if she understood little of what he was showing her. After another chauffeured drive out to Buckeye Lake, he took her sailing in his gaff-rigged catboat, the aptly named *TomCat*. Josephine tried to tease him about the name, but Townsend just laughed and swore that was the name of the boat when he'd bought it.

It was a perfect day for sailing, warm and clear with a light zephyr chasing over the surface of the lake. She was new to sailing but took naturally to the trim wooden boat; Townsend showed her the ropes, and even gave her a turn at the tiller.

"See that area over there, the ripples on the water?" Townsend said. "There's more wind over there, try to steer toward it." And when she did, the little boat picked up the fresh breeze and accelerated over the surface.

The visit to the lab and the adventure on the lake gave Josephine a better sense of her suitor. "We talked about everything that day," Josephine later told Linda. "I kept watching him and noticing how wonderful and blue his eyes were. He was very handsome and so tanned and when he smiled at me I just lit up inside. My previous impressions of him just melted away that day."

Tacking toward the far shore of the lake, Townsend told Josephine about dreams he'd been having and the ideas that came to him in his sleep that inspired him to experiment in his laboratory.

"He didn't have anyone who would just listen to him, so that was my role from the first," Josephine told Linda. "I didn't understand half of what he was trying to explain to me. It took a couple of weeks before it began to sink in. I just knew that it was the most important information that I probably would ever hear, and here was a man who was going to need me."

As the little sailboat skimmed across the lake, Josephine tried to lighten the mood.

"OK, Mr. Smarty, if you could travel through time, what do you think you will find in the future? Will there be more wars? What will become of Mankind in the future?"

The young dreamer with the tiller in one hand and the mainsheet in the other knew it was time to share the vision he had seen in his dreams.

"We will just sail away," he said.

"What do you mean?"

"Someday, men will travel in space, just as easily as we are sailing now. Great ships will silently push away from the Earth just as easily as this sailboat pushed away from the dock."

Josephine lingered in silence, listening to the water lapping against the hull. She closed her eyes and tried to imagine their little boat sailing across the void of space. In her heart she knew she was hearing something not only strange and fantastic, but also true.

She opened her eyes and smiled. "Mr. Brown, you are different, aren't you?"

Townsend smiled back.

"That was pretty much it for me," Josephine recalled. "I was a gone goose!"

When they got back to the yacht club, Townsend took Josephine home, and left her on the doorstep without so much as a kiss on her cheek.

"That night, I couldn't sleep," Josephine recounted. "So I knew what I was going through!"

"Yes," Linda thought to herself, as she listened to her mother that morning as the sun rose over Ashlawn. In her tangled feelings for Morgan, Linda knew exactly what her mother was talking about.

15

A Pineapple and A Pea
(Notes from the Rabbit Hole #4)

"Only a few find the way, some don't recognize it when they
do – some... don't ever want to."
– Lewis Carroll, Alice's Adventures in Wonderland

More than a decade after I first heard and wrote the words, "We will just sail
away..." I still don't know if the vision Townsend Brown shared with Josephine
as they sailed across Buckeye Lake is scientifically viable, but the vision is hard
to ignore.

Rereading Townsend's prediction reminded me of a passage from *The Boy
Who Invented Television,* my biography of Philo T. Farnsworth.

In the final years of his life, long after he was done with television, Philo
Farnsworth turned his attention to the riddle of controlled nuclear fusion: How
do you bottle a star?

My journey to that riddle started when I first heard of Philo Farnsworth in
the summer of 1973. As I was getting ready to relocate to Los Angeles to seek
my fortune in the TeeVee business, I picked up a magazine[25] with a story about
Farnsworth. I was surprised I'd never heard the name, nor had any idea that the
industry I wanted to work in could trace its origins to a sketch he drew for his
high school science teacher in 1922 – when he was just 14 years old. The imagery
in the article – photographs of televisions and cameras from the 1920s and 1930s
– was all new to me. I wondered why I'd never seen any of it before, as I had seen
photos of Edison with his first phonograph or the Wright Brothers hovering above
Kitty Hawk in the original 'Flyer.'

Later that summer I took a trip up the Pacific Coast Highway and stopped
to visit a public access TV advocate in Santa Cruz who called himself 'Johnny
Videotape.' Johnny was friends with Phil Gietzen, who edited the magazine where
I'd found the article about Farnsworth. Gietzen knew Philo T. Farnsworth III,
eldest son of the TV inventor, who told Gietzen stories about his father's pursuit
of controlled nuclear fusion in the 1950s and 60s.

Nuclear fusion is the same process that powers our sun and all the stars. If
fusion could be harnessed on Earth in the same manner as its evil twin – nuclear
fission – it could offer a clean, safe, and virtually unlimited source of electrical

power. But there's a catch: Just like a star, a fusion reaction is so hot – millions of degrees Centigrade – that it cannot be allowed to touch the walls of its container. That would either destroy the reactor vessel or cool and extinguish the reaction.

This is the celestial magic that Philo T. Farnsworth – who "breathed life into all our living-room dreams[26]" – tried to perform in the 1960's.

In 2022, when I returned to the Townsend Brown story after my long hiatus, I recalled a passage from the Farnsworth bio that describes his vision of how fusion energy would change the world:

> **He believed that fusion would alter the basic relationship that hinders current space travel – the weight ratio between launch vehicle and payload. He used the analogy of a pineapple and a pea: Today, what little space travel we do is conducted with payloads the size of a pea that are lifted into Earth orbit by launch vehicles the size of a pineapple. The reason for this inefficiency is because so much fuel has to be consumed in the initial thrust just to get the rest of the fuel off the launchpad. Farnsworth predicted the reversal of these ratios, with small fusion-engines gently lifting enormous payloads into orbit. He predicted that once in orbit, fusion-powered spacecraft could make it to Mars on as much nuclear fuel as could be stored in a tank the size of a fountain pen.**
>
> **In the realm of interstellar travel, Farnsworth hinted at the truly daring cosmology behind his fusion work. He dared to question our whole concept of distance as it relates to travel through outer space, asking aloud on many occasions, "Why do we assume that we have to exert so much energy to cross something which is actually nothing?"**

Farnsworth proved his unorthodox theories with the Fusor – a device not much larger than a soccer ball. But he stopped short of his goal of producing useful energy. He became suspicious of his corporate benefactors and withheld certain information. The funding ran out and the research ended in 1967.

And then he took the secret to his early grave[27].

I was first drawn to Philo Farnsworth because he invented electronic video. The harpoon didn't sink in until I started hearing about his unfinished work in fusion energy.

Thirty years later, that chance encounter in Santa Cruz led me to Townsend Brown.

Now here I am – another twenty years farther on – seeing the similarity between Philo Farnsworth's 'pineapple and pea' scenario and what Townsend told Josephine: that voyagers of the future will just "push away from the Earth as easily as we pushed away from the dock."

And wondering if the combination of fusion energy and gravity control offers a glimpse into the Universe of Magical Things.

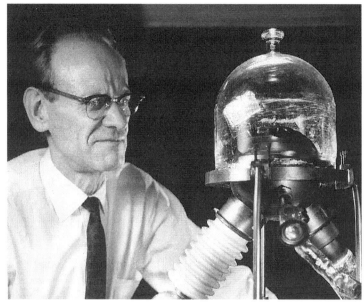

Philo T. Farnsworth and an early 'bell jar' iteration of his Fusor, ca. 1959

16

A Great Disappointment

(1926)

The staff of L.K. Brown's offices in Zanesville ca. 1930. Townsend on the far left, his father third from right, Grace Redmond to his right.

Townsend and Josephine kept their romance to themselves for more than a year, not only to keep Josephine's girlfriends' tongues from wagging, but also to avoid any interference from Townsend and Brown families.

Townsend's mother Mary – 'Mame' to friends and family – had already selected a bride for her only son, a young woman from her own patrician circles, Miss Cornelia Smith. Mame and Cornelia's mother were already making plans for a big church wedding that would surely be the highlight of the Zanesville social season. Recalling her own wedding – attended by more than 600 guests when she married Lewis Brown in 1898 – Mame expected nothing less for their son and heir.

Townsend, happily exploring the mysteries of the universe in his laboratory, hadn't really given Miss Cornelia much thought. He was quite certain that Josephine was the woman he could confide in and trust to protect his innermost secrets.

Townsend's laboratory was funded entirely by his father's largesse and operated in a corner of the elder Brown's offices in downtown Zanesville. Townsend would have been left entirely to his own devices were it not for the meddling of one Grace Redmond, his father's secretary and the unofficial holder of the purse-strings for the various family enterprises. Miss Redman did not share her boss's deference to his son's scientific inquiries. She considered the younger Brown's experiments to be "utter nonsense," and never missed an opportunity to make Townsend beg her for the funds he needed to purchase equipment and supplies.

In her churlish way, Grace Redmond embodied the expectations descending onto the shoulders of T. B. Townsend's only grandson. On his twenty-first birthday, Townsend received a letter from his Uncle Orville, Mame's brother:

Dear Nephew,

You are now twenty-one years old and don't want to be a chauffeur or a loafer all your life. You will never be happy unless you get into active business so you will be independent. Your parents are not well, you will not always have them with you, so you should start now to earn something, while you have the benefit of their advice, instead of everlastingly spending and looking for ways to spend money.

We want you to distinctly understand that all of the families have nothing but the kindest wishes for your success. You must realize that you are the only man out of the three families to hold together the business and financial interests that your uncles and your father will leave. Naturally, all of us wish that you will be a successful businessman. You are now of the age and you should appreciate what your father and mother have done for you in the way of education. Now it is up to you to repay them and the families that are interested in you, to show them whether or not you are capable. Unless you tie down to business at once, you will be a great disappointment to us all.

Kindly keep this letter for future reference. You may thank me in later years for writing you as I have, as it is all intended for your personal good.

Your affectionate uncle,

Orville N. Townsend

Rather than tying himself down to the family business, Townsend was pondering his escape from the midwestern confines of Zanesville.

First, there was the matter of a wedding to attend to.

17

Wagner In The Trees

(1928)

*Josephine and Townsend on their honeymoon
at Green Cove Springs, Florida.*

On September 8, 1928, more than one-hundred guests gathered for what they thought was just another late-summer picnic and swimming party at Hawthorne Farm – the Brown family's estate on the outskirts of Zanesville. Some were still dripping wet, fresh out of the pool, when the sound of Wagner's wedding march suddenly began to radiate from loudspeakers that Townsend had hidden among the pine trees.

The ensuing nuptials were described in the society column of the next day's *Zanesville Times Recorder*:

> **Surrounded by members of their own families and intimate friends and in the midst of tall trees through which the setting sun shone in benediction, Miss Josephine Beale, daughter of Mr. and Mrs. C.A. Beale of Merrick Avenue and Townsend Brown, only son of Mr. and Mrs. Lewis K. Brown of Adair Avenue, were united in marriage, Thursday afternoon at the Brown farm on the Newark Road.**
>
> **The marriage was to have been a surprise, but some of the many birds who live in the trees on the Brown farm must have heard the**

young couple whispering their secret and made haste to tell it to their friends for everyone was expecting "something to happen."

After a delightful picnic supper had been served to the guests who numbered over five score the music of the Lohengrin wedding march was heard faintly at first, as though from a great distance, then as the voices of the guests were hushed, more clearly. The music seemed to be wafted from the tops of the trees by angel voices in the most entrancing fashion and had been so arranged by the young bride and groom and as the guests all arose and moved up to meet them, the young couple appeared walking together over the brink of the wooded hill and proceeded to the place where Dr. Austin M. Courtenay of Delaware, a personal friend of the Brown family and a former pastor of Grace church awaited them.

Dr. Courtenay read the beautiful ring service of the Methodist Episcopal Church without a book and made it seem by so doing a peculiarly intimate and personal service performed for those whom he loved.

It was a picture seen by those present which will never be forgotten. The youth of the principals, the beauty of the woods and sunset sky and the solemn hush which stole over the scene as they made the responses uniting them for life, all created an atmosphere of dignity mingled with simplicity which was most appealing.

The bride was attired in a simple grey traveling frock with little grey hat and shoes and hose to match and carried a huge shower bouquet of pink and lavender flowers with a long pink and lavender shower. She was graduated last year from Senior High School and is a member of the Putnam Presbyterian church. She is unusually popular with her classmates and members of the younger social set.

Townsend Brown is one of the most interesting young men in Zanesville and has been widely known as an inventor and experimenter and has made some unusual discoveries which will work changes in theories of gravitation and electrical mechanism. He is engaged with his father in the sand business, but his chief interest is in his laboratory where his research and experiments are conducted.

After two weeks in the East the young bride and groom will live at the Brown home on Adair avenue, although they plan during fine weather to spend a great deal of their time at the Brown farm, where Mr. Brown has built himself a little house right by the edge of the large swimming pool. Both Mr. and Mrs. Brown are greatly

interested in swimming and water sports and out-of-doors life of all kinds, and the farm offers an alluring spot on which to spend an early fall honeymoon.

The newlyweds spent their wedding night at Hawthorne, in the little poolside cottage that would serve as their first home together, which they dubbed 'El Nido' – 'The Nest.'

Before departing for their honeymoon in New York and Florida, Townsend presented Josephine with a gift: A mint-green ceramic teapot, hand-painted with delicate, cursive gold lettering that read simply 'El Nido.' As Josephine placed the little green teapot on a shelf, she had no way of knowing how many different shelves she would place it on in the years ahead.

18

Anniversaries

(1964)

Linda Brown had her own reasons for remembering the date of her parents' wedding. On September 8, 1964, her parents went into the city to celebrate their 36th anniversary. Linda stayed home in the solitude of Ashlawn, preparing for her departure the next day for a college in Western Virginia called Southern Seminary.

When it was founded in 1867 as the Bowling Green Female Seminary, the word 'seminary' just meant a school for girls or women. Now it was a finishing school – a place for young women to find a suitable husband and take their place in proper society. Linda chose Southern Sem only for its outstanding equitation program, having loved all things hoof-and-bridle since she was nine years old. She wasn't interested in the school's social pretensions. She just wanted to spend as much of the next two years as she could in the company of horses.

Linda expected her parents would be leaving Ashlawn soon, too. Her father had honored the bargain he made with Josephine when they moved in: that they would stay put long enough for Linda to finish her last two years of high school in a single location.

"Hattie and Taft were still on vacation," Linda recalled, "and I knew that Dad had arranged for them to take another position when they got back." Indeed, after Josephine found a situation for them with the neighboring Asquith family, Townsend informed Mr. Asquith that he had been paying "his couple" a sum that was double their actual salary at the time – and had promised them a substantial raise as well. When Mr. Asquith accepted the terms, "Hattie and Taft were beside themselves" at the prospect of their new positions.

"I was alone in that big house," Linda recalled of her last night at Ashlawn. "Charles had driven them into town, left the car with Dad and took a train to Washington. I'd already said my goodbyes to him, and he slipped a hundred-dollar bill into my hand, saying 'This is for anything extra you might need.' I didn't actually stop to think that it might be years before I would see him again."

Linda wandered around the house, "just sort of saying goodbye to everything. That's a trick I'd learned long before, with all the moving we did, to take a very hard and long last look, so that I would not be homesick later for things left behind."

Linda was still confused with the way things stood with Morgan. After the night of their long talk, he came by and "grabbed his guitar out of my hands, mumbling something about being late for work and took off. I was still grieving over what I figured was a lost cause."

And then the phone rang.

Linda started a fire in the downstairs rec room and put some music on. "I hadn't really intended to make it such a romantic setting," Linda remembered, "but… well, maybe…"

Morgan had his guitar with him when he entered the room.

"You better be careful you don't leave that thing here again," Linda teased.

"Oh? And why is that?" Morgan asked.

"Because we're all leaving in the morning and there won't be anybody here for you to retrieve it from."

They small-talked for a while, sitting next to each other on the sofa and staring a bit uncomfortably into the flames. The situation felt awkward and cold despite the warmth of the fire.

"What's wrong?" Morgan finally asked.

"Look," Linda said after a long silence, "I thought that maybe there was something going on between us. I guess I just thought, maybe, that you and I had something a bit more important than whatever you've got with all those other girls you spend time with. But now I don't know. Now it all just feels…."

Linda stopped herself. In the silence, she first felt vulnerable, and then, suddenly… safe.

"It just seems very one sided," she confided. "Like I'm the only one that feels this way. I guess I'm just sad because it really meant something to me. And now it's coming to an end."

Morgan jumped to his feet and put out his hand. "Let's dance."

Linda stood slowly and waited to feel him pull her closer. Morgan put his hand around her waist. Their bodies pressed together, and they swayed back and forth. It wasn't really dancing. It didn't need to be.

Morgan brushed his lips against Linda's ear and whispered, "What you feel… I feel it too. I had to stay away because I knew that there was a chance that things would go too far too fast. That's not the kind of going away present that I want to give you."

Linda pulled slightly away from Morgan, just far enough that they could look into each other's eyes.

And then he kissed her.

Linda's delight was suddenly consumed with dread. "But all this is going to be over tomorrow," she sighed.

"Oh no," Morgan said, "You're kinda stuck with me now."

19

Tapping Cosmic Energy
(1929)

After his humiliation at Cal Tech in 1924 and the unexpected publicity about his inventions, Townsend Brown maintained a low profile – until early 1929, when Ohio newspapers reported that he had been granted a patent.

One headline read, "Method for Deriving Power from Gravity Is Devised by T. Townsend Brown." Another said Townsend had invented "a relativity engine." A headline in the February 18 edition of the Cincinnati *Enquirer* declared, "Zanesville Inventor Applies Einstein in New Electrostatic Pendulum Motor."

Enquirer reporter Wilmer Mason had witnessed Townsend's invention, and wrote:

> That power is inherent in normally inert matter is proved, and that it is possible to release and utilize such power is demonstrated by an apparatus devised and set up by T. Townsend Brown.
>
> Brown's concepts prove Dr. Einstein's recently propounded theory of a relationship between the electric field and the gravitational field, for Brown uses electrical means to release what he describes as a gravitational force.
>
> Brown grasped the essentials of his development and began its improvement four years before Dr. Einstein published his formulae purporting to show such a relationship. Brown says that whereas Dr. Einstein deals with such a relationship as theory, Brown treats it with the mechanics that apparently verify the connection.
>
> "Tapping cosmic energy" is the way Brown summarizes his system.
>
> The apparatus demonstrates the principle of making mass move by virtue of power within, [which] eliminates power losses due to heat and friction and therefore holds enormous possibilities for commercial economics.
>
> The invention consists simply of surrounding or impregnating a mass of any non-conducting material with an electro-static condition by applying high-voltage current to opposite ends of material that does not transmit electrical force, i.e., a dielectric or insulator.

Brown had sandwiched a layer of a material that *does not conduct* electricity – called a 'dielectric' – between two layers of a material that *does conduct* electricity – the 'electrodes.' This is the first published account of Townsend Brown's most controversial invention: a gravity-defying pendulum he called the 'Gravitator'[28]:

To demonstrate the liberation of force Brown suspends a block of insulating material with its accompanying electrodes to permit it to move as a pendulum. When the current is turned on, this unit moves in one direction, endwise, until its weight overcomes its own force, until the current is turned off or until it loses temporarily its inherent power characteristic.

In other words, when the current is applied, the pendulum rises to one side of its arc, and then remains suspended there for...

...38 to 80 seconds, after which the unit is unable to release its apparently inherent energy for several minutes...

Had Mason reported that the direction of movement was toward the positive pole, he would have accurately described the Biefeld-Brown effect. Because the dielectric layer interrupts the flow of electricity in the apparatus...

...the circuit is not completed, and this is one reason why Brown and scientists called in by him to test his results unite in saying the electrical energy present is not the cause of the force liberated...

...which affirms Brown's contention that his invention liberated some kind of 'cosmic energy.'

The patent also described how an array of eight to ten pendulums could mimic the dynamics of an internal combustion engine, some units...

...giving off power and carrying themselves and their companion units forward, while the first exhausted cells would be recuperating, "recharging from space..."

The *Enquirer* article then addresses one of the themes that would preoccupy Townsend Brown for the rest of his life, his determination to find the source of the fluctuations in the 'cosmic force' his apparatus released that he called 'Sidereal Radiation.' He wanted to use his invention to...

...measure changes in the gravitational field caused by the motion of the earth and the relationship to the earth of the sun, moon and planets.

The greatest distortion in the gravitational field comes when the sun and moon are in the line of horizontal action of his gravitational cells – that is, at the time of the rising or setting sun or moon. The

exception to this is when sun and moon are opposite and therefore neutralize each other in part. The maximum distortion comes when the sun and moon rise or set together, thus acting in conjunction. It is the effect of these varying factors that Brown calls "distortion of the gravitational field."

Finally, the *Enquirer* article dispels the notion that the Gravitator was some kind of 'perpetual motion' machine,

Either a power line must be tapped to provide the small amount of electrical energy necessary to release his "cosmic force", or a generating unit operated in conjunction with it.

In other words, the Gravitator may be tapping into some kind of 'cosmic energy,' but it still needs an external power source to do so.

20

Gravity & Electricity, Space & Time
(Notes from the Rabbit Hole #5)

> "I am not crazy; my reality is just different from yours."
> — *Lewis Carroll, Alice's Adventures in Wonderland*

Modern science tells us that there are four fundamental forces – called *interactions* – at work across the universe: gravity, electromagnetism, the 'weak force' (the energy released when unstable atoms decay, producing nuclear radiation) and the 'strong force' (which binds like-charged protons into atomic nuclei; also, the energy released when atomic bombs go bang).

Mankind has achieved some measure of control over three of these forces. Only gravity remains untamed. Despite hydrogen bombs and trips to the Moon, despite computers and satellites and hand-held geo-positioning systems, gravity remains pretty much a mystery. Any attempts to actually harness its motive power have gone for naught or been the subject of ridicule.

In the seventeenth century, Isaac Newton did a heroic job of calculating the mechanics of gravity. He determined that gravity is a function of mass: the more massive a celestial body, the more gravity it has; the greater the distance from that celestial body, the less the effects of its gravitational field. In his *Principia Mathematica,* Newton also asserts that "The powers of gravitation arose from the impulses of a subtle medium that is diffused over the universe and penetrates the pores of grosser bodies." In other words, every object in the Universe, from the smallest particle to the largest planet or star, is somehow connected to every other object in the Universe – an idea that laid the foundation for quantum mechanics 250 years later.

For more than three centuries, mankind utilized Newton's equations to predict planetary movements and put men on the moon. But even Newton could not really explain what exactly makes gravity work. The how/why of gravity remains a mystery.

In the late nineteenth and early twentieth centuries, mankind's experiments with electricity presented myriad challenges to scientific precepts that originated with Newton. The fixed foundations of the Newtonian universe began showing cracks.

With the publication of his *General Theory of Relativity* in 1916, Albert Einstein turned Newton's universe inside-out. In Einstein's telling, massive objects like stars and planets bend, or warp, the space around them, and other planets or moons are held in their orbits by the resulting curvature. The most common illustration of this theory depicts a celestial body like our sun suspended in the elastic fabric of space, as a rubber membrane would stretch if a ball were placed on its surface. In the resulting curved space, planets assume their orbit around their stars, and moons assume their orbits around their planets[29].

Einstein gave us an explanation of how gravity works in the cosmos, but *General Relativity* lacks the kind of practical utility that men like Faraday and Maxwell gave us with the electromagnetic force. A century later, we can still do little with gravity besides fall down or drop things.

In the remainder of his life, Albert Einstein struggled to articulate a *Unified Field Theory,* the mathematical commonality in all the known forces in the universe. In particular, he sought to find the theoretical link between gravity and electromagnetism. Such a linkage would infer the ability to produce artificial gravity with electricity, and consequently the synthetic means to 'bend' space.

In his *General Theory of Relativity,* Einstein unified the three dimensions of space with the fourth dimension of time, redefining the fabric of the cosmos as 'the spacetime continuum.' So: if one can manipulate gravity with electricity, and that infers the bending of space, does it not also stand to reason that electrically induced gravity also implies the bending of time?

21

How I Control Gravitation

(1929)

How I Control GRAVITATION

By THOMAS T. BROWN

An article written exclusively for this magazine, dealing with the meaning of the Einstein "Field Theories" and the relation between electro-dynamics and gravitation. Actual experimental confirm- ation and practical results are given.

After the Gravitator patent was issued, an article appeared in the August 1929 issue of *Science and Invention* magazine, with a headline that suggested that electricity and gravity had found their Faraday:

How I Control Gravitation
by Thomas T. Brown

Writing for the first time in his own words, Brown starts with an echo of Einstein's efforts to define the Unified Field:

> There is a decided tendency in the physical sciences to unify the great basic laws and to relate, by a single structure or mechanism, such individual phenomena as gravitation, electrodynamics and even matter itself. It is found that matter and electricity are very closely related in structure. In the final analysis matter loses its traditional individuality and becomes merely an "electrical condition."

Brown is stating that matter is a manifestation of electrical energy, extrapolating from the notion that atoms consist mostly of electrically charged protons and electrons.

> In fact, it might be said that the concrete body of the universe is nothing more than an assemblage of energy which, in itself, is quite intangible. Of course, it is self-evident that matter is connected with gravitation, and it follows logically that electricity is likewise connected.

The reasoning is simple: if matter is a form of concentrated electrical energy, and if large celestial objects exist within their own gravitational fields, then it "follows logically" that there is some connection between electricity and gravity.

Brown then offers a brief explanation of Einstein's "distorted space" theory of gravitation and addresses the question of field theories and the difficulty even Einstein has encountered in coming up with a "Theory of Combination." But...

Einstein's new field theory is purely mathematical. It is not based on the results of any laboratory test and does not, so far as is now known, predict any method by which an actual demonstration or proof may be made.

Dr. Einstein's recent work has spirited the physicists of the entire world to locate and demonstrate, if possible, any structural relationship between electrodynamics and gravitation. It is not that they questioned or doubted Einstein's reasoning or his mathematics, (for they have learned better), but that they realized that a relation should exist and were eager to find it.

Brown then claims that as early as 1923, he had discovered and "constructed the... bridge between the two then separate phenomena, electricity and gravitation" and offers some speculation as to just where such a discover might lead:

Multi-impulse gravitators weighing hundreds of tons may propel the ocean liners of the future. Smaller and more concentrated units may propel automobiles and even airplanes. Perhaps even the fantastic "space cars" and the promised visit to Mars may be the final outcome. Who can tell?

Who indeed. But is that all there is? Planes, trains, and automobiles, maybe big boats and space cars? If we can 'bend' space, what, then, of time?

22

Closing Ashlawn

(1964)

*The Brown family's 1960 Cadillac convertible parked
behind Ashlawn, waiting for the next mission.*

The morning after Morgan told Linda she was stuck with him, the Brown family loaded a footlocker into the trunk of Townsend's big green 1960 Cadillac convertible and headed south for Virginia.

Linda loved watching her father get the Cadillac ready for a road trip. "He'd go under the hood and check the oil and water levels, walk around the car and check the tires and all the lights and turn signals. The interior was decked out with an elaborate instrument panel, and the way it lit up while the car was warming up for an early-morning departure always reminded me of some kind of spaceship."

Adding to the Caddy's space-age allure was another feature rare for its day: a car phone. With the electrical guts stashed in the trunk and just a handset in the front seat, "It worked like a ship-to-shore radio; you had to ring up a mobile operator to make a call, and then all this gear in the back would clatter into action." Linda always wondered what it was about her father's work that required such an exotic accessory.

As the Cadillac roared out from Philadelphia, through Maryland and onto the Blue Ridge Parkway in Virginia, the temperatures were cool, but the late summer sun was warm enough for Townsend's preferred mode of travel—with the top down, all the way to the Shenandoah Valley.

After spending an evening in historic Leesburg, Virginia, Townsend piloted the Cadillac up to the focal point of the Southern Sem campus: a four-story, red and white gingerbread building that originally served as a resort hotel, complete with Victorian gables, turrets, towers and onion domes. As her father found help unloading her footlocker, Linda and Josephine ascended the grand entrance to find Linda's room and her new roommates.

By the time Linda and Josephine got back to the car, Townsend was already anxious to get back on the road. Goodbyes were said, and the Cadillac headed back to Philadelphia – though Linda was pretty certain they would take a couple of days and the scenic route to get there. "He never went in a straight line," Linda said, "at least, not if he could help it."

Linda flourished in her new environment. She exchanged letters with Morgan, who was likewise exploring his own new station as a freshman at Antioch College, a liberal arts school in Ohio with a Bohemian streak.

Linda was pleasantly surprised that she "fit right in among the heiresses of what some called 'the mink and manure set,' though I hardly considered myself one of them. We were the only ones allowed to wear our breeches and boots into the classrooms, and that always gave us a special feeling, like we were the elite of the elite."

Linda also exchanged chatty letters with Josephine, but she didn't realize what was going on at Ashlawn until one night after nearly a month at Sem, when she called home. Expecting to talk to her mother, Linda was surprised when Charles Miller answered the phone.

Charles' two year "tour of duty" with the Browns had turned out to be far more pleasant than he had anticipated when he was first instructed to "look over the family." He hadn't taken into account what that would mean on a personal level. Charles was really not the kind of person who ever acknowledged that he even *had* a personal level. His body lean and wiry, his countenance dour and unrevealing, Charles was well trained for any physical challenges the job might present, but he was not prepared to become, literally, a part of the Brown family and their life at Ashlawn.

When Charles answered Linda's call, Ashlawn was empty except for a cat named Heidi. The moment Townsend and Josephine returned from Virginia, Josephine found her little green teapot with the hand-lettered 'El Nido' and carefully packed it away. By the end of September, all of the fine furniture, rugs, and personal effects were packed and gone.

With the big stuff accounted for, Townsend and Josephine packed their personal stuff in the back of the Cadillac and headed south for Homestead, just east of the Everglades, at the very southern tip of Florida.

An hour later, as Charles was checking off the last details in his head – the phone rang.

"Oh, Linda," Charles said, "your Mom and Dad left here about an hour ago. They're on their way to Florida. I'm closing up the house now." He gave her a phone number in San Francisco where he could be reached by the end of the week.

Linda hung up the phone, lingering a few moments with her hand on the receiver. She really had no idea what her parents had been planning or what they had been up to. In the few weeks that she'd been in Virginia, she hardly thought about Ashlawn. Now she realized how much she was going to miss the place.

And then it suddenly dawned on her: If she wasn't going back to Philadelphia, where and when was she going to see Morgan again?

23

A Vague and Unscientific Report
(1929)

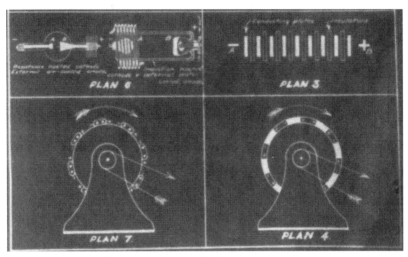

Patent drawing of a Gravitator motor

Townsend and Josephine Brown spent their honeymoon summer of 1929 at the beach resort of Ocean City, New Jersey, where Townsend served as a lifeguard and Josephine taught swimming to the children of the resort's wealthy patrons. Their summer was as light-hearted, elegant and carefree as any time the two would ever spend together.

Returning to Zanesville at the end of the summer, the newlyweds took up residence at the Brown family's stately home on Adair Avenue, where Josephine quickly found herself at odds with her mother-in-law. Josephine wondered if Mame still harbored some resentment that her son had not married the woman of higher standing that she had chosen for him.

Townsend returned to his laboratory, determined to understand the fluctuations he observed in his instruments, and trying to develop a practical application of the gravitator. Josephine chafed under Mame's watchful eye as Townsend's activities continued under the scrutiny of Miss Grace Redmond, who insisted it was time for this young heir to make something useful out of his nonsensical work and his father's swelling investment.

The mounting tensions at home and work eventually took a toll. As Linda Brown recalls, "Mother never really confirmed what happened. We only ever spoke of lost babies one time. My best guess is that they returned to Zanesville in the fall of 1929 expecting, but something happened. We only ever talked about after I'd suffered a miscarriage of my own. I don't think Mom ever told Mame what happened. If she told anybody it would only have been her own parents. In my grandmother's defense, Mame was deprived of the information that might have made her more accommodating. Mom was vulnerable, and Mame probably interpreted that as weakness."

Then the stock market crashed.

The Brown family was more fortunate than some, but the crash had an impact on Lewis Brown's willingness to continue pouring funds into his son's weird experiments. In the spring of 1930, Lewis Brown asked a family friend and business associate, John H. Hislop, to call upon his business contacts to help his son find an industrial-strength source of funding. Mr. Hislop already had some prior knowledge of the young man he had been asked to mentor, whom he first encountered as a ten-year-old using electricity to harvest earthworms for a fishing expedition.

Hislop called on Edward H. Deeds, a native of Granville, Ohio, and a graduate of Denison University who had built his first fortune electrifying the mechanical products of the National Cash Register Company (NCR). Deeds later formed a life-long partnership with another inventor and engineer, Charles Kettering. Kettering invented, and with Deeds developed the first electric self-starter that replaced the tiresome and dangerous hand-cranking system that fired up the first horseless carriages. When the Cadillac Company acquired that innovation, Deeds and Kettering created the Dayton Engineering Laboratories Company (DELCO). After a series of fortuitous acquisitions, Deeds and Kettering found themselves among the largest shareholders in the world's largest industrial corporation: General Motors.

Drawing on their mutual Ohio roots in a letter dated March 13, 1930, Deeds introduced Townsend Brown and his discoveries as best as he could understand them, occasionally resorting to name dropping to lend credibility to the presentation. He mentioned Dr. Millikan and Brown's time at Cal Tech, where…

…he conceived this new theory of gravitation, which, as nearly as I can understand, is based entirely on the Einstein theory. He has developed through his experiments a mechanism which demonstrates Einstein's uniform field theory, that is, the same mathematical equations and laws that govern the electromagnetic field also govern the field of gravitation.

Citing Brown's collaboration at Denison with Dr. Biefeld, "who was a classmate of Einstein's," Hislop continued:

I have had a number of scientists view the Gravitator and they have all been absolutely amazed by its action, frankly stating that whereas they see the results and the movements of the gravitator, it is absolutely unexplainable by any laws of physics that they know.

Finally getting to the point of his letter on page three, Hislop writes:

I am wondering if you are interested or intrigued enough by my vague and unscientific report to send a competent man to investigate his claims with the idea (if they prove worthwhile) of taking Brown into the research laboratory of some of the large corporations you are connected with, so that he might develop his Gravitator into a commercial success.

Two months later, at Deeds behest, Hislop contacted Charles Kettering directly, telling the industrialist – who had built an empire out of an invention he had knocked together in an Ohio barn – that...

...I truly believe that this young man, after years of study and experiment, has discovered a new source of power which, with the facilities at your command, could be brought to commercial success.

...and invited Kettering to Zanesville to see what the young man had on his workbench. Kettering passed Hislop's lettering to H.W. Asire, the head of the Electrical Section of the GM's Research Laboratories. On May 20, 1930, Asire replied to Hislop's letter with something like, "Does the device operate on direct or alternating current?" and "What is the approximate output of the unit and what is its overall efficiency?" After expressing his interest in having "a personal discussion with Mr. Brown", the letter ends with Asire inviting Townsend to bring a Gravitator to Detroit for a demonstration in June.

There is no evidence that Brown ever made that trip or demonstrated a Gravitator for any auto industry executives in Detroit. Rather, surviving correspondence[30] suggests that Brown may have had an ulterior motive. On June 10, 1930, Brown wrote to Asire about the "phenomenal variations" he had observed in his invention's performance:

As you probably know, Zanesville is located in an exceedingly hilly district where large gravitational masses produce field distortions and introduce considerable error in the readings. For this reason, we are glad to have the opportunity to take readings where the land is comparatively level.

The "field distortions" Brown wrote about – the phenomenon he called 'sidereal radiation' - is the curiosity that would occupy him until the last weeks of his life. His interest in taking readings from alternate locations may indicate that he believed his experiments were manifesting something more than an ability to control gravity. Brown was starting to believe that the fluctuations he observed bore some resemblance to radio waves and might be suitable for transmitting Morse code or audio signals through the ether. He was looking for evidence that in addition to a new means of conveyance, he had also discovered a new means of communication.

Whatever interest Kettering or GM might have had in a 'new form of locomotion' faded quickly: the company never offered Brown any form of material support, nor has it – or any other company – produced any kind of vehicle or vessel with a Gravitator engine.

Townsend Brown's next letter was addressed to an institution that pioneered the use of wireless communications: the United States Navy.

24

Opportunities for Technicians and Scientists
(1929)

*The future Lt. Townsend Brown, displaying an early
affinity for all things nautical ca. 1908.*

In the short autobiography that he dictated to Josephine, Townsend Brown said that he "always loved anything to do with the Navy." There is a photograph taken of young Thomas when he was three years old, cradling a toy battleship in his arms. The model ship looks to be about as long as the child was tall at the time. And we know of the summers that he spent on Buckeye Lake, sailing his cat boat or cruising around in his refitted motor launch, the *Viking*.

The 1929 article in *Science and Invention*, "How I Control Gravitation," includes two potential nautical applications of the gravitator: an elegantly tapered "model Gravitator boat 12 feet long" and a bulkier "model commercial Gravitator for marine use" that is sometimes referred to as the "Gravitator barge."

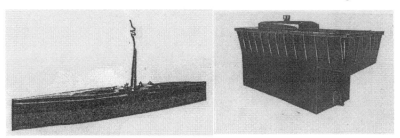

Early prototypes of the Gravitator Boat and the Gravitator Barge ca. 1929

After the stock market crash, Townsend found it harder than ever to obtain funds from Grace Redmond, his father's unyielding keeper of the purse-strings. "Grace thought all of his work was nonsense and she made him practically grovel for the funds to keep his research going" according to one family friend. "Of course, he could over-ride her by going directly to his parents, but he despised doing that."

On December 4, 1929 – just a few weeks after the crash – Townsend wrote to the Navy Department in Washington, inquiring about "opportunities in the Service for technicians and scientists."

The Navy replied, recommending that Brown apply for a commission with the Naval Station at Great Lakes, Illinois, noting that "the Special Service branch of the Naval Reserve is open to specialists of high professional qualifications for special service in the Navy in time of war."

There being no war at the time, Townsend kept working in his lab for most of the following year – including the visit from Dr. Paul Biefeld found in his Navy records. On September 3, 1930, with Biefeld's affidavit in hand, he slipped away from the disdainful gaze of Miss Redmond, and reported for Basic Training at the Great Lakes Naval Station.

The proud mother and her sailor son, ca. 1930

For somebody who had chafed through most of his academic career, Townsend Brown turned out to be an outstanding apprentice seaman. In November, the base newspaper reported that the boy who couldn't finish college was chosen "Honor Recruit of Company Seven" and was assigned to the Naval Radio School in San Diego, California. Josephine enrolled in a nursing school there and accompanied her husband to San Diego.

Despite his professed affinity for ships and sea, weighing anchor was really the furthest thing from Townsend Brown's mind. That he sought assignment to the Radio School indicates that he was angling for a way to continue his own scientific inquiries, starting by learning all he possibly could about wireless communications under the aegis of the U.S. Navy.

After a few months in San Diego and a fortuitous meeting with the base chaplain, base Commandant Capt. Sinclair Gannon ordered the newly promoted Seaman Second Class to report for further shore duty at the Naval Research Laboratory near Washington, DC.

Brown's personal motives come to light again in a letter he wrote to the NRL before reporting, attaching a copy of the Biefeld affidavit and offering to donate his experiments to the Navy:

> **For the past six years I have been engaged in experimental research work in my laboratory in Zanesville, Ohio. During this time, I secured funds to carry this work through various friends, universities, and the Research Foundation. The recent depression made it impossible for me to continue my work so that it became necessary to close my laboratory and store its equipment, its value probably $20,000. Since I am in the Naval Service, I will be glad to offer this equipment to the Navy for experimental research in this field, should the Navy Department find it possible and desirable to carry on such research.**

Brown's letter – and the offer of his equipment – bounced around Navy brass, ultimately resulting in an endorsement from Capt. Gannon addressed to the Chief of the Navy's Bureau of Navigation:

> **– The offer of his experimental electrical equipment to the Navy is decidedly out of the ordinary but I am convinced of Brown's sincerity in the matter as well as of his interest in his chosen but interrupted field of research.**

> **– To transfer a man of Brown's attainments and natural bent to a seagoing ship where he would in all probability become a radio or electrical engineer would be a lack of appreciation of his latent value**

when that value can be employed in the Naval Research Laboratory, and I recommend that Brown be so transferred.

Townsend wrote home, asking that his laboratory be shipped ahead, and reported for duty at the Naval Research Laboratory in Anacostia, Maryland on March 16, 1931.

25

A Seagoing Sailor At Last

(1932)

Brown wrote that arriving at the Naval Research Laboratory was "a happy event" that "combined my two interests in life – the Navy and scientific research." At the NRL he hoped to find a sympathetic ear for his unorthodox ideas – particularly the possibility that a gravitator-powered vessel might propel itself through water.

The NRL traces its origins back to the days before the United States entered the First World War. In May 1915, a correspondent for the *New York Times* asked Thomas Edison for his thoughts on the war in Europe, and Edison advised that "the Government should maintain a research laboratory to develop all the technique of military and naval progression without any vast expense."

Josephus Daniels, the Secretary of the Navy under President William Howard Taft, enlisted the Wizard of Menlo Park to chair the Naval Consulting Board – a civilian panel formed to advise the Navy on science and technology. Congress approved the Board's proposal with a $1.5-million appropriation in 1916, but America's entry into The Great War delayed the construction of a facility until 1920.

The Naval Research Laboratory opened on the outskirts of Washington DC in the summer of 1923 with two divisions. The Radio Division pioneered in the new art of wireless communications; the Sound Division worked on underwater sound propagation. The Labs produced communications equipment, direction-finding devices, sonar sets, and (according to NRL reports), the first practical radar equipment built in this country. The operations expanded over the next two decades to include new divisions dedicated to the study of Optics, Chemistry, Metallurgy, Mechanics and Electricity, and Internal Communications.

After a warm reception from NRL Commander Capt. E. D. Almy, Brown asked to be assigned to the Heat and Light Division under Dr. Edwin Hulbert, citing their mutual interest in radiation, "especially cosmic radiation, which was Dr. Hulbert's specialty." Brown later expressed his delight with the situation, writing:

> **I wore a white lab coat, had my own room with my name on the door, and carried on the experiments I had started in Zanesville. Experiments were conducted which seemed to prove the concept of Gravitation which I had hypothesized at Cal Tech.**

But not everybody at the NRL was thrilled with Brown's experiments.

Equipment was built and all manner of tests were conducted. But, as the history of science always seems to show, the results were controversial – even with Dr. Hulbert and Dr. Ross Gunn (Hulbert's assistant). I even heard it remarked at one point that "Brown's work wasn't worth the powder to blow it up." I never quite knew his reasons.

*

Early in 1932, the NRL offered Seaman Brown his choice of two cutting-edge expeditions. He could either accompany Admiral Robert Byrd's final expedition into the Arctic, or volunteer for the Navy-Princeton Gravity Expedition to the West Indies. The choice was easy for a sailor who'd spent half of his formative years in Florida and California. "It sounded warm," the newly promoted Seaman First Class recalled, "and I dislike the cold." He packed his duffle accordingly and headed for the Caribbean.

Vening Meinesz with his gravimeter (from the collection of the Utrecht University archive/museum)

The 1932 Expedition was one of a series conducted on behalf of Princeton's Department of Geology beginning in 1926. Geologists at Princeton were looking for data from the oceans that could advance their theories of the origins and formation of the Earth. The focus shifted when anomalies observed during a 1929 expedition near the Bahamas raised questions about gravity's role in the formation and structure of the islands.

The voyage that Brown signed on to was spearheaded by a world-renowned geophysicist, Dr. F. A. Vening Meinesz of the Netherlands, who had spent the past decade aboard submarines measuring gravity fluctuations at sea. On a voyage in the mid-1920s, Meinesz detected anomalous gravity belts running parallel to the deep-sea trenches near Indonesia, which phenomenon are known to this day as the "Meinesz Belts."

Dr. Meinesz made his discoveries using a device of his own invention that measured fluctuations in the earth's gravitational field. The Vening Meinesz Pendulum suspended oscillating arms in a specially gimbaled and counter-weighted housing. When operated at depths between 100 and 400 feet, the Pendulum could accurately measure gravity at sea.

There was just one hitch: These sensitive measurements could only be conducted at considerable depth in order to minimize the interference of wave action on the surface. That meant somebody had to come up with a submarine. When Meinesz explained this to the Expedition's organizers, Princeton President Emeritus John Hibben called on Secretary of the Navy Charles F. Adams, who provided a submarine known only as *S-48*.

S-48 was one of a new line the Navy built to achieve parity with the more advanced submarines produced in Europe during the First World War. The S-Class subs were larger and faster than their predecessors, could dive deeper, cruise farther, and carried more torpedo firepower.

The submarine S-48 barely survived her initial sea trials.

Despite her advanced design and construction, *S-48* had a checkered history. On a test dive during her initial sea-trials in 1921, an improperly sealed ballast tank filled with water and the whole boat sank tail-down, her props settling into the sand in sixty feet of water. The crew managed to bring the bow to the surface just long enough for all hands to scramble to safety through a torpedo tube. Two weeks later the sub was towed back to the builder's yard. After a year of refitting, *S-48* was returned to service.

A decade later, *S-48* ferried Dr. Meinesz and his pendulums into the Caribbean to study gravity. When Dr. Meinesz insisted on taking someone who could be trained to take charge of future expeditions, Seaman Townsend Brown was selected to serve as Dr. Meinesz assistant. NRL Commander Almy noted that the selection of Townsend Brown over other physicists was a recognition of his superior skills as a 'lab man' – he was not only good with ideas, he was good with machines and instruments, too.

While the S-48 was outfitted for the mission at Guantanamo Bay in Cuba, the scientific crew lodged about 30 miles away in the city of Santiago.

At 1:17AM on the morning of February 3, 1932, all hands were awakened by a frightening encounter with gravity – and the impact it has on buildings when their masonry foundations are shaken by a severe earthquake. The ground shook for nearly a minute, during which, Brown recalled,

> **We were awakened amid indescribable terror. It seemed everything was either roaring or cracking. The lightly built Spanish walls of the Casa Grande Hotel where we were staying were parting in big cracks and crashing together again every two seconds. The floor was heaving and the furniture rolling.**

After the shaking stopped, Brown fumbled through the darkness for a flashlight. He and Harry Hess (another member of the scientific team) stumbled their way down a "twisted and shattered stairway in a series of jumps." When they reached the second floor, they discovered that a large section of one wall had fallen into one of the hotel rooms, scattering plaster and lath across the bed. Pushing the rubble aside, peering under the bed with their flashlights, they were startled to find Dr. Meinesz huddled beneath the bed frame. Hess and Brown pulled Dr. Meinesz to safety, shaken but uninjured. Just as they reached a vacant park across the street, they turned around to see the roof of the hotel come crashing inward, crushing what was left of the space they had just escaped.

*

On the deck of the S-48 l-r: Lt. Cmdr Rosnell, Dr. Venig Meinesz, Harry Hess and Seaman 1st Class T.T. Brown.

Four days later, on February 7, 1932, *S-48* and her surface tender departed from Guantanamo Bay. Over the course of the next six weeks, the *S-48* traced a serpentine route through the Caribbean and North Atlantic: Jamaica; Cabo San Antonio; Puerto Rico; the Bahamas; Miami Every sixty miles or so, the S-48 submerged to take readings from Dr. Meinesz pendulums, measuring fluctuations in the Earth's gravitational field.

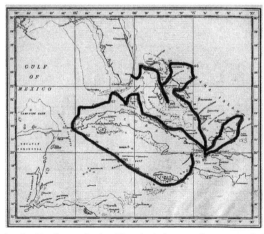

The route of the S-48 through the North Atlantic Ocean and Caribbean Sea.

Brown wrote that he was "delighted, not only to go on a history making expedition, but to be 'a seagoing sailor, at last!'" He also recalled some of the mission's perils: "Most dives approached the crush-depth of the submarine" – the depth at which the pressure of the surrounding seawater would cause the steel shell of the sub to implode. "There were several instances when, due to automatic valves out of control, we actually exceeded the crush-depth. It was a frightening moment, but by blowing all the ballast tanks we came shooting to the surface like a cork."

Over expedition's six weeks, *S-48* performed as many deep dives as most submarines of the day performed in an entire year. When the sub finally put in for service at the Naval Yard at Key West, the commander recorded in his log that his vessel was acting "like a wounded whale."

Nevertheless, the voyage was considered a scientific success. An extensive journal of the expedition was published by the Hydrographic Office of the Navy, with Seaman T. T. Brown providing much of the text.

Between Brown's performance as the science officer on the expedition, and his exploits in rescuing Dr. Meinesz from the rubble of the Casa Grande, an even more significant impression was made. Dr. Vening Meinesz, as it turns out, was a man with friends in high places, and he applied his quiet influence in the background to recommend Seaman Brown for his next assignment at sea.

26

A Complete System

(1932)

After the Gravity Expedition aboard *S-48*, Seaman Brown returned to the NRL, expecting to resume his assigned duties while continuing his research on the side.

Despite becoming "a seagoing sailor at last," one irony of Brown's assignment to the Gravity Expedition was the Navy's refusal to consider the assignment a form of the actual sea duty. Never mind that the expedition was dubbed the 'Navy-Princeton' expedition or that the entire voyage was conducted aboard a commissioned Naval vessel. In his role as a scientist, Townsend Brown might just as well have been a civilian. The Navy's mandate that all of its personnel spend some time on a boat created a tug-of-war among his superiors.

Chief among Brown's benefactors was NRL Commander Almy, who made the case for Brown's indispensability in a letter to the Bureau of Navigation, which kept pressing for his requisite time at sea. Stressing Brown's unique talents – and recommending a salary increase from \$2,000 to \$2,600/yr. – Almy wrote:

> **Brown has an engaging personality and obviously is capable of development. To be of value to the Navy however, a special disposition should be made of his case. He would be of no special value at sea in the usual rating and duties, but on shore in a laboratory of scientific endeavors he not only will be valuable for the work accomplished, but will have potential value as a source of creative effort in Naval science.**

Almy's recommendation fell upon deaf ears. In July of 1932, F.B Upham, writing on behalf of the Bureau of Navigation, dismissed Brown's service on *S-48*, informing Commander Almy that:

> **– An examination of the record discloses that Brown has approximately one year ten months service, during which time he has performed no sea duty.**
>
> **– The Bureau considers that Brown has already received special consideration in the matter of promotion and does not desire to promote him further at the expense of enlisted men afloat. All in the service must be employed in manning the ships and stations as required by naval operations.**

Upham asserted that the Bureau categorically opposed the assignment of enlisted personnel to posts that would more properly be the purview of civilians.

He offered that if Brown would just resign from the Navy, the service would respond favorably to his request for a special discharge.

Brown stayed in the Navy for another ten years.

Rather than peeling potatoes in a ship's galley, he began presenting ideas that could revolutionize those ships' basic means of propulsion. On August 5, 1932, Brown sent a memorandum to Commander Almy proposing the study of *Electromagnetic Reaction: Application to the Propulsion of Ships, the Pumping of Fluids, and the Measurement of Flow.* The study summarized what he had been working on at the NRL, leading him to believe that...

> **...a model ship can be propelled through water at a comparatively high rate of speed and with fair efficiency. The electromagnetic device is installed inside the hull and the mechanical reaction is induced outside the hull directly in the water. The movement of the model is controlled by the magnitude and direction of the electrical current supplied to it. The method requires no propeller or paddles, in fact, employs no moving parts. No vibration or sound is created by the source of the motive power.**
>
> **The direct reaction drive has the unquestionable strategic value of being absolutely noiseless. It is suggested that the latter type of drive may be employed to advantage in submarine warfare, both as a means of propelling submerged submarines and for surface ships on patrol duty engaged in listening for submarines.**

A half century later, a Tom Clancy novel called *The Hunt for Red October* features a renegade Russian submarine propelled by a silent 'magneto hydrodynamic drive' that sounds suspiciously like the very thing Townsend Brown proposed to the U.S. Navy in 1932.

Another illustration in the 1929 Science and Invention article shows this "gravitator boat... 12 feet long." This is the only known illustration of this gravitator application.

Brown's silent electrical propulsion system is just one facet of the proposal. Later in this letter he suggests a pair of corollary applications of the same principal.

First:

> **When the electromagnetic propelling device is held stationary, the liquid is caused to flow. It is conceivable in this connection that a silent, non-corrosive pump having no moving parts could be developed.**

Conversely:

> **When the electromagnetic device is held stationary and conductive fluid is forced past it, usable electric current is generated. The method [might be] practical for the generation of electric power on a commercial scale . . . in connection with tidal power ideas.**

There it all is – for the first time and in considerable detail – *a complete system of power generation and utilization:*

> **1. Place a "gravitator" type device on a vessel, and the vessel moves through water.**

> **2. Hold the vessel stationary in the water, and the Gravitator will serve as a pump, forcing the water to flow past the mechanism.**

> **3. Hold the Gravitator stationary and force water past it, and it will generate an electric current.**

Townsend Brown's proposal to the Navy was as revolutionary to mid-20th century science as Nikola Tesla's introduction of the polyphase electric system was to the late 19th century. Tesla's system provided alternating current to a world of industry. Brown proposed to do it all with no moving parts, no vibration, and no sound.

*

The inter-bureau squabble over Brown's status as an enlisted sailor persisted. Over the next several months, letters flew between the NRL and the Bureau of Navigation, with Commander Almy continuing to argue for Brown to remain ashore at the NRL.

At one point, Townsend's father tried to intervene. L.K. Brown solicited letters of commendation from at least one Senator and one Congressman on his son's behalf. Representative James M. Beck of Pennsylvania wrote to the Secretary of the Navy, insisting that Townsend's "knowledge and experience in research endeavors would prove especially valuable to the Department were he retained in his present assignment."

The dispute reached the highest echelons of the Navy Department. In a letter dated August 3, 1932 Secretary of the Navy Charles F. Adams repeated the Navy's unwavering position:

I regret that it is not in the best interests of the service to accord Brown special consideration in regard to promotion or assignment to duty...It is not desirable to maintain enlisted men on permanent shore duty.

Two weeks later, Commander Almy received direct orders to ship SFC Brown out on the *USS Bridge*, a supply ship which he would find taking on provisions at the Naval base in Norfolk, Virginia.

Almy still had one ace left up his sleeve. He appealed to the Navy's Bureau of Engineering to keep Brown ashore, insisting that Brown's services were required by the Hydrographic Office in order to complete the report on the *S-48* Gravity Expedition.

The day that Brown was expected in Norfolk, S. M. Robinson, Chief of the Bureau of Engineering, countermanded the orders of the Bureau of Navigation, recommending instead that "subject man be retained in his present duty for a period not exceeding a year." How the director of the Bureau of Engineering managed to effectively overrule the Secretary of the Navy we'll never know. We can only surmise that as an engineer, Robinson was surely keen on Brown's proposals, writing:

The possibilities of the investigation being conducted by Brown are of extreme importance if investigation discloses that there is a scientific foundation to Brown's claims.

At last, somebody was taking Townsend Brown seriously.

27

A Deeper Draft Vessel
(Notes from the Rabbit Hole #6)

When the day becomes the night and the sky becomes the sea,
when the clock strikes heavy and there's no time for tea;
and in our darkest hour, before my final rhyme,
she will come home to Wonderland
and turn back the hands of time.

— *Lewis Carroll, Alice's Adventures in Wonderland*

I met Townsend Brown's daughter Linda for the first time at a Holiday Inn in Las Vegas in the spring of 2003.

Before that, we had been corresponding – first through the U.S. Mail and then by email – getting to know each other as Linda worked through her reticence to revisit the mysteries that had governed her life.

In April 2003 I flew from Nashville to Las Vegas for the annual convention of the National Association of Broadcasters, where I participated in a panel discussion about Philo T. Farnsworth, the subject of my first book.

Linda drove in from her home in the California desert, the trunk of her car filled with two large Rubbermaid tubs that contained all that remains of Townsend Brown's personal papers, notebooks, and photographs – the collection referred to in these pages as the "family archives."

Once we'd settled into my room, there were fewer than ten minutes of preliminary banter – How was the drive up? How was the flight in? Isn't Las Vegas ridiculous in the daylight? – before we started foraging through the tubs.

I turned on a tape recorder.

When I left Las Vegas two days later I had nearly ten hours of conversation on tape.

Among the documents Linda pulled from the Rubbermaid was a comprehensive file the FBI had compiled on her father in the 1950s, which Andrew Bolland had obtained some years earlier through a Freedom of Information Act filing with the Bureau. Flipping through the report prompted a discussion about how her father had come to be associated with the UFO fringe – and our mutual reluctance to chase the rabbit down that particular hole. But I could tell that Linda found the material equally fascinating and discomfiting.

Other documents in the tubs turned the conversation toward Brown's service in the Navy. Linda wondered why her father had resigned from the service in the fall of 1942. It seemed odd to both of us that an officer with valuable skills in radio and radar was discharged barely a year after the United States was drawn into World War II.

"What are the possibilities," Linda wondered, "that he was working on something highly classified, that he was experimenting with things that even the Navy didn't know about?"

That statement did not compute. If her father was in the Navy, stationed at the NRL, and working on classified projects, then who could have classified them besides the Navy?

"Look at it this way," Linda said. "You've got somebody working on important projects for the Navy. We're neck-deep in a World War and suddenly he's not in the Navy anymore. Do you think that the work would have stopped?"

Linda then used an expression which meant little at the time but which would come to have increasing meaning in the months and years ahead. "We're talking about military classifications," Linda said, "but there's another possibility – that somebody with an even 'deeper draft' than the Navy came along and said 'we need that man...' Who, or for what, I don't know."

At this moment in the recording there is a long pause as I scanned the room. I noticed the lamps, the telephone, the switch plates, the clock radio by the bed, the TV remote control – and wondered if somebody might have been listening in to our conversation.

Linda continued, sounding just the slightest bit nervous. "I would just as happily leave this stuff alone. It's interesting, but I don't want to steer you in that direction because you can get yourself so totally lost. Somewhere there could possibly be..."

Linda caught herself in mid-sentence, veering off in an entirely different direction – a tactic no doubt learned in the course of a lifetime confronting these abstractions and recognizing how weird and twisted a tale they could tell.

28

A Gentle Breeze, A Mattress – and Mr. X

(1964)

The 'remote lab' at Homestead Florida ca. 1964-65.

After packing up Ashlawn and putting much of the furniture in storage, Townsend and Josephine loaded up the Cadillac, put the top down, and headed south to Homestead, Florida – a sleepy town thirty-five miles south of Miami on the edge of the Everglades, where US Highway 1 dips toward the Florida Keys. The house where Josephine unpacked her teapot was small, but behind the house was a larger building Townsend called his Remote Lab.

As Linda's Thanksgiving break approached, Townsend arranged some business in the Philadelphia area. He and Josephine drove up from Florida, collecting Linda at Southern Sem along the way.

"We went to some shows, and we shopped at Wanamaker's Department Store, which was right across the street from where we were staying," Linda said. "It took the whole weekend to tell them about everything going on at school. We had a lovely time and enjoyed the snow that swirled in the canyons of the city that weekend."

Her parents asked about Linda's social life. Townsend in particular was curious of news of Morgan – who Linda had mentioned more than once in her letters home.

Thru the fall, Linda and Morgan had exchanged a few letters. Linda wrote about her snooty classmates; Morgan wrote about the classes he was taking in Russian at Antioch College in Ohio. When Linda learned that her parents had shipped out to Florida, she wrote Morgan "a panicked letter saying that I wouldn't be coming back to the Main Line, how would we ever see each other again?"

Morgan wrote back a simple note saying, "I have two weeks off for the holidays. Shouldn't take me that long to hitch down."

*

A few days before Christmas, a tall young man with chestnut hair – and a full, thick, Eric-the-Red beard – was seen along the highways between Ohio and Florida waving a large white cardboard sign:

**I am going to visit Linda in
FLORIDA
please give me a ride**

In mid-December Linda took the train from Virginia to Florida. On the third day of her visit in Homestead, as the family was gathering in the kitchen for dinner, they heard someone whistling in front of the house. Josephine peered through the window, turned to Linda, and with a knowing smile said, "It's Morgan!"

"I ran straight out into the front yard, straight to him," Linda recalled. "He had grown a beard that I thought was terribly sexy." Morgan was just grateful to have arrived in time for dinner, and Josephine was more than happy to set another place at the table.

"Morgan and Dad were laughing about one thing or another," Linda said. I didn't realize it at the time, but Dad was watching this fellow very carefully."

After dinner, Morgan volunteered for cleanup duty. "I've got lots of experience cleaning tables and washing dishes," Morgan said. Townsend and Josephine nodded to each other, taking their cue to leave Morgan and Linda alone in the kitchen. On her way out, Josephine pulled Linda aside, and whispered, "He will probably break your heart, Sweetie. But he is probably worth it."

Once they had laughed and splashed and pretended to dish-wash all they could, Linda showed Morgan the place she had set up for him to spend the night – a sleeping porch on the far side of the house, a spot that had all the prerequisites for what she knew they both had in mind. There was a gentle breeze, a mattress, and as much privacy as the small house could afford.

After Morgan rolled out his sleeping bag, he grabbed a flashlight, and turned anxiously to Linda.

"You wanna go for a walk or something?"

"Walking wasn't what I had on my mind," Linda recalled, "but I was nervous, and walking was probably a good idea."

They found a garden bench at the foot of an enormous royal palm tree, where they sat back-to-back, propping each other up. After an awkward minute, Morgan finally broke the silence.

"So, have you decided? Yes or no?"

Linda laughed nervously, "Maybe."

"Linda, there are only two answers to this question. 'Maybe' is the same as 'yes.' But I would rather hear 'yes.'"

Linda was grateful that the decision was hers to make. "He had made up his mind a long time before that," she said, "and was just waiting for me to come to the conclusion that this was my idea in the first place. I was not about to let him leave before we became lovers," Linda said. "Of course, my answer was 'Yes.'"

When they returned to the house, "I was so nervous," Linda recalled. "All this was new to me, so I tried to take some small comfort knowing that Morgan was more experienced. We tried to be quiet and discrete. I knew we had 'permission,' but it was a very quiet thing, lots of whispering. I could hardly contain myself. At the most intimate moment, I suddenly got very talkative."

Morgan assured Linda that she had nothing to worry about – and Linda finally lost interest in talking.

*

The following days were filled with leisure. One day the foursome – Townsend behind the wheel, Josephine riding shotgun, Linda and Morgan in the back seat – put the top down and took the Cadillac down the Rte 1 causeway to Key West. While Josephine and Linda strolled in and out of the picturesque shops, Morgan and Townsend checked out the boats in the nearby marina. "It was really a wonderful time, Linda recalled, "and I was amazed at how completely at ease both my parents seemed to be with Morgan."

Back in Homestead, Morgan hung around Dr. Brown's laboratory, soaking up more detailed explanations of fan/loudspeaker that Morgan had first scene a year earlier at Ashlawn.

One day Townsend received a spry, distinguished, white-haired gentleman who had flown in from Nassau in the Bahamas. Linda knew her father had some business contacts in the Bahamas and the family had lived there briefly a few years earlier – when Charles Miller first became a fixture in their lives. Linda knew nothing of the elderly gentleman, whom she referred to only as "Mr. X."

A couple of days before Linda and Morgan were scheduled to leave Florida, Mr. X extended an invitation to Morgan and Townsend to join him for a day trip to Coral Gables, where the three of them spent an afternoon sailing around Biscayne Bay.

Watching the three of them driving off in the Cadillac, Linda recalled "standing there, wondering why it was suddenly a 'boys club' and I wasn't invited."

29

The Caroline

(1933)

Eldridge Johnson's 279ft private yacht, the Caroline.

With his usual deliberate stride, Seaman First Class Townsend Brown searched the docks of the Brooklyn Navy Yard in January 1933 until he found the gleaming white hull of a palatial motor yacht with the name *Caroline* emblazoned across her broad stern.

At the recommendation of Vening Meinesz, Brown was once again on loan from the Navy, to serve as the radio and sonar engineer on a voyage called the Johnson-Smithsonian Deep Sea Expedition. Through the winter of 1933, the *Caroline* would ply the waters of the tropical Atlantic dredging for samples of the flora and fauna at the bottom of the ocean, in roughly the same region where Brown had helped Meinesz measure gravity fluctuations the previous year.

At the Navy Yard, the *Caroline* was undergoing final preparations for the voyage, installing a heavy-duty winch with 6,500 feet of 3/8" wire rope to lower a dredging bucket to the ocean floor.

At 279 feet length-over-all, the *Caroline* was the second largest private yacht in America – one whole foot shorter than J.P. Morgan's *Corsair*. The *Caroline* boasted eight luxurious staterooms, each with a private bath; a mahogany paneled library, a sumptuous dining room attended by five stewards, a complete laundry room, a state-of-the-art radio room, a drawing room complete with wood-burning fireplace, and an after-deck large enough for a tennis court. With a pair of 1,500 horsepower diesel engines capable of steaming at 15 knots, her tanks carried enough oil to cruise half-way around the world without refueling.

*

The 'Johnson' in the expedition's name was the *Caroline's* owner, Eldridge Reeves Johnson. The vessel was named for Johnson's mother, who died in the 1870s – long before her son became one of the world's wealthiest industrialists.

Eldridge Reeves Johnson ca. 1892.

Thomas Edison invented the tinfoil phonograph in 1877, but Eldridge Johnson created the modern recording industry. Amid the railroad tycoons, steel magnates, oil barons and financiers of the Gilded Age, Eldridge Reeves Johnson became the era's first media mogul when he started an outfit called The Victor Talking Machines Company.

Despite graduating from the Dover Academy at the age of 15, young Johnson was deemed unsuitable for higher education and served four grueling years as a machinist's apprentice in Philadelphia before opening his own shop in 1886. Two years later, Lady Fortune walked through Johnson's doors in the form of one Emile Berliner.

Berliner was a German-born inventor who had experimented with sound recording while working on improvements for another new-fangled machine, the telephone. Berliner determined that the quality of sound recordings could be improved by etching the vibrations into grooved surface of a flat disk, rather than the cylinder of Edison's design; the result was a machine that Berliner called the

Gramophone[31]. Berliner also developed an early technique for producing multiple copies of a recording from a single original.

An early prototype or Emile Berliner's gramophone ca. 1888.

The Gramophone was cheaper to produce and boasted better sound quality than Edison's cylinders but suffered from one major shortcoming. To spin the disk, the user had to turn a hand-crank at a continuous and steady rate of 150 turns per minute. An unsteady hand made the sound waver and the needle skip.

At Berliner's behest, Eldridge Johnson came up with a spring motor that, once cranked, would spin the turntable at a uniform speed long enough to play an entire record. That innovation made the Gramophone practical enough to find a place in millions of American parlors.

In October of 1901, Johnson and Berliner formed the Victor Talking Machines Corporation in Camden, New Jersey. In 1906, Johnson's company added a new word to the lexicon when a smaller model of the Gramophone with a built-in speaker horn was introduced as the 'Victrola' –the first brand name to become synonymous with its product, like Xerox or Kleenex today.

Along with the Victrola, the company introduced one of the most famous advertising campaigns ever: The image of Nipper – Berliner's white terrier – poised in front of the horn, his head cocked, listening intently to 'His Master's Voice.'

*'His Master's Voice' was Emile Berliner – until
it was Eldridge Reeves Johnson.*

The Victrola was an instant hit in the marketplace, but Johnson realized that even greater success could derive from selling not just the machines, but by selling what people played on them.

Johnson expanded on Berliner's duplication process, adding a production layer of multiple sub-masters from the original master recording– giving the Victor Company the means to press large numbers of copies of a recording and sell them to the public.

The Victor Company's general manager, Leon Douglass, created the first international pop star when he signed the Italian tenor Enrico Caruso to a contract and began releasing his records by the millions to a public eager for new things to play on their Victrolas. Other artists were signed to similar contracts, and Johnson and Douglass devised the concept of paying a royalty to the artists and songwriters for each record they sold – a concept that also empowered the manufacturers to hang on to the largest share of the proceeds.

Over the next two decades, sales of Victrolas and the records played on them soared into the millions of units, making the Victor Talking Machines Company one of the most successful enterprises in the world, and making both Eldridge Johnson and Leon Douglass wealthy magnates with an empire that circled the globe. Their business introduced Johnson and Douglass to the highest levels of business, finance, and international politics. In the fast-growing field of electrical communications, Eldridge Johnson and Leon Douglass were two of the most well-connected men in the world.

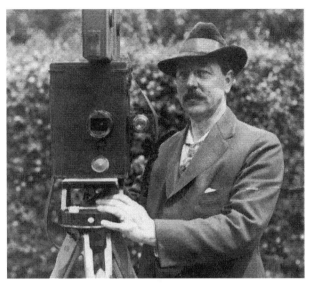

Leon Douglas, motion picture pioneer.

Around the time of World War I, a new medium called 'radio' began to compete for the attention of the Victor Company's customers with the lure of free entertainment transmitted through the ether. This new technology brought Johnson to a momentous decision: In January 1927, he and Douglass sold their interests in the Victor Talking Machines Company to the new Radio Corporation of America, which then morphed into the RCA/Victor Company and became the dominant player in both wireless communications and recorded entertainment.

Johnson walked away from the deal with a fortune of roughly $25 million – a portion of which he dedicated to the building of a proper yacht. The boat's keel was laid at the Bath Iron Works in Maine in August 1930, and the *Caroline* was launched on the 18th of July, 1931. The cost of construction was quoted at $1,567,410.90.

Another of Johnson's retirement indulgences was *Alice In Wonderland*. Johnson was so enamored with the story of the young girl and her surreal world that he acquired several copies of the first printed edition. His obsession culminated with the purchase – at no small expense – of the original manuscript of *Alice's Adventures Underground*, written in the hand of its author Charles Lutwidge Dodgson, who scribbled under the pen-name of Lewis Carroll. During one visit to England, he went to the trouble of having himself photographed with the elderly Alice Liddell Hargreaves, who, when she was a child, had been Dodgson's inspiration for Alice.

Johnson so treasured the original Alice that he had it housed in a steel cabinet, constructed to look like "fine mahogany... with unbreakable glass" so that he could keep the manuscript with him and share it with his guests whenever he went aboard his yacht – a practice his son observed [32]"really did render him the enjoyment which was proportional to its cost."

Eldridge Johnson's yacht was named for his mother
Caroline, who died in the 1870s.

In his retirement, Eldridge Johnson became one of the nation's most generous philanthropists. In 1929 he pledged an endowment of $800,000 to the University of Pennsylvania to establish what is now the school's Department of Biochemistry and Biophysics. And in 1932 he offered the use of his yacht, all 42 of its staff and an endowment of $50,000 to the Smithsonian Institution for a series of marine explorations of the tropical Atlantic.

The science portion of the Johnson-Smithsonian Expedition was directed by Dr. Paul Bartsch, the Smithsonian's leading authority on mollusks and deep-sea invertebrates. Bartsch brought along several other experts from the Smithsonian and related institutions. [33]

The *Caroline's* first-class cabins were occupied by Johnson's personal guest list,[34] which included Johnson's former business partner Leon Douglass, his wife, and their two very eligible and attractive daughters, Miss Ena Douglass and Miss Florence Douglass.

Eldridge Johnson and Dr. Paul Bartsch on the deck of the Caroline.

With all hands on board, the *Caroline* slipped from her moorings at the Brooklyn Naval Yard at 9:00 AM on January 23, 1933 and set sail under fair skies over calm seas for the lower latitudes. After a brief stop in Miami, she headed east into the Atlantic to anchor for a night at Nassau in the Bahamas – where one more distinguished guest came aboard to dine at the owner's table.

The Caroline at sea.

30

Intrepid

(1933)

The Caroline's stopover in the Bahamas was recorded in the *Nassau Daily Tribune* on January 26, 1933:

Oceanic Scientific Expedition Arrives In Nassau

Eldridge Johnson's Yacht *Caroline*
Equipped With Special Apparatus

The article describes Johnson's "$2,000,000 yacht," it's scientific mission, and the illustrious personnel onboard, including...

> **Dr. Townsend Brown, U.S. Naval Reserve, who is in charge of an electric sounding apparatus lent by the Navy Department.**

This is the first instance where Townsend Brown – officially a 'Seaman First Class' – is referred to in print as "*Dr.* Townsend Brown."

Despite listing every guest and staff member on the Expedition, the article in the *Tribune* does not record the one additional guest who dined aboard the *Caroline* during its stop in Nassau.

*

By the time it was acquired by RCA, the Victor Talking Machines Company owned subsidiaries on both sides of the Atlantic and Pacific. This global reach put Eldridge Johnson near the center of the most influential business and political circles in the world. Among his close contacts was a Canadian, operating mostly out of Britain in the 1930s, whose name was William Samuel Stephenson.

Like so many of the people who populate the Townsend Brown story, William S. Stephenson emerges from a misty nether world between Man and Myth. There are at least three published biographies[35] of the man, but the details of his life vary from volume to volume. They don't even agree on the date of his birth. As one biographer put it, "most of the information on Stephenson's life is bogus." The differing versions of Stephenson's story that emerged in the 1970s all served to support the legend – the fictional back-story that accompanies the kind of double life that William Stephenson led.

By most accounts, he was born William Stanger in 1897. At the age of four, when his widowed mother was unable to care for him, William was taken in by family friends Kristin and Vigfus Stephenson. There is no record of an official adoption, but young William Stanger became William Stephenson.

The boy demonstrated a photographic memory at an early age. He left school after the sixth grade and found work as a delivery boy for the Great North West Telegraph Company. He taught himself Morse Code and was promoted from delivering telegrams to actually keying them. Stephenson was still working for the Telegraph Company when the Great War broke out in 1914.

William S. Stephenson ca. 1918

In 1916, he enlisted in the 101st Battalion of the Winnipeg Light Infantry. After basic training at an icy camp near Winnipeg, Stephenson's unit was shipped to England aboard the *SS Olympic* (sister ship to the sunken *Titanic*). He arrived in July 1916, was sent directly to the front in France and barely survived a poison gas attack. He was sent back to England, where he was diagnosed as disabled for life.

Despite the dire prognosis, Stephenson recovered to the point of seeking his return to combat. When his doctors told him his lungs were too badly damaged for infantry duty, he asked if he could fly instead. His request was granted with a transfer to the Royal Flying Corps, which ignored Stephenson's medical record in order to fill their diminished ranks. He was given five whole hours of flight instruction and sent into the sky in what was generally regarded as the 'suicide service' – a testament to the number of pilots who never returned.

Instead of flying himself into an early grave, Stephenson distinguished himself, starting with his pursuit of Lothar von Ricthofen. While the rest of the RAF pursued Lothar's more famous and flamboyant brother – Manfred,

'The Red Baron' – Stephenson observed that Lothar was the more effective pilot, causing more damage by shooting down British observation balloons. In March of 1918, Stephenson observed a German Fokker execute one of Lothar's signature maneuvers, and "spun, dived, looped, and tried every trick" with his Sopwith Camel until his quarry was lined up in his sights. He fired his twin, through-the-propeller machine guns, and watched Lothar's plane spiral into a controlled crash in a thicket of brush and trees. Lothar never flew in combat again.

Depending on which account you go by, 'Billy' Stephenson shot down between twelve and twenty enemy aircraft, was awarded the Distinguished Flying Cross, and earned his superiors' special admiration for supplying "valuable and accurate information on enemy movements."

During a mission in July 1918, Stephenson took a bullet in his leg, survived the crash behind enemy lines and was taken prisoner. While incarcerated in the German POW camp at Holzminden, Stephenson befriended his captors and gathered valuable information. After two failed attempts, his third escape attempt succeeded, and he delivered to the Allied command the sort of detailed report for which he was making a name for himself.

Stephenson's report fell into the hands of Admiral Sir Reginald Hall – nicknamed 'Blinker' for a twitch that made one eye flicker like a marine signal beacon. Admiral Hall was the Director of British Naval Intelligence and a colleague and occasional drinking companion of a certain Winston Churchill. After reading Stephenson's report from behind the lines, Admiral Hall took the young pilot under his wing.

*

Military intelligence was not the only thing that Stephenson spirited out of that POW camp. According to one version of 'the legend,' Stephenson allegedly stole a new kind of can opener, a "twin handled, clamp-style" gadget that cut a smooth edge around the rim of the can.

What excited Stephenson about the can opener was not just the device's novelty, but the fact that it had been patented in Germany in 1915, after the start of the war – which meant that there were no patents for it in Britain, the U.S. or Canada. When he escaped from the POW camp, he smuggled that can opener out with him. When the war ended, he obtained patents for it in "every other country in the world" – or so the legend says.

After the war, Stephenson, still in his early twenties, started a company in Winnipeg with his friend Charles Russell to manufacture and sell the 'Kleen Kut' can opener. The firm also obtained licenses to market a variety of hardware, cutlery, and automobile accessories. But after an ill-conceived attempt at further expansion, the company faltered and filed for bankruptcy in 1922.

Stephenson left Canada and returned to Britain. Somehow, within months, according to one biographer, "the unsuccessful Winnipeg can opener salesman was being hailed as a 'brilliant scientist' by the London Daily Mail." Another newspaper story in mid-1923 heralded the arrival of "this young man to his Mother country from the far Canadian west, who in a remarkably short space of time has established himself as a brilliant scientist and a leader of industry. A rare combination."

There is no hard evidence that explains Stephenson's remarkable reversal of fortunes, only a suggestion between the lines of his various biographies that Stephenson returned to England to resume his relationship with Blinker Hall. He also joined forces with the British inventor T. Thorne Baker, who had achieved some success transmitting photographs over telephone lines. Stephenson and Baker upgraded the process into one that could transmit photos by wireless. In 1922, the *London Daily Mail* published the first photograph ever transmitted via wireless, by means of an apparatus devised by Stephenson.

William S. Stephenson with his wireless photo transmission device ca. 1930.

William Stephenson's patent on wireless photo transmission made him a millionaire before he was thirty. By the early 1930s, "he controlled a score of companies," which he managed from "an impressive office on St. James Street" in London and lived in a "house on fashionable New Cavendish Street. He also acquired a country squire's farm in the Chilterns," where he and his wife, the former Mary French Simmons, a tobacco heiress from Springfield, Tennessee, "entertained on a generous scale."

Like Eldridge Johnson, Stephenson's ascent afforded him easy access to the major business, social and political centers across Europe. During the late 1920s and early 1930s, Stephenson traveled extensively through Europe and North America. With his photographic memory hardened from years of military experience, he was among the first to observe the rise of militarism in Germany. He reported his findings to his friend Blinker Hall, who introduced him to the web of scientists and businessmen gathering around Winston Churchill in anticipation of the threats to come.

The evidence of an affiliation between William Stephenson and Eldridge Johnson is largely circumstantial, owing to their common international interests in the field of electrical communications. But knowledgeable sources[36] assert that William Stephenson dined with Eldridge Johnson and his guests aboard the *Caroline* while she was berthed in Nassau in January of 1933.

Given his own unique skillsets and insights, it would be equally unsurprising to learn that Townsend Brown was introduced to Stephenson, and drawn into whatever network of international scientific, business and political interests these titans of industry occupied the center of.

On January 30, 1933 – a few days after the Caroline steamed out of Nassau – Adolf Hitler walked into the office of Germany's president Paul von Hindenburg and assumed the office of Chancellor of Germany.

Another forty years would pass before the world learned of the wartime exploits of William S. Stephenson, Winston Churchill's master spy, the quiet Canadian on whom Churchill bestowed the code name 'Intrepid.' The intelligence operations that Stephenson spearheaded were instrumental in the Allies' victory in Europe.

But in December of 1964, a decade before the world ever heard of *A Man Called Intrepid*[37], William Stephenson invited a bearded, chestnut-haired college student to join him for an afternoon of sailing on Florida's Biscayne Bay.

31

Reflections on Biscayne Bay
(1964)

Our family dynamic changed radically when we lost my little sister in a swimming pool accident. No family should ever have to go through that. Dad was supposed to be watching her, but my brother and I felt the blame too. My Mother took that loss in the worst way. She blamed my Dad and she never got over it. After that summer there was never peace in my household.

I've often thought that if I had the power to alter the past, the one thing I would do is go back and save my sister. But then I realize that her death was the thing that started me on the road to being who I am…

– Morgan[38]

"Looking back," Morgan recalled, "it seems that Dr. Brown was surprised to see me when I first showed up on his doorstep, but maybe not entirely. It was hard to tell. He knew that Linda had decided to 'go in my direction' physically, and he didn't seem to have any objection to that. I guess that I made her happy, and that's what he wanted.

"Late at night in his lab he and I would talk, often past dawn, about his propulsion system and the possibilities for it. He talked often about the impossibly high voltage required to get the full effect. He described the challenges he faced with his work in Philadelphia and why he'd left the area so abruptly.

"And I confided my thoughts about becoming a spy. 'Dangerous business' was all he said."

"Now that I've had all these years to think about it, I don't know who was seducing whom. During the day, Linda and I were taking these side trips around Homestead, having a wonderful time with each other. She was like some kind of gift from the ocean. We swam once at the Venetian Pool in Coral Gables, while Dr. Brown had an appointment with 'some people.' I didn't realize at the time that he was setting up a meeting with one of the most influential men in my future life – Sir William.

"Not long into the visit this slightly built, white-haired gentleman visited the lab. He was accompanied by guys with sunglasses who were just 'there.' My nose was sniffing, 'danger, danger!' Who were these guys? Not one of them smiled at me when I walked past.

"Linda told me one afternoon when they were all there that her father wanted to see me at the lab, so off I went, a lion-shocked lamb, heading into the den.

"I knew right away from the deference that Dr. Brown showed his visitor that this man was important. His men were clean shaven, and suddenly I was very aware that my hair was long and I was sporting a full beard. Linda said it was sexy and that was cool, but I suddenly wished it was all gone.

"Dr. Brown showed a great deal of respect for this gentleman, and I could tell that the feeling was mutual. I was the only one that didn't have any kind of past history or standing. Sir William – I didn't know that was his name then – asked where I was going to school. When I mentioned that I'd be taking part in my school's work study program in New York City he seemed familiar with it. Now I realize the mark of a true gentleman, as he deliberately put me at ease.

"And then he then he turned to Dr. Brown and said, 'Tell you what. Let's show this young man a little bit of the Biscayne Bay!'"

"Dr. Brown took off like a shot. 'Great idea!' He caught Linda on the way out and said something like 'Sweetie, we'll be back after dark.' The scene still reminds me of a Chinese fire drill as we all cleared out of the lab and piled into the limo that was waiting, with Dr. Brown's Cadillac as the backup car. I am not even sure I had a chance to say goodbye to Linda, who was still standing there as we drove off.

"For several hours, it was just Dr. Brown and this gentleman and me day-sailing around Biscayne Bay. I hadn't ever done much sailing. I dug the tacking back and forth, and then out in the center of the Bay. Dr. Brown just let her rip and we took off. I'd never known quite that kind of thrill. And I could see they were enjoying my reaction. The whole time, the two of them laughed and enjoyed the wind and the salt in the air.

"It wasn't until much later that I realized that I was being vetted. I poured out all kinds of stuff about myself, just trying to hold up my end of the conversation. I told them about my family, my grades at school, cleaning stalls for my Dad's horses, running the tractor in the summer, my high-school wrestling and my introduction to martial arts at the local YMCA, being on the Chess Club at school, learning Russian from my Grandmother. Other than my experiences with the girls in my life, I told him just about everything.

"We returned to the marina at Coral Gables and left 'Mr. X' behind.

"As we got into the Cadillac for the drive back to Homestead, Dr. Brown said something to me that had as much of an impact as anything that was said or suggested that day. I remember *exactly* how he phrased it. He was speaking of

Linda when he said, 'She needs… not to know.' It wasn't 'Don't tell Linda.' It was, 'She *needs*… not to know.' "That was the first whiff I got of that this wonderful new opportunity, this exciting job that included travel and the hint of danger – was not going to be Linda's life also.

"At the end of the day, I was nearly wiped out mentally. But then I had to make things right with Linda. That was the most difficult – and most rewarding – part of one of the most interesting days I have ever spent.

"The next evening, or early morning – I wasn't getting much sleep on this trip! – I found Dr. Brown at his desk. By then he was making me feel welcome, as if in his mind he had already 'married me' to Linda and I was his son. I remember thinking how *weird* all that was. After that afternoon on Biscayne Bay, we started to cover more topics than our previous conversations had covered. And then he dropped a bombshell on me.

"He said, 'If it turned out that it would be possible to travel in time, what would you chose to do?'

"I'd go back and save my little sister."

"He nodded and, after a bit of a pause he said, 'But, if there are some natural rules against that, then what would you want to do?'

"All I could think to say was 'I'd help whoever I would be allowed to help – and enjoy the adventure.'

"Dr. Brown just smiled. I finally asked him, 'Is time travel possible?' and he very simply answered, 'Yes, I believe it is possible. In your lifetime.'

"Suddenly I was compelled to say, 'I want to do that. Is there a list?' I was half kidding, but only half.

"He was not kidding at all. 'You will be on that list, if you want to be,' he said, and when I looked him in the eye, I realized he was being dead serious.

"That was a life-changing moment. After that, there is no going home again."

32

Dredging The Depths

(1933)

Florence Douglass, the siren of the Caroline.

After her one night in Nassau, the *Caroline* steamed off to dredge the depths of the tropical Atlantic. Eldridge Johnson's son Fenimore reported that "useful observations began when Lt. Townsend Brown[39], U.S.N. put the sonic depth finder into operation."

Fenimore Johnson was an amateur oceanographer but cared little for the kind of aristocratic cruising that a long voyage aboard the *Caroline* offered. He described a long cruise on a big yacht[40] as "Nothing to do, all day in which to do it, and fifty people to do it for you."

Profoundly loyal to his father, 'Son Fen' spent the weeks prior to the departure helping Dr. Bartsch turn his father's luxury yacht into a research vessel – installing nets, spools of cable, and a crane to lower the dredge thousands of feet to the ocean floor. After supervising the outfitting, he realized that "there were many problems still to be solved." Concerned about the "great weights and strains which some of the gear" would place on the vessel, he "consented to join the expedition for the early part of it." He was soon to regret his decision because he "got stuck with the whole of it."

Fen's concerns were justified when the voyage started out on rough seas. Dr. Bartsch reported to the Smithsonian, "The *Caroline* encountered swells and winds that drove smaller vessels to harbor. We have lost more gear in this short interval than I have ever seen expended on any previous expedition."

Despite the "rough following seas," Eldridge Johnson's diary commends his yacht's seaworthiness, which he attributed to one of the *Caroline's* many state-of-the-nautical-arts features, her gyro stabilizer – a horizontally-mounted 20-ton wheel "spinning like a top" at 1,300 rpm, that kept the *Caroline's* roll and pitch to less than two degrees in most conditions. Johnson's diary recorded on January 31, that the expedition had "...lost all the nets but got fine specimens."

Townsend Brown (l) and Fenimore Johnson in
the radio room of the Caroline.

When Fenimore instructed the *Caroline's* Captain Andrew Peterson to "run day and night on a sounding survey of the Puerto Rican Deep, Lt. Brown, who was in charge of the sonic depth-sounding device, cheerfully sat and operated it for twenty-four hours straight."

Documents found in the Expedition's records attest to Eldridge Johnson's preoccupation with social protocols. In a pre-departure letter to Charles G. Abbott, the Secretary of the Smithsonian, Johnson asked about the status of the scientific personnel:

> **Are all of these people first class passengers? Would they dine with the owner? You have to be a careful on a yacht. There is the owner's dining room, which he and his guests use; the captain dines alone, unless he has guests; there is the officers' mess; the general crew, and there is also a special dining-room where valets, maids, and aides-de-camp dine.**

In the only photo of the owner's dining room, we see three guests who were not listed among Mr. Johnson's personal entourage. Closest to the camera is the only Naval personnel on the voyage, Townsend Brown – dressed in civilian clothes and being treated as one of the first-class passengers.

Just another evening of fine dining aboard the Caroline.

Also seated among those first-class passengers were Leon Douglass's attractive and eligible young daughters, Ena and Florence. Florence took a particular interest in the sonar operator on loan from the Navy and was photographed assisting him launch a weather balloon from the *Caroline's* afterdeck.

The expedition conducted most of its work during the daytime, anchoring each night in Puerto Rico's San Juan Harbor. The night of February 10th, the *Caroline* anchored in the lee of Mona Island – a flat, rocky outcropping some forty-two miles north of Puerto Rico that is considered the 'Galapagos of the Caribbean' for its diverse indigenous habitation. The morning of February 11, members of the scientific team along with both Ena and Florence Douglass, set off in the *Caroline's* launch to explore the island's white sand beaches.

If the photographic evidence of that landing party is any indication, Lt. Brown was not engaged in any scientific work. He and Florence had a fine time, swimming in the surf, beach combing and playing pirate, pretending to be ship-wrecked together on their desert island.

Florence's father had encouraged his pretty daughter to "talk to this young man and tell me what you think of him." After she had socialized with him above and below the decks of the *Caroline* and played pirate on Mona Island, Florence reported to her father [41] that "This Townsend Brown is a true gentleman, a man of honor and courage – and a man of his word."

Later, she told friends that she found him a brilliant and engaging conversationalist – and admitted that she was disappointed to learn that he was married.

When the voyage ended in early March, Townsend returned to Josephine and his duties at the Naval Research Laboratory. As he regained his footing ashore, the young scientist was simultaneously setting sail on his life's defining adventure: aboard the *Caroline* he was drawn behind the curtain of an international industrial intelligence initiative.

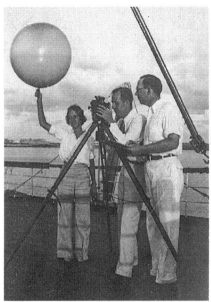

Florence Douglas (r) assists Seaman Brown (c) launching a weather balloon.

The Dread Pirate Brown takes a break from pillaging the beaches of Mona Island.

33

A Deeper Draft (Redux)
(Notes from the Rabbit Hole #7)

"It was much pleasanter at home," thought poor Alice, "when one wasn't always growing larger or smaller, and being ordered about by mice and rabbits. I almost wish I hadn't gone down that rabbit-hole – and yet – and yet – it's rather curious, you know, this sort of life!"

– *Lewis Carroll, Alice's Adventures in Wonderland*

President Woodrow Wilson was re-elected in 1916 partly on the promise that he would keep American boys out of the trenches of Europe.

That changed when Allied codebreakers deciphered the Zimmerman telegram.

In February 1917, Germany's Foreign Minister, Arthur Zimmerman, sent a coded telegram to the President of Mexico. Herr Zimmerman promised to return to Mexico those territories in Texas and California that had been annexed by the United States in the nineteenth century – after Mexico formed an alliance with Germany and the U.S. was defeated by their combined forces.

Zimmerman's telegram was transmitted through a relay station in Wales, from whence Blinker Hall and his team of codebreakers in 'Room 40' routinely intercepted international communications. It took more than a week to decrypt and translate the message, but on February 24, Britain's ambassador to the United States presented the document to Wilson. News of Zimmerman's telegram leaked to the American press, the tide of public opinion turned, and on April 6, 1917 – a month after Wilson's second inauguration – the United States Congress declared war on Germany.

The Assistant Secretary of the Navy – an ambitious young man named Franklin Delano Roosevelt – sailed to England, met with Blinker Hall, and observed first-hand the operations of British Naval Intelligence. By the end of the war, Roosevelt's Office of Naval Intelligence had its own network of agents that reached into Europe, Latin America and the Orient.

Six months after the Armistice in November 1918, the U.S. set up a new installation to eavesdrop on foreign diplomatic communications, under the direction of Herbert O. Yardley. Operating out of a brownstone in midtown Manhattan, Yardley's 'Black Chamber' was sanctioned by the U.S. State Department but operated so secretly that it could circumvent the Communications Act of 1912 – which stipulated harsh penalties for any interception of private communications.

Yardley's facility was so covert that when the administration of Herbert Hoover took over in Washington in March of 1929, the new Secretary of State, Henry Stimson, was not aware of its existence. Stimson was his boss, but Yardley kept it all a secret for several months. When Stimson finally learned of the Black Chamber, he ordered the operation dismantled, famously admonishing Yardley that "Gentlemen do not read each other's mail."

As the 1920s slipped into the 1930s, America's foreign policy apparatus became effectively deaf and blind. A similar vacuum formed in Britain, but when Blinker Hall retired from the Admiralty, he maintained a shadow network of businessmen, financiers, politicians, diplomats, and scientists. Public sentiment on both sides of the Atlantic weighed heavily against further cloak-and-dagger operations. But Hall knew – and his protégé William Stephenson agreed – that the channels had to be kept open.

In this vacuum between the World Wars, when governments' intelligence capabilities atrophied, private networks[42] formed to keep a finger on the pulse of international political and financial affairs – giving us the first real clue to what Linda Brown was thinking of when she spoke of a 'deeper draft vessel' during our first meeting in Las Vegas in the spring of 2003.

34

A Time of Peace, A Tug of War

(1933)

(l) Joseph T. Robinson (D-Arkansas), U.S. Senate Majority Leader 1933-1937; (r) Claude A Swanson, Secretary of the Navy 1933-1939.

Seaman Brown received his promotion to Lieutenant shortly after the voyage aboard the *Caroline*, but his status with the Navy became uncertain as soon as he returned to the NRL. He came ashore during the most difficult years of 1930s, when the NRL's budget had little room for the work that Brown wanted to resume – a dilemma which sparked a tug of war between the civilian and military authorities that oversaw the Navy.

On one side of the struggle was the Majority Leader of the United States Senate, Joseph Robinson, Democrat of Arkansas, who, for reasons unknown, intervened on Brown's behalf. On the other side was Secretary of the Navy Claude Swanson and various admirals, who insisted in that there were simply insufficient funds to continue Brown's tenure at the NRL. In early May, 1933, a memorandum directed to the attention of one Rear Admiral Henry Brisner insisted:

> **The Laboratory operating under reduced expenditures does not have sufficient funds to carry on all the work that they would like to do on strictly Navy problems [therefore] the Research Laboratory stated that they have no intention of requesting the recall to active duty or requesting the services of Mr. Brown at the laboratory.**

Secretary Swanson passed that memorandum on to Senator Robinson, adding in a cover letter addressed to "My Dear Joe,"

> After my telephone conversation with you, I directed that a full investigation be made into the recall to active duty of Mr. Thomas Townsend Brown. I informed those who made this investigation of your interest in Mr. Brown, and my desire to have your wishes carried out if possible.
>
> I enclose herewith a memorandum ... which fully explains itself.
>
> I am sure you will appreciate that it would not be proper to recall Dr. Brown to active service for the work referred to while we are preparing to furlough and dismiss regular and active officers in the Navy.

'Dear Joe' Robinson had not risen to Leader of the Senate Majority by taking "no" for an answer. On May 12, he wrote to Swanson again on Brown's behalf:

> The whole point in my suggestion has been overlooked or at least not taken into account. Brown is a genius. It is a misfortune to the Government of the United States to lose his services when the same can be secured by merely calling him into active duty.
>
> You will recall that great inventors have gone to other countries solely by reason of the fact that administrative officers did not possess the foresight or breadth of vision to secure the services of such men and they were compelled to secure recognition abroad.
>
> From time immemorial it has been the practice of both our Army and Navy to commit such blunders as that indicated in the memorandum.

Three days later, Secretary Swanson stood firm with 'Dear Joe':

> In view of your special interest in this young man and high esteem for his professional abilities, I have caused further investigation to be made as to whether it would not be possible to assign him to the desired duty.
>
> I am satisfied that this duty cannot be justified within the drastic cuts administered to the Naval establishment during the coming year.

The die was cast, so newly-minted-but-now-discharged Lieutenant Brown began preparing to take his experiments elsewhere. He wrote to the director of the NRL, recounting his contributions of time and materiel, and asking for the return of the equipment he had donated as well as new components he had built:

> During the period of 1 November 1932 to 31 January 1933 I was under contract to the Naval Research Laboratory to "investigate phenomena and application of electromagnetic reaction of fluids."

In pursuance of this investigation, special equipment was designed and built.

I am particularly interested and qualified in this field and am anxious to continue the investigation. The experimental apparatus is of little or no value outside of the use for which it is intended.

I respectfully request that the apparatus listed below be turned over to me until the research work is finished or until such time as its return to the Laboratory is requested:

1 electrostatic generator

2 electrostatic rotors with recording drums

1 electromagnetic speed indicator with cables

Lt. Brown is asking the Navy, "Can I have my stuff back?"

Unsaid is what he intends to do with it.

35

Never Heard of the Guy
(Notes from the Rabbit Hole #8)

"You may have noticed, I'm not all there myself."
— *Lewis Carroll, Alices Adventures in Wonderland*

The further I fell down the rabbit hole, the more frequently I described my task as writing "the biography of a man whose story could not be told." The quandary was never more apparent than when I corresponded directly with the Naval Research Laboratory.

In the family archives, I found correspondence between Brown and the NRL that began in 1931. Typical of those documents is the exchange between two high level officers cited in the previous chapter: One admiral insisting that Brown's work was indispensable at the NRL while another admiral was equally adamant that it was high time he serve on an actual boat.

In September 2004, I attached copies of those letters when I filed a Freedom of Information Act (FOIA) request through the NRL's website seeking "any and all information regarding the service of Thomas Townsend Brown at the Naval Research Labs between the years of 1932 and 1942 and possibly beyond."

Six weeks later, I received a one-page response from Richard L. Thompson, writing for the NRL's archives. One page was all it took for Mr. Thompson to say "We are unable to process your request; NRL has been unable to find any record of Thomas Townsend Brown, or any other rendering of that name."

Translation: "We've never heard of the guy."

Thompson's letter included instructions for filing an appeal through the office of the NRL's General Counsel.

I marched down to my neighborhood Kinko's and made copies of the twenty-some pages of correspondence between Brown and the NRL. On December 6, 2004, I sent my appeal with all the documentation to the General Counsel.

On December 21, 2004, I received another one-page letter, this time from William A. Molzahn, the Deputy General Counsel of the Department of the Navy, conveying the "final administrative adjudication" of my FOIA appeal:

> Upon review, I conclude that the search for the responsive records met the standard of reasonableness as set forth in Oglesby v. Department of Army, 79 F.3d 1172, 1185-7 (D.C. Cir. 1996).
>
> The NRL Records Manager conducted searches of both the laboratory research notebooks database and the NRL telephone directories from 1937 to 1944 without locating any information about Mr. Brown. After the appeal was received, the records you provided were reviewed but did not assist in locating information at the NRL about Mr. Brown.
>
> Accordingly, this letter constitutes final denial of your appeal by the designated appellate authority for this matter.

Translation: "We've never heard of the guy, and don't ask again."

I knew I was writing about an obscure twentieth century scientist, but this was getting ridiculous.

*

The task of retrieving Townsend Brown's comprehensive Naval records fell to Linda Brown, who, as next of kin, was entitled to whatever the National Archives held of her father's service records.

In April 2004, Linda received a thin report on Brown's service as an enlisted man, beginning with his enlistment as an apprentice seaman in September 1930 and describing his basic training at the Great Lakes Naval Station and subsequent promotion to Seaman First Class. Nothing new there, but that was just the 'rank and file' records. Linda filed another request for her father's records as a Naval *officer* from 1932 until 1942.

Another month passed before Linda received a thick pile of papers from the National Archives detailing the service of… the wrong guy. Instead of the records of Thomas Townsend Brown, we received the records of a Lt. Commander Townsend (n) Brown,[43] an Annapolis graduate and naval aviator who began active duty in 1937 and served until his honorable discharge in 1949. A charming, dedicated, and patriotic fellow, no doubt – but not the droid we were looking for.

I tried to follow up with several calls to the Archives that went unanswered for several weeks. Linda finally got a call from a supervisor named Mrs. Painter who told Linda, "The technician has been looking for the past five weeks and can't find anything."

Mrs. Painter added, "this is impossible, this can't happen." She then volunteered to "personally walk down to the archives and go through the files. He has to be there somewhere. This is very unusual, and very frustrating. This is a very unusual name, he ought to be right here – and he is not."

A couple weeks later Mrs. Painter called back. She had finally found what she called Brown's "personnel file."

"She made kind of an aside," Linda told me. "She asked, 'Who is Brian Parks?'"

Linda told Mrs. Painter, "I don't know."

And then, under her breath Mrs. Painter said, "Oh…that's another agency" – inferring that a researcher from another agency had gone through the files.

Linda asked her, "Is this something that just happened recently?"

"No," Mrs. Painter replied. "It was years ago."

Mrs. Painter told Linda that she would send what records she had found, adding a caveat:

"Understand," Mrs. Painter said, "there will not be anything in that record that refers to anything classified."

Linda asked, "Are you saying that if there is classified material in the file, or anything in the file that refers to classified material, then both the classified material and anything that referred to it…"

"Would be not there."

Translation: "We've never heard of the guy. If we have heard of the guy, we don't have any records. If we do have any records, anything that you really want to know is classified. And if it is classified, then we can't even tell you that it exists."

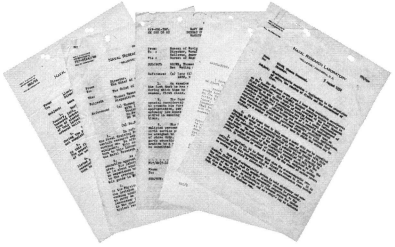

All these letters to-and-from the NRL but "We've never heard of the guy"?

36

Back to Ohio

(1934)

Father and son Joseph at Hawthorne ca. 1934

The impact of the Great Depression on the Brown family fortunes was reported as "a tragic accident" in the *Zanesville Times Recorder* on February 20, 1932:

> **Zanesville's business, industrial and commercial life was given one of its greatest shocks when news of the tragic death of Orville N. Townsend 72, retired capitalist and financier, became generally disseminated today. He plunged to his death at 11 o'clock this morning from a window of his office on the fourth floor of the First Trust and Savings bank building at Main and Fifth streets, alighting on his head.**

A forensic accounting of Uncle Orville's finances suggests a different likelihood for his alighting: When family patriarch T. B. Townsend died in 1916, his half-million dollar[44] estate was divided into equal shares between three heirs: Uncle Orville, Thomas Townsend's mother Mary Townsend Brown, and Aunt Hattie, wife of Rufus C. Burton. When Orville died in 1932, his estate listed assets of slightly more than $65,600 – and liabilities of nearly $63,000. In other words, at the time of his death, Uncle Orville – the man who had told 21-year-old Thomas

Brown in 1926 to "tie down to business or be a great disappointment to us all" – had dwindled his own estate down to a mere $2,600.

Granted, the man was 72 years old, had a history of asthma and a heart condition. But at least one eyewitness supported the *Times-Recorder*'s account that "Mr. Townsend had been leaning from the window of his office when he suddenly lost his balance" before landing headfirst on the pavement.

Into such diminished fortunes the next generation of Townsend Browns returned to Ohio in March 1934.

*

While Townsend was working at the NRL near Washington, Josephine was living at her in-laws' big house near Green Cove Springs in Florida. On his departure from the Navy, Townsend joined her there. The quality time they spent together is manifest in the birth of their first child, Joseph Townsend Brown, on March 13, 1934.

Joseph's birth certificate lists Adair Avenue in Zanesville as the parents' address. After her hospital stay, Josephine and the baby went back to Adair Avenue, where Josephine placed her 'El-Nido' teapot on a shelf under mother-in-law Mame's roof. The baby's father, meanwhile, looked for gainful employment in the area.

Lieutenant Brown was placed on inactive duty pending the creation of a new department in the Navy, the Gravity Section of the Hydrographic office – presumably an extension of the *S-48* expedition, which Lt. Brown would lead. When that opportunity was slow to materialize, he accepted a job with the state of Ohio, supervising a harbor protection project. His work kept him away through most of 1934 and '35, while Josephine tended to her baby and endured life as a new mother.

An opportunity to return the teapot to the cottage where Townsend and Josephine spent their wedding night arose in the spring of 1936. When the family of tenant farmers who occupied Hawthorne decided not to renew their lease, Townsend prevailed upon his father to let he and Josephine make something of the estate. The young couple transformed Hawthorne Farm into Hawthorne Pool, an upscale swim and social club for the affluent citizens of Zanesville.

The Host and Hostess of the Hawthorne Pool Club ca. 1936.

Throughout that spring, Townsend and Josephine got the property ready for summer. When relentless rains impeded the work, the *Zanesville Times Recorder* reported,

> **Mrs. Brown, with a determination that would not be drowned by more rain, climbed aboard the tractor and leveled the parking lot herself. She and her husband put their hands and heads to work, converted an old hen house into a charming party house seating 60, added shuffleboard, tennis courts and numerous other improvements to make the Hawthorne farm one of the most attractive swimming spots in central Ohio. Even cabins have been provided for those who like to spend a day or week there under the cool shade of the huge trees.**

*

This item appeared in the December 24, 1936, edition of the *Zanesville Times Recorder*:

Finger Amputated

Townsend Brown of 733 Adair Avenue underwent amputation of the second finger of his left-hand Wednesday afternoon in Bethesda Hospital following an accident which occurred at the Wise Foundry,

Machine & Supply Co. on North Sixth Street. Brown was having some work done in connection with an experiment when his finger was caught in a lathe operated by another man. He was removed to the hospital in the Dean ambulance.

*

Despite all the work that they put into developing the property, Hawthorne Pool closed its doors after just one season. The property was placed in receivership, and on May 6, 1937, the *Times Recorder* reported:

The old L.K. Brown property on Adams Lane, better known as the Hawthorne Pool, will be offered for sale on the club grounds at 2 o'clock Monday afternoon May 17. C. M. Gibson of No. 9 East Long Street, Columbus, receiver of the property, will be in charge of the sale.

Noting that "Last year the pool was conducted with success by Mr. and Mrs. Townsend Brown," the article lists various "property and chattels" appraised at more than $24,000 that were sold for only $21,000 to John K. Hislop of Columbus.

37

Too Big A Word

(1965)

As the Virginia mountains began to thaw in March of 1965, Linda's classmates at Southern Sem were making arrangements for spring break. Some would head for the beaches and boys in Florida; others headed for home and hearth, to friends and family.

Linda received several invitations to join friends in places like Fort Lauderdale and Palm Springs. But she had only one destination in her mind, and it wasn't a place. It was a person. Her parents' hometown may not have had much to offer in the way of beaches or sun, but it had one distinctive merit: it was in the same state where Morgan was at school.

Linda found another classmate who lived in Zanesville. She called her mother in Florida and mentioned how convenient it would be to catch a ride and visit with Grandmother Beale and Aunt Sally, Josephine's mother and sister. Josephine thought that was a terrific idea. The conversation then turned to some discussion of Townsend's lingering difficulties with the firm he'd been working with in Philadelphia, and the prospect of a new organization forming in the Bahamas in the summer, but Linda wasn't thinking that far ahead.

Shortly after Linda returned to her room, the hall phone rang again. When the girl who was on phone duty knocked on Linda's door, "she sounded surprised that there was another call for me. Unlike the other girls on our floor, I was not one to use the phone often. And suddenly I had two calls in one night."

Linda made the long trek down the creaking hardwood floor to the phone, wondering what Josephine might have neglected to mention. She sat down on the hard wooden chair with a curious "Hello?"

Her heart skipped when she heard Morgan's voice. "Hello there."

"I'm at a loss for words," Linda said softly.

"I know what you mean," Morgan said with a soothing chuckle on the other end of the line. "I'm feeling the same way. Don't worry though. I have a sack full of quarters."

"We could talk until dawn," Linda said.

"That's been done before," Morgan replied.

When the call ended – well before dawn – Linda was amazed that her plan had fallen into place: Morgan would meet her in Zanesville at the end of the month.

*

Linda stayed at her Grandmother Beale's home and spent some time with her Aunt Sally. But her mind drifted, recalling "the feel of Morgan's skin on mine.... the sound of his voice... how much I just wanted to be with him, without anyone else to think about or consider."

Morgan's part of the plan included transporting some furniture to Zanesville in his brother's pickup truck. In a letter to Linda, he promised to pick Linda up at her grandmother's house "in the early afternoon – so that we can spend some time together without causing a moral outrage."

The truck full of furniture proved useful as the young couple checked into a motel on the outskirts of town. The clerk behind the desk looked Morgan straight in the eye, and with a voice of parental authority said, "You both look pretty young to me. How do I know you two are really married?"

Morgan motioned to the clerk to join him near the office window and pointed at the loaded pickup truck in the parking lot.

"See that?" Morgan asked, "what single guy would have a ride like that?"

The clerk apologized and handed Morgan the key.

"Oh, you are so bad," Linda giggled as Morgan slipped the key into the lock.

"No," Morgan replied, "I'm not bad. I just get what I want."

*

Linda had promised her grandmother she'd be home by 9:00 PM. By 8:30, the domestically camouflaged pickup was parked outside the house, and Linda felt the time slipping away.

"I had been studying Morgan's face in the darkness," Linda wrote, "trying to form the words that I had been wanting to say since our first kiss back at Ashlawn. Suddenly the words just spilled out.

"Morgan, can I tell you that I love you – or do I have to keep hiding it?"

Morgan looked at Linda for a long time, his eyes darting feverishly around her face, avoiding her eyes.

"No, you don't have to hide it," Morgan said, kissing Linda gently on the lips. "But 'love,' is too big a word for me..."

"Poor boy," Linda said faking a laugh, "a college student and still all those big words are beyond his comprehension!"

Linda leaned over and gave him a "a really good kiss" – one that she wanted to make sure he would remember. When their lips parted, Linda looked Morgan in the eye and said firmly "Good night. See you in Nassau."

In the month that followed, Morgan and Linda exchanged a flurry of letters and phone calls in what Morgan would later refer to as the 'Do You Love Me? Panic of '65' – Linda seeking verbal reciprocation, Morgan just unable to form the words she wanted to hear.

"The whole thing just blew up in my face," Morgan recalled. "I realized that I was going to have to make some kind of commitment. She was asking for some kind of assurance that I was as emotionally involved as she was. But I just couldn't answer her. I was afraid of losing control of my life. We would have split up if she had insisted on an answer. But what I was feeling and what I could admit to were two different things."

The panic eased when Morgan confessed in one letter that ignoring the impasse "would have meant losing you…"

As she read his words, Linda savored Morgan saying, in his own way, what she longed to hear. Even if Morgan could never say "I love you" it was enough to know that he never wanted to lose her.

"By summer," Linda said, "we had put all of this behind us and it just seemed that we just folded into each other's arms. No questions. No demands."

Another decade would pass before Linda recognized in herself the same qualities that enabled Josephine to stay with her ever moving and frequently absent husband.

38

Parallel Lives

(1965)

Ilya Tolstoy, grandson of War And Peace author Leo.

In the summer of 1965, Morgan hitch-hiked to Homestead again.

"We had a wonderful visit," Morgan recalled. "We were both outrageously in love. The question she asked when we were in Zanesville scared the bejeezus out of me, and I had back-pedaled like a champ. She hadn't heard exactly what she wanted to hear, but by the time summer rolled around we were both a little gun-shy about broaching the subject again. I knew that Dr. Brown and Josephine had accepted me – or at least, had accepted their daughter's decision to go in my direction."

Morgan also knew – from the moment back in December when he'd stepped off the sailboat on Biscayne Bay and Dr. Brown told him that "Linda needs…. not to know" – that he and Linda Brown would be living parallel lives that would truly converge only in their hearts.

Morgan spent plenty of time with Townsend in the Remote Lab, "talking about his loudspeaker array and what it was really capable of, and the role of this 'organization' that he said was shielding certain aspects of his work."

After Morgan had been in Homestead for a few days, Townsend invited Morgan and Linda to join him on a business trip to St. Augustine. The three of them piled into the top-down Cadillac and made the scenic drive up Florida's Atlantic coast, from Homestead to Marineland of Florida, 'the world's first oceanarium.'

Long before Disney World drew all of Florida's theme-park traffic to Orlando, Marineland was Florida's most popular tourist destination. The founders of 'Marine Studios' – established in 1938 to serve the motion picture industry – were an unlikely quartet with backgrounds in adventure, filmmaking and privilege: W. Douglas Burden and his cousin Cornelius Vanderbilt Whitney were descendants of the Vanderbilt dynasty; Sherman Pratt was heir to one of the founders of Standard Oil; and Count Ilya Tolstoy was the grandson of the iconic Russian novelist Leo Tolstoy. Though a pioneering attraction in its heyday, by the mid-60s the park's glory days were well behind it.

The trio from Homestead arrived at Marineland in time for a late lunch. While sitting at a patio table, Linda recalled, "This man just walked up. He already had a sandwich, so he just sat down with us and started talking with Dad like they were old friends."

The surprise lunch guest introduced himself as one or the park's founders.

"Ilya Tolstoy," he said, extending a hand to Morgan.

"That's certainly an illustrious name," Morgan said.

"Indeed," the man said. "My grandfather."

After a bit more small talk around the table, Townsend made a suggestion. "Morgan here has been studying Russian for a couple of years. Maybe he could put some of that to use?"

Tolstoy nodded, and suddenly Morgan found himself conversing in Russian with the grandson of the author of *War and Peace*.

"It sounded to me," Linda recalled, "like the first couple of sentences were chit-chat. Then all of a sudden, the dialog took on a very menacing tone. I couldn't understand what they were saying, but from their body language I could tell that it was not a friendly discussion and it made me very uncomfortable."

Townsend leaned over to Linda and whispered, "let's go for a walk."

"When we got back, the entire attitude had changed," Linda said. "They were laughing and I could tell Morgan was elated."

Morgan had just passed another test.

*

Two days later, Townsend and Josephine and Morgan and Linda boarded a chartered Grumman 'Flying Goose' seaplane for the short flight to Nassau for what Linda thought was just another day's pleasure trip.

After the seaplane docked in Nassau, a private car took the party to lunch at the historic Graycliffe Hotel. In its prior life, the tropical Victorian mansion was the winter home of Mr. and Mrs. Izaak Walton Killam – a Canadian financier who built a fortune from wood products and hydroelectric plants throughout Canada and South America. Killam was believed to be the richest man in Canada – and was a good friend of Sir William Stephenson.

"For Stephenson's group," Morgan said, "the Graycliffe was the command center where important men gathered and smoked fine cigars" and played a free ranging version of a card game called Russian Bank while conducting their business.

To Linda, the Graycliffe was just an elegant hundred-year-old hotel with a fabulous buffet. As they finished their meal a distinguished looking gentleman, an attorney named Peter Graham, approached the table, at which point Townsend turned to the girls and, gesturing toward Morgan said, "will you ladies excuse us?"

Townsend and Morgan went with Mr. Graham to downtown Nassau, to a place called the Rootes Building – named for Lord William Edward Rootes, an inventive and acquisitive soul who turned his father's bicycle shop in Kent, England into an automotive empire that included the Hillman, Humber, Talbot and Sunbeam marques. Over the course of World War II, the company converted its operations to the manufacture of tanks and aircraft engines, supplying Britain with 14% of its bombers, 60% of its armored cars, 35% of its scout cars, 50,000 aero engines and 300,000 bombs.

"And that's just what they were doing on the surface..." Morgan said.

At the Rootes Building, Morgan had his second encounter with Sir William Stephenson. Morgan expected a long and arduous interrogation, but Stephenson asked Morgan only one question.

"What would you do if you found yourself in a life and death situation? Would you be able to draw and fire?'"

"I would do whatever it takes to stay above ground," Morgan quickly replied.

In the years to follow, whenever their paths crossed again, Sir William would greet his young apprentice by saying, "Still above ground, I see..."

Before summer's end, Morgan was offered a job. "I was shocked," Morgan said. "I would be an 'international security agent' based out of Nassau, New York, Philadelphia, Boston and San Francisco. They gave me a chance to consider, but the offer was contingent on passing muster with somebody in Boston."

"If I cleared that hurdle and still wanted the job, I'd report to a place called Camp Peary. That's the training facility the CIA calls 'The Farm.' I was going to train alongside other CIA recruits, but would not actually work for the Agency. The training couldn't start for almost a year, which was how long it would take to get my affairs in order, which meant disengaging from the rest of my life as I had known it."

The foundation for that understanding was laid, "When Ilya Tolstoy and I first started speaking to each other in Russian – the part of the conversation that Linda overheard and found 'menacing' – he was making it perfectly clear to me what was at stake."

"You will be offered an opportunity," Tolstoy told Morgan, "that will change your life. But it will be a life-long commitment. You must either commit yourself to this opportunity now or walk away now – because if you try to walk away later, somebody will kill you."

*

After the meeting at the Rootes building, Townsend and Josephine flew back to Florida on the seaplane. Morgan and Linda stayed overnight in Nassau, "doing touristy things," Linda remembered, "finding secluded beaches and marveling at the warm, pink, sand beneath our toes. We stayed up all night, wandering the streets and the beaches. And we talked about everything." They flew back to Florida together the following afternoon.

Morgan knew he had only a few more days before he'd have to hitchhike back to school in Ohio. "Once Linda was asleep, I would slip over to the lab to join Dr. Brown. He encouraged me to accept the offer. He said I had the right temperament for it, and that I was sorely needed. But he also said that it was something that only I could decide.

"And I tried to fathom how any of this was going to work with Linda. I envisioned going off and doing my secret agent thing for weeks at a time, and then Linda was just going to be happy to see me come home. I hadn't figured yet that 'Linda needs… not to know' actually translated into 'You have to walk away. It's part of the job.'"

On the day of Morgan's departure, Josephine found him rolling up his sleeping bag and slipping things into his duffel.

"Are you going to marry Linda?" Josephine asked.

Morgan kept stuffing things in his bag. Maybe he could find the answer for Josephine's question there.

"Well," Morgan said, "If I were to get married, I would marry Linda."

"If you're going in that direction," Josephine said quietly, referring to the offer from Nassau, "then you have to let Linda go. You have to break it off with her."

39

Remember, Dear...

(1937)

Joseph Townsend Brown, 2 years old in 1936

Townsend Brown's annual Navy Reserve Fitness Report, filed in July 1937, shows that he was dividing his time between two addresses: 900 19th Street NW in Washington, D.C., and 733 Adair Avenue in Zanesville.

While still living part-time under her mother-in-law's roof, Josephine never faltered in her conviction that she was married to "a rare force of nature." And Townsend knew that he could trust Josephine with the mysteries that nagged his soul. The question now was, just how much could he confide about the clandestine world he was slipping into?

In later years Townsend would sometimes say with a grin, that he "got her young and trained her." When the laughs subsided, Josephine would smile slyly and add, "Remember, Dear, you will always have me!"

So, what are we to make of Petition #29634, filed on September 10, 1937, in the Court of Common Pleas of Muskingum County Ohio, in which Josephine attests that her husband...

...has been guilty of gross neglect of duty toward this plaintiff in that he now refuses to maintain a place where they might reside and live together as husband and wife and has advised her that he is no longer desirous of continuing any of the marital relations or duties and refuses to perform same.

Wherefore plaintiff prays that she may be divorced from said defendant, that she may be granted custody of the minor child of the plaintiff and defendant herein, and for such other and further relief to which this plaintiff may be entitled.

A subsequent filing grants Josephine's divorce from Townsend Brown on December 3, 1937.

The *Zanesville Times Recorder* reported that in the fall of 1938, recent divorcé Mrs. Josephine Beale Brown served on the Bethesda Hospital Junior Assembly Dance Committee. The following year she chaired the hospital's Junior League. In late 1939 she served on a committee to organize a benefit card party for the Junior League, then chaired the League's New Year's Eve Ball. An article in April 1940 said that "a large contingent of prominent Zanesville citizens attended the Jorg Fasting Annual Dance program in Columbus, Ohio" and among the mentioned guests were Mr. and Mrs. Lewis Brown and their ex-daughter-in-law Mrs. Josephine Beale Brown.

None of the printed accounts mention a Mr. Brown.

That her parents had been divorced came as a complete surprise when Linda Brown first learned of it in the spring of 2006.[45] For all the years that she had spent sharing confidences with her mother, Josephine had never said anything about having been divorced in 1937.

"The wagging tongues of Zanesville would have zeroed in on mother," Linda said. "I think that picture of Joseph sitting on the nail keg was probably taken around the time that Mom and Dad divorced. I can hear Aunt Sally now, the 'Tsk, tsk, isn't it a shame. What kind of Mother is she? And the little boy cried...' Divorce was failure and a scandal in those days."

After learning a family secret that had been hidden for more than sixty years, Linda pondered the parallels with her own experience.

"Did Stephenson tell Dad what Morgan was told?" Linda wondered. "Cut away from every social situation? Did Mom and Dad have to give each other up? Was it a requirement that they end their marriage, or was it something that Dad staged for Mom's protection? Did she see a similar pattern ahead for Morgan and me? And, even if it had been possible for us to somehow be together, what kind of personal life would that have been?"

*

In January of 1938, Brown pooled what remained of his family assets into the "Townsend Brown Foundation" – a non-profit organization named not for himself but in honor of his parents' families' surnames, 'Townsend' and 'Brown.'

Writing on Naval Research Laboratory stationery on March 22, 1938, Brown approached the Board of Trustees of Denison University in Granville, Ohio with a recap of the work he'd been doing at the NRL, some of which went with him to Zanesville:

> **Expensive instruments were constructed at the Laboratory and operated over a considerable period of time. The observations indicated the presence of an external (perhaps sidereal) effect. The results were so encouraging that decision was made to extend the investigation to a field station some distance west of Washington.**
>
> **Since no appropriations were available for the rent of space at a field station, I offered to provide suitable space rent free at my home in Zanesville.**

The Navy had given him the gear, but by 1938 the family's financial situation was such that the home was put up for sale. Brown wrote to Denison to ask if the University would house his instruments.

> **In casting about for desirable space, it occurred to me that the constant temperature vault at Barney Science Hall would indeed be an ideal location to continue the observations.**
>
> **Fortunately, thru the cooperation of the Townsend Brown Foundation, a non-profit Ohio corporation for the promotion of scientific research, financial assistance is available. Funds can be employed to cover costs of reconditioning the space, installing instruments, for the payment of rent, charges for electric service, technical assistance and other maintenance items.**

Brown seems to be saying on the one hand, "we have to sell the family home," but on the other hand, "we've got enough money to pay the expense of moving and housing this equipment." Perhaps the real reason Brown is casting about for "desirable space" is found in his Navy records describing his activities during the 1930s:

> **Since leaving the Naval Research Laboratory I have continued independently a pure research problem relating to the isolation and**

measurement of an apparently new-found radiation from space. Because of pronounced maximum intensity at 16h Sidereal Time it has been named Sidereal[46] radiation. The investigation appears to be of considerable value[47] to science.

Brown was investigating the anomalous fluctuation he detected in his Gravitator devices, and he believed the source of those fluctuations was a form of radiation coming from deep space, ergo "Sidereal Radiation[48]."

Nevertheless, the reply from Denison University's Board of Trustees declined Mr. Brown's generous offer of exotic equipment and the funds necessary to install and operate it.

40

Golden Galleon

(1938)

The Brooklyn-class cruiser U.S.S. Nashville, Lt
Brown's home-at-sea in the summer of 1938

In March of 1936, Hitler scrapped the Treaty of Versailles when he sent an occupying force into the Rhineland, the area along Germany's border with France, which had been established as a demilitarized zone.

In Britain, First Lord of the Admiralty Sir Winston Churchill turned to his friend William Stephenson, who began supplying intelligence gleaned from his business activities on the continent. When Stephenson advised Churchill that Hitler's military expenditures were approaching the equivalent of a billion pounds sterling, Churchill began organizing opposition in Parliament to the appeasement policies of then Prime Minister Neville Chamberlain – making Churchill one of the first to sense what he would later call 'The Gathering Storm.'

*

Now divorced, Townsend Brown returned to his other first love, the U.S. Navy. Still on inactive duty with the Naval Reserve, he learned in April 1938 that he was eligible for promotion to full Lieutenant. He submitted an application, received his promotion, volunteered for sea duty and was assigned to spend the summer on a newly commissioned cruiser, the USS *Nashville*.

Lieutenant Brown stepped aboard the *Nashville* for her shakedown cruise through familiar waters in the Caribbean, where he performed "special duty in

[the] Fire Control and Radio Divisions.[49]" In August, the *Nashville* embarked on her maiden voyage across the Atlantic for a 'goodwill visit' to European ports including Cherbourg, France and Portsmouth, England.

Of the voyage, Brown wrote:

> **Chamberlain was trying to stop Hitler. We visited Stockholm, Sweden and Gothenburg, Germany. We listened to gunfire of Germans at practice getting ready for World War II. We were exposed to the German Navy while we were in the Baltic Sea, but no incidents occurred.**

The *Nashville* steamed on to Portsmouth, where Brown observed an unusual dockside activity:

> **Before we left Portsmouth, we loaded $50-million worth of gold bullion from the Bank of England that arrived shipside in three garbage trucks. No escorts, motorcycles, or convoy. We had it carried aboard and placed in the magazines of the ship. It was in ingots, encased in wooden boxes; each gold ingot in a wooden box with numbers boldly stamped on each box, each box worth a quarter-of-a-million, and weighing so much it was all one man could do to carry it.**
>
> **One man stood at the foot of the gangway, making entries in a ledger as each box was unloaded from the trucks. Another man with similar ledger waited at the head of the elevator, which lowered the gold into the magazine. These two ledgers naturally had to check. The gold was consigned to the Chase Manhattan National Bank of New York.**

How did a Lieutenant who was officially assigned to the 'Fire Control and Radio Divisions' know exactly what was in those 200 unmarked crates – where it came from, and where it was going?

*

Lieutenant Brown left one other record of his voyage aboard the Nashville – a bit of verse entitled *A Sailor's Life*[50] that includes these reflections on his true feelings for Josephine:

> **There is only one I will not leave behind...**
> **she cannot be here now**
> **but will sail with me later**
> **We will stake our lives on a compass true**
> **and we will make our home on this wild bounding Blue...**

Her love and faith I mean to share
but her future dreams I care! I care!
Where to place the blame for what may be a great loss?
I cannot say
perhaps the blame was before my day
Like an act of God in one respect
In another a random coin toss.

Returning stateside at the end of September, Lieutenant Brown submitted *A Sailor's Life* for publication in the service periodical *Our Navy*. In his submission, he lists his return address as

USS *Nashville*,

Navy Yard Brooklyn, NY.

A few weeks later, Brown wrote to *Our Navy* again, to order a subscription to the magazine. This time, he lists his address as...

T. Townsend Brown

Physics Department

University of Pennsylvania,

Philadelphia, Pa.

...which is the first indication we have of where his equipment may have gone when the offer to Dennison University was declined.

*

British Prime Minister Neville Chamberlain returns from Munich on September 30, 1938 to declare "Peace in our time."

Lieutenant Brown's tour of duty aboard the USS *Nashville* ended on September 30, 1938 – the same day Neville Chamberlain returned to London after conferring with Adolph Hitler in Munich.

As he stepped off the plane in London, Chamberlain famously waved before the waiting throng the following statement:

> **We, the German Führer and Chancellor, and the British Prime Minister, have had a further meeting today and are agreed in recognizing that the question of Anglo-German relations is of the first importance for our two countries and for Europe.**
>
> **We regard the agreement signed last night and the Anglo-German Naval Agreement as symbolic of the desire of our two peoples never to go to war with one another again.**

Returning to the Prime Minister's residence at 10 Downing Street in London, Chamberlain read the statement again to a cheering crowd, this time adding,

> **My good friends this is the second time in our history that there has come back from Germany to Downing Street peace with honor. I believe it is peace in our time.**

Which would have been true, if by "our time" Chamberlain meant "less than a year."

On the first of September in 1939, Adolph Hitler launched his blitzkrieg into Poland. When the British and the French honored their alliance with the Poles and declared war on Germany, Europe became engulfed its second World War.

The initial invasion was followed by eight months of relative calm. Some in Britain believed that their government had conjured up a 'Phoney War,' but those with foresight used the period to marshal resources at home and abroad. For several years already, William Stephenson – in league with Winston Churchill's shadow government in London – had been building a network through which he folded is private resources into the British intelligence community.

The calm ended in the spring of 1940, when Hitler launched invasions into Denmark and Norway. Another German blitzkrieg slammed into the low countries and spread into France. Neville Chamberlain resigned in May, Winston Churchill became Prime Minister of Great Britain, and Stephenson's nascent network went into overdrive.

In *The Quiet Canadian*[51], Stephenson biographer Montgomery Hyde writes,

> **Stephenson traveled to America ostensibly as a businessman promoting the interests of his various companies. His secret instructions were explicit but limited to furthering Anglo-American**

co-operation in one specific field. He was required to establish relations on the highest possible level between the British Secret Intelligence Service (S.I.S.) and the U.S. Federal Bureau of Investigation.

At the time, the FBI was the closest thing America had to a unified intelligence agency. Stephenson met with the Bureau Director J. Edgar Hoover, but there was little Hoover could offer: his hands were tied by an official US policy of neutrality with regard to the hostilities in Europe.

The meeting with Hoover was strictly perfunctory. The important communications were conducted through back channels with President Franklin Roosevelt, who, according to Hyde,

> **...welcomed the idea enthusiastically, while the fact that it had to be kept from even the State Department provided a striking illustration of the strength of American neutrality during this period.**

With Roosevelt's quiet consent – and without J. Edgar Hoover's knowledge – William Stephenson began laying the groundwork for an intelligence network unlike anything the world had ever seen.

41

Shadow Trails
(Notes from the Rabbit Hole #9)

> "But I don't want to go among mad people," Alice remarked.
>
> "Oh, you can't help that," said the Cheshire Cat: We're all mad here. I'm mad, you're mad."
>
> "How do you know I'm mad?" said Alice.
>
> "You must be," said the Cat, "or you wouldn't have come here."
>
> *— Lewis Carroll, Alice's Adventures in Wonderland*

Once Townsend Brown stepped off the yacht *Caroline* in 1933, his life began to fade into the shadows. After 1937, Townsend and Josephine's divorce left two shadow trails. Like outlaws in a black-and-white Hollywood western, they split up in order to make their trail harder to follow.

We know where Townsend went. He re-upped with the Navy, sailed off to Europe, and as a mere Lieutenant witnessed the covert loading of $50 million in gold bullion into the cargo holds of the USS *Nashville*. In those shadows there is a connection between that gold shipment and Lieutenant Brown's mailing address in care of the Physics Department of the University of Pennsylvania.

Elsewhere in those shadows, The University's Department of Biochemistry and Biophysics became home to the Eldridge Reeves Johnson Research Foundation, which since 1929 has awarded fellowships "for adventurous and innovative research in structural biology."

Corroboration is found in Brown's Annual Fitness Report, filed June 10, 1939:

Since being detached USS *Nashville* on Sept 30, 1938, I have been engaged in building and installing a new sidereal radiation recorder in the Physics Department University of Pennsylvania, and in computing the records for 1937 and 1938.

Little more is known of what became of the equipment, or the data it generated. When he did refer to it, Morgan would only speak of 'stuff,' and say that 'stuff' went in a couple of different directions once it left the University.

*

In the two years following her divorce, Josephine's shadows show up at 4447 Greenwich Parkway in the fashionable Georgetown section of Washington, DC – not far from the C&O canal that runs parallel to the east bank of the Potomac River. I was told:

> **The house that Josephine moved to was arranged for her by Stephenson himself. She worked directly for him, or more precisely, for his executive secretary, who ran a group of women as couriers from New York to Washington. Josephine was one of them. Later, she joined a secretarial pool, again directly under that lady's supervision.**

"That lady," was Evelyn McBarnet, a subordinate to Stephenson's executive secretary, Grace Garner. Though it merits little mention in any of his published biographies, as his network expanded, Stephenson hired a large number of women who served not only in the traditional support roles, but also as couriers, liaisons, and, ultimately, as operatives in the field.

That Josephine worked for McBarnet, who worked closely with Stephenson, is the only evidence we have that connects Josephine directly to Stephenson apart from her (then ex-) husband. We will never be able to prove that Josephine herself was in league with Stephenson, but we do know what initially attracted Townsend to his future wife: She could keep secrets.

The last years of the 1930s find Josephine ferrying secret documents back and forth to New York and Washington, DC, where she had at least one secret of her own: clandestine meetings on the banks of the Potomac with a certain Lieutenant in the United States Navy.

Josephine in Washington, D.C. ca. 1940.

42

Your First Lesson

(1965)

Schlachtschiff Tirptz in 1942.

When Morgan left Florida in the summer of 1965, after his encounters with Ilya Tolstoy in St. Augustine and William Stephenson in Nassau, "I basically packed my old life up and never went back to it. I was given an address in Boston and told to expect to stay several weeks. 'Training,' it was called. A special school. I had visions of some kind of training camp, with others. I knew a little about the camp where CIA officers were trained, and I figured I was going someplace like that.

"When I got to the address in Boston, I was the only one. It was just me and this short, red-headed Irishman. He introduced himself as Mr. O'Riley – I never did learn his first name – and told me in no uncertain terms that he was going to be giving me his full attention. I didn't realize until later how dangerous that could be."

*

Like all the people Morgan met during his vetting and training, O'Riley had his own history as a soldier, a sailor and a spy.

Desperate to escape his hard-scrabble Irish roots, O'Riley lied about his age to enlist with the British Navy and volunteered for a top-secret operation. "They were looking for smaller guys who were strong," he recalled. "I fit the bill. I'm pretty sure 'expendable' was one of the qualifications, too."

O'Riley was assigned to a secret mission to deploy small submarines to take on the mightiest ships of the German fleet. "The crews were assembled and trained in Scotland," O'Riley said. "They had only one question when we got there: 'Do you swim well?' Naturally, I lied about that, too.

"When they finally showed us our boats, I started to think again. They were these tiny, bathtub-sized submarines. And we were supposed to go after German battleships. In a fucking submerged bathtub! The entire sub weighed less than a German battleship's anchor. When we went out on trial runs, we came back drenched, half drowned. Even on the surface, the damned things sweated so much that we had to wipe the bulkheads down."

O'Riley's doubts persisted until he and his crew mates learned the target of their mission: the *Tirpitz* - the battleship that Churchill called 'The Beast.'

Like her sister ship the *Bismarck*, the *Tirpitz'* mere appearance was a threat to the Allies' supply lines. After the *Bismarck* was sunk in the spring of 1941, Churchill turned his sights on the *Tirpitz*, which patrolled the coast of Norway in defense of Hitler's misplaced conviction that any invasion of the continent would come through Scandinavia.

Of the *Tirpitz*, Churchill wrote in the winter of 1942, "The destruction or even crippling of this ship is the greatest event at sea at the present time. No other target is comparable to it. The whole strategy of the war turns at this period on this ship. I regard this matter of the highest urgency and importance."

O'Riley said, "When we heard that we would be going after the one battleship that Churchill himself had called the biggest threat to Britain, we thought to ourselves, 'Maybe that would be worth it.' That's youth for you."

The dreadnought Churchill wanted sunk was one of the largest warships ever launched. Nearly a thousand feet long and displacing 50,000 tons, the *Tirpitz* could steam at speeds up to thirty knots despite her foot-thick armor. She carried eight 15" guns, twelve 6" guns, almost a hundred smaller guns, eight torpedo tubes, six aircraft, and a crew of 2,400 sailors.

Against all this tonnage and firepower – which had already withstood five attacks by RAF bombers – the British Navy proposed to launch a fleet of tiny submarines manned by crews of water-logged sailors who could barely swim.

An 'X-Craft' midget submarine undergoing sea trials ca. 1943.

Called 'X-Crafts,' the midget subs' mission was to maneuver close enough to the *Tirpitz* to place explosive charges alongside her hull. That was the easy part of the mission. The hard part was getting the leaky subs into the same ocean as their target. To find the *Tirpitz*, the six miniatures had to be towed by a conventional submarine – while both were submerged – from their secret base in Scotland toward the coast of Norway.

Each X-Craft had two crews. An 'operational crew' of four men responsible for the actual mission had the luxury of riding on the big subs during the crossing. O'Riley was assigned to one of the smaller 'passage crews' – assuming the arduous task of holding the little submersibles together while they were towed beneath 1,500 miles of the frigid Norwegian Sea.

The X-Craft were not designed to spend more than a few hours submerged, but the passage took more than a week in September 1943 – the little subs surfacing every six hours for fresh air. One of the subs and its three-man crew were lost when its tow cable snapped. Another had to be cut loose when it became ensnared in mine cables while enroute.

The engine room of an X-Craft midget submarine.

Once they found the *Tirpitz* in Norway's Alta Fjord, one of the crews maneuvered its charges directly onto the big ship's hull; another managed to place hers close enough that when the combined charges were detonated, the *Tirpitz* was said to have blasted six feet out of the water. The huge warship didn't sink but was sufficiently damaged to spend the next six months in dry dock. The commanders of the two X-Craft that placed the explosives were awarded Britain's most prestigious military honor, the Victoria Cross.

As difficult as the crossing must have been, O'Riley was fortunate to be on the passage crew. The X-craft that he had successfully navigated to its destination was lost during the *Tirpitz* operation. Neither the vessel nor any of her four-man crew was ever found.

After the *Tirpitz* mission, "strange things began happening" for O'Riley. "Soon I was sitting at a desk, learning the ropes and meeting people I needed to meet. I didn't understand where this was taking me at the time, but it satisfied my craving to do something important."

Twenty-some years later, the ropes he learned and the people he met led the midget submariner to training the next generation.

*

Morgan recalled that the first thing O'Riley did when he arrived was "walk completely around me as I stood at what I figured was attention. Not ever having had any kind of military training, it must have been pretty obvious I didn't know how to do even that. He walked around me slowly. And as he looked me over, I figured I already had him by maybe a whole foot and a whole lot more muscle."

O'Riley pointed to a chair in front of his mahogany desk and said sharply, "Sit down."

As Morgan took his seat, O'Riley shuffled through some papers, finally handing Morgan a thick file.

"That's you," O'Riley said. "Get to know yourself."

Opening the file, Morgan found "an entire history of… this other person. There was a passport picture that looked like me. Sorta reminded me of the old expression, 'If it looks like shit, smells like shit, it must be….'"

O'Riley had compiled a dossier on his young recruit, including a list of every girl that Morgan had ever slept with and the fact that there were occasional incidents with more than one. The dossier also revealed that Morgan had seen a psychiatrist to deal with his grief over his sister's drowning. There were even statements from boys who had propositioned Morgan with homosexual liaisons – and a notation that Morgan had turned them all down "graciously."

O'Riley fired off a barrage of questions, some of them personal to the point of embarrassment. "They knew everything, down to the smallest details. Sexual preferences, practices. I answered, but it's pretty rough when you're sitting across from a total stranger. I started to get the feeling that the interview was going downhill, but I couldn't really figure why."

O'Riley then asked Morgan a variation of the question that Stephenson had posed. "If someone put a gun to your head, with his finger going white with the pressure on the trigger, would you kill him?"

Morgan said, "I guess so…" and immediately realized his mistake. And then he compounded his error by smiling.

"I guess so!?" O'Riley roared, getting right in Morgan's face. "Look, Mister. I've decided I don't like you a whole hell of a lot. You are a smart ass! You think too much of yourself. That makes you a liability. And I have decided this interview was a mistake."

Morgan just stared at O'Riley, unable to keep his smile from turning into what O'Riley swore was an outright smirk. "After all," Morgan recalled, "I was taller, I was stronger, and I knew how to handle myself."

O'Riley walked over to a wooden box on a bookshelf near his desk. He opened the box and pulled out a large, bone-handled knife. He took the knife out of its leather sheath, and then threw it on the carpet near Morgan's feet.

"Pick it up," O'Riley yelled, with what Morgan thought was "an awful lot of noise from such a short guy."

"Pick it up," O'Riley shouted again. "Pick it up and defend yourself, because I have decided I am going to kill you."

As Morgan bent down to pick up the knife, something blunt and hard struck his head. There were more blows to his shoulders, to his back, and all over his body.

Morgan crumpled to the floor.

O'Riley had rolled up a magazine from his desk and beat the living daylights out of Morgan with it. In O'Riley's powerful and experienced hands, the wad of paper took on the force of a sawed-off baseball bat.

Morgan tried to defend himself, but "he beat me up so badly that I was bleeding from parts of my face I didn't even know I had." When he was done pounding on Morgan, O'Riley went to a washroom and came back with a wet towel. He handed the towel to Morgan and sat next to him on the floor.

"That was your first lesson in staying alive," O'Riley said. "Never underestimate your opponent."

"After the 'training' in Boston," Morgan said, "I started shutting down my life. I started pulling away from personal friendships, closing off other contacts. Creating a new 'legend' takes a certain amount of time, but the old 'me' was starting to fall away…"

Morgan sold his motorcycle – "too dangerous," Dr. Brown said, without even a hint of irony – and replaced it with an MG convertible, in British racing green.

Then he started to think about Linda.

Giving up his motorcycle, walking away from friends, even getting the holy crap beat out of him by a little man with a rolled-up magazine. All that, Morgan suddenly realized, was the easy part.

43

For The Good Of The Service

(1940)

When William Stephenson arrived in America in the spring of 1940 at the behest of Winston Churchill, his first objective was to establish a base of operations for an espionage network in a place where it could survive if Britain fell to a Nazi invasion. The headquarters for British Security Coordination (BSC) were setup in offices at Rockefeller Center in New York City.

Official accounts will trace the formation of BSC to the weeks immediately following Churchill's occupancy of #10 Downing Street. But we know from the unofficial account of Townsend Brown's voyage aboard the yacht *Caroline* in 1933 that Stephenson's operations preceded the onset of the war by at least half a dozen years. In New York that spring and summer, Stephenson's real work was converting his private web of business and financial interests into a classified network of political and military capabilities.

*

Lieutenant Townsend Brown remained in the Navy through the first year of the war. In another Annual Fitness Report, filed on June 10, 1940, Lt. Brown listed his occupation as "Materials and processing engineer" for the Glenn L. Martin Aircraft Co. in Baltimore MD, where his duties included being "in charge of inspection and testing of aircraft materials and construction, shop processes and special research problems." He also mentions conducting a "special study of corrosion prevention" for the Navy's flying boats.

But the most important news Townsend Brown's life was found not in the Navy records, but, once again, in a Zanesville newspaper, which reported on September 24, 1940:

> **The marriage of Mrs. Josephine Beale Brown and Lt. Townsend Brown took place Thursday, Sept. 19, in Alexandria, Va. The Rev. Mr. Ashby officiated, and the couple will reside at 4447 Greenwich Parkway, Washington D.C.**
>
> **Mrs. Brown has been district supervisor of the W. P. A. housekeeping aid project of District No. 3. Mr. Brown is with the Navy department of the United States in Washington.**

Josephine in a photo possibly taken after the Browns'
remarried in 1940. The inscription in the lower right corner
reads: To the man I love with all my heart, Jo.

Brown's official Navy records begin to show heavy redactions during this period, but the story in the newspaper also reports that his work for the Navy included acoustic and magnetic mine sweeping – a subject addressed in some detail in the short autobiography that Townsend dictated to Josephine many years later:

> **Some way was needed to sweep mines from the Channel, and this required exploding them where they were. One way to do this was by placing a huge coil on a barge and passing current thru the coil to produce a magnetic field which spread to the bottom of the seabed. The trouble was, when blowing up the mine, it was invariably under the barge and blew up both barge and coil.**
>
> **Someone suggested that if we could trail a wire behind a converted tugboat and put current in that wire of several hundred amperes, that would do the job.**
>
> **But the wire being heavier than water, would sink to the bottom. A way had to be found to keep the wire at the surface. Plastic floats were tried. Only, when the mine was detonated, it blew up all the floats and the wire sank to the bottom.**

> That is when I got the idea of putting floats *inside* the wire, like sausages. Wire wrapped around the sausages so the cable floated. It was 3 1/2" in diameter and conducted 300 amps, which was more than enough to blow up the mines. When the mines blew up, the explosion merely tossed the cable in air without damage.
>
> I took out a patent on this idea. It was immediately classified. I heard nothing more, but understand it is still in use today, still accepted as the best method of minesweeping.

Those heavily redacted Navy records say nothing of this. But several times over the years, Josephine told Linda a story about a night she and Townsend spent at the Mayflower Hotel in Washington. Linda had no reason to suspect that she may have been hearing a story about her parents' second honeymoon:

> Daddy had been away a lot. Months. Mother simply missed his company (in and out of their bedroom!). When they were reunited, she was looking forward to a long weekend behind locked doors at the Mayflower.
>
> She admitted they had already had a pretty good time, so she was surprised when she felt his hand brush against her hipbone. Mother was fashionably thin in those days. His hand stopped on one hipbone, and slowly traced across the flat of her tummy, and then up the other hipbone, where his hand paused again….
>
> Mother was thinking, "Oh boy…." and then…. "Huh? What the heck?"
>
> Suddenly Daddy yelled, "That's it!" and threw the bed sheets aside. He scrambled into his uniform and was out the door with barely another word. He was gone for months, and it was not until years later that she discovered that her hipbones were responsible for a breakthrough in mine-sweeping cable design that saved many lives during the war.

Lieutenant T. Townsend Brown was still on active duty when the Japanese attacked Pearl Harbor on December 7, 1941, drawing the U.S. into World War II. His superior officers continued to commend him with glowing praise, as in the 1941 Fitness Report in which the commanding officer commented that:

> This officer is well educated, intelligent, and adaptable. He is well informed in theoretical and practical electricity and physics. He is particularly suited to research rather than engineering. His value to the Service will increase with experience. He is recommended

**for retention on active duty during the present emergency and for
promotion when due.**

In the first months of 1942, Lieutenant Brown was assigned to the Atlantic
Fleet Radar School at the Norfolk, Virginia Naval base as a Radio Officer,
Ship's Service Officer, and Educational. Another Fitness Report, dated June 25,
1942, states,

**Lieut. Brown is thorough, energetic and possesses exceptional
initiative. Has performed his duties in a thoroughly satisfactory
manner of excellent professional and personal character. Is
recommended for promotion when due.**

Despite the glowing commendations and consistent recommendations, there
were no promotions. To the contrary the Navy records contain a letter dated
September 30, 1942:

ATLANTIC FLEET SCHOOLS
NAVAL OPERATING BASE
NORFOLK, VIRGINIA

September 30, 1942

From: Lieut.Comdr. T.T.Brown E-V(S) USNR.
To : The Chief of Naval Personnel
Via : Commanding Officer, Atlantic Fleet Schools.

Subject: Resignation from the U.S.Naval Service.

1.   I herewith submit my resignation from the navy for
the good of the naval service in order to escape trial by
General Court Martial.

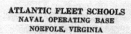

Thomas Townsend Brown

Five days later, on October 5, Lieutenant Brown received his final orders in a
telegram addressed to the Commanding Officer:

**LIEUTENANT COMMANDER THOMAS TOWNSEND
BROWN EVS USNR HEREBY DETACHED -X- WHEN DIRECTED
BY COMMANDING OFFICER REPORT FOR PHYSICAL
EXAMINATION –X- UPON COMPLETION PROCEED HOME
UPON ARRIVAL RELEASED FROM ALL ACTIVE DUTY X
CHARGES PSANDT X FORWARD COPY OF THESE ORDERS
BEARING ALL ENDORSEMENTS TO BUPERS...**

There is no explanation for the termination of Brown's service anywhere in the file. The statement "CHARGES PSANDT" is not an explanation for his dismissal but is rather an instruction to the bursar of accounts to pay the departing sailor his "Pay, Subsistence and Travel" expenses until he got home.

It is hard to fathom why the United States Navy, so recently engaged in a global war, would part company with one of its most qualified radio and radar specialists.

Less than two weeks later, the recently discharged Lieutenant assumed a post as a 'research engineer' for the Vega Aircraft Corporation[52] in Burbank, California.

44

We've Lost Morgan

(1987)

Fast forward to the year 1987.

It is two years since Townsend Brown died, at age eighty, on Catalina Island off the southern California coast. Linda, her husband George, their daughter, and Josephine are living near a small town in the California desert, wedged between two mountains roughly midway between Los Angeles and Palm Springs.

"Mother was happy to be away from the island and into something new," Linda said. "She helped us pack. To this day, I can't wrap something in paper and put it in a box without thinking immediately of her."

A few weeks before Christmas, Linda felt a foreboding that something was not right in the Universe. In her journal, she wrote of "the strangest, most chilling emotion I have ever had, and it hung on for days."

George had no idea what to make of his wife when she just burst into tears in his arms one night. "I felt alone and hopelessly lost, utter despair," she wrote. "It felt like someone was calling my name."

Linda took a mental inventory of family and friends, finally concluding that all were safe and accounted – until she got to Morgan. And then "it was if all the tumblers in a lock slid into place."

It had been two years since she'd last seen Morgan, when he had come for a brief visit to Catalina and left her with the phone number of a colleague in San Diego. "If you ever need me," he'd said, "call Carlos."

She found the number on a slip of paper tucked in her wallet. With nervous fingers barely hitting all the right buttons, Linda punched out the numbers Morgan had scrawled out for her. She recognized the voice of Maryanne, Carlos' wife, when she answered the phone.

Linda asked, "Have you heard from Morgan? I've been thinking about him a lot lately. Do you know if he's OK?"

Maryanne sounded puzzled. "As far as I know, he's fine. He's still constantly on the move, you know. In fact, he was in California last week. We had lunch with him in Venice."

"Well, don't worry," Linda said. "It's nothing really. I just had this sudden urge to see if I could restore contact with him" and ended the call after giving Maryanne her phone number.

Linda and George spend the next day with a friend. When they got home, a houseguest, Michelle, came out to meet them saying, "you had a call from somebody named Maryanne."

Linda froze. "What did she say, did she leave a message?"

"She said something like, "We've lost Morgan.""

"My heart just stopped," Linda recalled. "George just stood there, stunned more by my expression than from the actual news."

Linda wrote in her journal, "I went through several days of real depression. If Morgan was gone, then an enormous page had been turned in my life and everything I had ever known or experienced had been wiped away. Morgan had been my touchstone, my other heart. Suddenly I felt very old in a world that didn't matter anymore."

Carlos called a few days later. He said something about an icy road in rural Tennessee. A tractor trailer braking for another car and jack-knifing on the ice, forcing Morgan's motorcycle off the road, internal injuries and his penchant for motorcycles finally catching up with him. Carlos took the first flight he could and spent the last three days with him, but there was nothing anybody could do.

"He wanted me to tell you…." Carlos said, and there was a long pause.

"He wanted me to tell you 'to keep a light in the corner of your soul' for him."

Linda burst into tears. Through his own muffled tears over the phone, Carlos added, "He also said something that might not make any sense to you. He said 'Just hold this in your hand if you can't read my writing.'"

Linda knew what it meant, and her tears turned into a laughing sob.

After she hung up the phone, Linda found the little scrap of paper where Morgan had written Carlos's phone number and remembered what Morgan had said when he gave it to her: "If you can't read my writing, just hold this paper in your hand and you will hear me saying 'I love you' in your ear and it won't make any difference if you can't read it."

Part 2:
Black

In all affairs it's a healthy thing now and then
to hang a question mark on the things
you have long taken for granted.

-- *Bertrand Russell*

Introduction to Part 2: Black

> Alice waited for a few minutes to see if she would shrink any further: She felt a little nervous about this; "for it might end, you know," said Alice to herself, "in my going out altogether, like a candle." And she tried to fancy what the flame of a candle looks like after the candle is blown out, for she could not remember having ever seen such a thing.
>
> *--Lewis Carroll, Alice's Adventures in Wonderland*

I wonder what imagery we would use today if Lewis Carroll hadn't blessed the literary canon with Alice going down a 'rabbit hole.' That oft-cited metaphor is perfectly suited for this tale, which at times is as baffling as the adventures that poor Alice encountered once she chased after the White Rabbit and started ingesting hallucinogenics.

Only this story is not an hallucination.

And this story comes by its *Alice* association quite honestly. In *Chapter 29 – The Caroline,* Eldridge Johnson...

...was so enamored with the story of the young girl and her surreal world that he acquired several copies of the first printed edition. His obsession culminated with the purchase – at no small expense – of the original manuscript of *Alice's Adventures Underground*, written in the hand of its author Charles Lutwidge Dodgson, who scribbled under the penname of Lewis Carroll. And during one visit to England, Johnson went to the trouble of having himself photographed with the elderly Alice Liddell Hargreaves, who, when she was a child, had been Carroll's inspiration for Alice's adventures.

When I first embarked on this undertaking, I envisioned a sequel to my first book, *The Boy Who Invented Television.* I expected I would be writing another conventional biography, presented entirely in the third person.

The first half of this text begins mostly with that intent. Whenever it seemed necessary to add some perspective – from my own experience or a tangential source – I stepped out of the conventional voice in chapters subtitled *Notes From the Rabbit Hole.* Thank you, Mr. Dodgson.

I labeled Part 1 of this book *White* because the narrative was easily drawn from Linda Brown's recollections, the family archive, military records, newspaper reports, and other sources readily available in the public domain.

Once Townsend Brown left the Navy in 1942, source material gets scarce. Brown disappears into the 'black' realm of classified military research and covert intelligence operations.

Which brings us to Part 2: *Black* – where finding the story becomes equal to telling the story. New voices come forward in the pages that follow. Besides Townsend's, Linda's and mine, you'll hear directly from two confidential informants: Morgan and O'Riley. Both were intimately involved in Townsend's life and work, but I've never met either of these men in person. All their input arrived in voluminous email exchanges that started in 2004.

Townsend Brown's life story might never have come to light if Morgan and O'Riley hadn't volunteered to get involved. But from here on it's impossible to separate their input from mine.

So, no more *Notes From The Rabbit Hole*.

Because it's all rabbit hole from here.

45

The Ghost At The Corral

(2004)

Linda Brown could be maddeningly circumspect at times.

Usually when we talked on the phone, Linda would eventually get around to whatever was on her mind. But during a call in late February 2004 – about a year into our collaboration – I sensed some resistance. There was either something she didn't want to tell me, or, more likely she was going to make me work for it.

She asked, "Does the name 'Norman Paperman' mean anything to you at all?"

"Nope."

"Nothing, huh?"

"No, not a thing."

"Damn. Well, OK then," and then she laughed that girlish giggle of hers, the one that told me not to give up so easily.

"What have you got?"

"Well, I got a postcard. All it says is 'Hi, remember me?' and it's signed 'Norman Paperman'."

As we were talking, I Googled 'Norman Paperman' and learned that is the name of the main character in *Don't Stop The Carnival*,[53] a Herman Wouk novel about the misadventures of an Eisenhower-era Broadway press agent who runs off to start a new life as the owner of a run-down resort on fictitious King George The Third Island in the Caribbean – known to the locals as "Kinja." I started reading all this to Linda over the phone.

From the other end of the line, I heard a slight gasp, followed by a brief pause and then Linda said, "I think we've heard from someone…."

"Someone? Like who?"

"I can't say – I'm having a hard time breathing right now."

"Do you think someone is finally going to start helping us make sense of this story?"

"I don't know," Linda said, "but this is very exciting. I'm dancing around in my kitchen here."

The conversation drifted off onto other topics, ending with something between a suggestion and a warning: "Whatever questions you've got, make sure you've got them at your command so that you can ask them quickly should the need arise."

"Hell," I thought, "I've got an armload of questions. Who am I asking?"

*

Later that day I ignored a phone call from an unrecognized number in Texas. When I played the message that was left, a honey-dipped female voice said, "Paul, Mr. Paperman would like you to send the questions that you have to…." a post office box in rural west Texas.

I glared at the phone. What the fuck?

I called Linda and asked, "Who did you talk to after we talked this morning?"

"Who did I talk to?" she mused, and mentioned a neighbor.

I cut her off. "Let me put it this way. Who knows that you and I have been talking about Norman Paperman?"

"Why?"

"Just answer the question. Who – that we know that we've talked to – as opposed to who might have been listening in?

"Well, I personally haven't mentioned the name since I talked to you."

"Well, I got a phone call." I described the voice-mail message.

"That's interesting," Linda said, sounding coy.

"So, tell me, why would whoever left that message think that I'd have any idea who Mr. Paperman might be?"

"That's a really good question."

"No shit, Sherlock. Somebody calls me out of the blue, and says 'Mr. Paperman would like you to send him your questions…' Why would that caller think I'd have any idea what they're talking about?"

Linda tried the opposite tack: "If you'd gotten a call like that, and we hadn't had that prior conversation, what would you think?"

"I'd think 'wrong number.' Except that she called me 'Paul'. They didn't leave a number, but I've got caller ID. Maybe I should call back and ask, 'Who the hell is Mr. Paperman?'"

Linda laughed. My guess is you're gonna get somebody that's gonna say, 'Huh?'"

*

A few days later I sealed up a priority mail envelope with two dozen questions about Townsend Brown and addressed it to "Mr. Norman Paperman," at a post office box in Texas.

A week later, the phone rang again. This time I recognized the phone number in Texas and picked up.

The now-familiar honey-dipped voice said, "Paul, this is Mr. Paperman's secretary. I have one question for you."

"Fire away."

"Mr. Paperman wanted me to call and ask you if Linda still has the token."

It took a beat to recall a story that Linda told me when we first met in Las Vegas: She and Morgan had celebrated New Year's 65/66 together in New York[54]. Knowing that it might be some time before their paths crossed again, Morgan reached into his pocket and handed Linda the only thing he could find, a NYC subway token. Morgan pressed the token into Linda's hand, like a talisman, 'Good for One Fare' if she ever needed to find her way back to him. Linda carried that token with her always and showed it to me in Las Vegas.

"Yes," I said, "She still has the token."

"OK," Mr. Paperman's secretary said, "I'll let him know that."

Ten minutes later, Linda Brown was working in the corral behind her house, under a cloudless blue high California desert sky, shoveling feed to her aging horse Shadetree, when a ghost emerged from the sagebrush, sauntered to the edge of the corral, and said, "Hello there…."

Without a word, Linda reached out. Morgan remained silent as Linda's fingers spread out and her palm flattened over his chest. This ghost had a heartbeat.

46

Hey Woodward
(2004)

From the start of my correspondence with Linda Brown in late 2002, she had been reluctant to talk about her lover who'd been dead for seventeen years. Once we'd signed our collaboration agreement, the first thing she sent me was an excerpt from her journals. "I feel strange dragging you through my romance with Morgan," she wrote, "but it really does figure into the whole picture, and Daddy interacted enough with our relationship to make it worth writing about, I hope."

Then in the spring of 2004, a ghost calling himself 'Norman Paperman' showed up in the California desert.

Per his secretary's request, the letter I sent to Mr. Paperman posed nearly two dozen questions.

For example: Was Townsend Brown a CIA officer? When did he first become involved in espionage? Did he work with the OSS during World War II? When was he recruited, and by whom? Was there a connection between those assignments and his own discoveries and scientific research?

And: What were the circumstances of Townsend Brown's discharge from the Navy? Why was he so suddenly dismissed, when the service acknowledged that he was one of their most knowledgeable scientists? And how does his dismissal reconcile with showing up at a top-secret aviation research facility just a few weeks later?

Ten days later came the first reply:

> **Paul,**
>
> **No need for formalities. I go by different names. Paperman works well now. Only hope I can live up to it.**
>
> **So, you are a Parrot-head. That will make some of my references easier to flesh out. "Kinja Rules" will have some meaning for you…**

'Parrot-head' is a reference to the fans of the recording artist Jimmy Buffett. I'd listened to a lot of Buffett when I lived in Hawaii in the 1980s, but was less familiar with his more recent work, which included *Don't Stop The Carnival* [55] – a musical based on the Herman Wouk novel. In a track entitled "Kinja Rules," a local kingpin on King George III Island advises Norman:

> You gotta play by Kinja rules
> Forget about da tings you learned in school
> We use a different box of tools
> And you gotta play by Kinja rules

The letter continued:

> On this end, I have a very simple box of tools. Forget about the things you learned at school. Answers will come, but as you have guessed, not everything can be approached.

> Yes, Dr. Brown was a valued member of our community and still has more awards at the agency than anyone is ever going to know. They are sometimes called "Jockstrap Awards" because that's about the only place you could ever wear them.

Mr. Paperman explained that Brown's credentials had come to the attention of a "certain organization" during the early 1930s; that he'd been invited to join a cruise where he was "vetted and recruited" by Florence Douglas on behalf of Eldridge Johnson and joined the organization immediately.

> He stayed with them, intermittently, for years. He was always awarded the freedom to work on his own projects but occasionally was pulled in other directions by the needs of what you have come to call the 'Deeper Draft Vessel.' For my own purposes I have called it the 'Caroline Group.'

> These connections will prove nearly impossible to substantiate. Your knowledge of the connections might enable you to make other connections. Only Time Will Tell.

Only Time Will Tell[56] was another Buffett lyric.

Three pages later, the now-slightly-less-mysterious Mr. Paperman ended by acknowledging the code name that I'd given him:

> **"I guess it's…. Morgan."**

*

Morgan and I corresponded via 'snail mail' for several months. I sent direct questions. Morgan sent oblique answers. I tried to read between the lines.

In his letters, Morgan often referred to Linda Brown as "Desdemona" – a name he lifted from another Jimmy Buffett song, *Desdemona's Building a Rocket Ship*[57]. I wanted to get into the cloak-and-dagger spirit by asking if I could have a code name, too.

In May of 2004, Morgan sent me the first email I received from him, which started with the subject header, "Hey Woodward.[58]"

The message that followed touched on everything from Brown's vetting by the Caroline Group to Morgan's own introduction to that network and his first encounters with 'Mr. X' – "a sharp eyed, white-haired gentleman who could blend in at a yacht party one moment and a boarding party the next."

After that first email, with the electronic channel established, the floodgates opened on an exchange of more than 2,000 messages.

47

A Universe Away

(1942)

Townsend Brown and his 1941Packard convertible.
That's mother 'Mame' riding shotgun.

The U.S. had been engaged in World War II for less than a year when Townsend Brown was discharged from the Navy in September 1942.

Josephine wrapped up her green 'El Nido' teapot and packed it into the trunk of a 1941 Packard One-Eighty convertible. She, Townsend, and eight-year-old Joseph headed west, where the Navy officer who resigned "for the good of the service" jumped into a new role at the Vega Aircraft facility, with free rein to pursue a line of top-secret research at the behest of the Caroline Group.

That connection was drawn for me by Morgan. First, he directed my attention to Brown's 1939 Navy Fitness Report, which describes his role as...

> **Research Physicist: since being detached USS *Nashville* on 30 Sept 1938 I have been engaged in building and installing a new sidereal radiation recorder in the Physics Dept of the University of Pennsylvania and in computing records for 1937 and 1938.**

...and suggested I make note of the mention of the USS ***Nashville***, where Brown witnessed (if he did not actually *supervise*) the delivery of a horde of gold bullion from the Bank of England to the Chase Manhattan Bank in New York.

Morgan also highlighted the installation at the University of Pennsylvania. On July 28, 1942 (two months before his discharge from the Navy), Brown received an order from the Commander of the U.S. Atlantic Fleet Schools to report to the University "to supervise the disassembling and packing of scientific equipment to be shipped to Atlantic Fleet Schools."

When I pressed Morgan for details, his response was typically opaque:

I can tell you[59] that the 'stuff' being moved from the University of Pennsylvania to the Atlantic Fleet Radar School was Dr. Brown's *own* development – backed by both the Navy and the Caroline group. The University site was set up originally by a Caroline member – Eldridge Johnson – while Dr. Brown was on the USS *Nashville*. Upon his return much of this 'stuff' was reorganized and consolidated into a central location at the University.

Money was there now to fund the project – some fifty million, which I think you already know about and can find the record of its transfer from England.

Later the 'stuff' was shipped to California, where it continued its development under the darkest of conditions.

*

On their way across the country, the Brown family stopped in Claremore, Oklahoma to tour the Will Rogers Museum. At the gift shop, Josephine picked out a handful of postcards to send to friends and family. Though she stashed the post cards in a coat pocket, they became slightly wrinkled by a light rain.

To her parents – still living in the Washington, DC area – Josephine wrote:

Dearest Folks,

We stopped here for lunch in Will Rogers' hometown. Weather is still good – much colder – will be half-way tomorrow nite. Joe is having a big time. We are now getting in the "Wide Open Spaces."

Love,

Jo

Josephine was excited about the prospects for their future, but also worried aloud about how far they were going to be from her folks.

"California," Josephine said to Townsend, "is a universe away."

Morgan described[60] what happened next:

Dr. Brown agreed that it was indeed going to be quite a change.

Then Josephine shuffled the damp cards into a neat stack, ready for posting. He watched her hand the stack of postcards to the clerk, their warped surfaces overlapping like rippled sheets of corrugated

steel, when it suddenly occurred to him that the Universe was formed just like that wavy stack of cards, one on top of the other; that the surfaces all had connections with each other, and that to describe one of those cards would describe the whole.

Once that thought hit, he and Josephine went back into the dining room and ordered some desert – apple pie, with ice cream. Joseph ate his pie quickly and ran outside to investigate some penned deer on display for the tourists outside. But Josephine stayed to listen to this 'different' man she had married as he excitedly explained to her this profound realization that an infinite number of universes exist simultaneously. And that what one knows, they all know. Instantly.

I wrote back to Morgan, "So you have this…universe of infinite universes? And one of them always occupies the space you are sending your message to, and is right next to the point of origin? In one of those parallel universes?"

I tried to fathom how that scenario might overcome the generally accepted velocity limit of the speed of light. Speed is not really a factor if you're merely wriggling from one parallel universe to another. If that's how gravity waves travel, then the distance between parallel universes can be crossed instantly – because *there is no distance.*

I posed the quandary to Morgan: "Please let me know if I'm hallucinating here, that I'm not having acid flashback, you know…??"

And Morgan assured me:

You are absolutely on the mark. Do you know how good that feels to type? Probably as good as it feels to read.

*

In much the same way that a submarine may not get its orders until it is already out to sea, Townsend and Josephine wended their way across the plains, waiting for the next transmission.

Arriving in Los Angeles in early November 1942, the family found a cozy bungalow on Wonderland Drive[61] in Laurel Canyon, deep in the eucalyptus-scented hollows of the Hollywood Hills.

Within days of their arrival, the FBI put a 'thirty-day cover' on the Browns. The Bureau wasn't reading their mail – that would have required a warrant – but the cover let the Bureau track from whom and to whom the Browns' mail was coming and going.

Why the FBI was interested in Townsend Brown remains an open question. The obvious explanation is J. Edgar Hoover was aware of Brown's affiliation with

William Stephenson – a foreign national who was known to conducting espionage operations on American soil, a realm that Hoover felt strongly should have been his own exclusive domain.

Whatever the FBI's interest, the Laurel Canyon address provided Townsend with an easy drive over the crest of Mulholland Drive into Burbank, where he went to work every day at the Vega Aircraft plant.

Lockheed's dual-fuselage P-38 Lightning – "the fork-tailed devil" – was a favorite among World War II fighter pilots.

A subsidiary of the Lockheed Aircraft Company, Vega was named for the parent company's first production aircraft, the Lockheed Vega. Produced in 1927, the Vega was one of the first monoplanes, a six-passenger model that was highly prized among top pilots for its durability over long distances. When Amelia Earhart became the first woman to match Charles Lindbergh's feat of crossing the Atlantic solo, she flew a Lockheed Vega.[62]

With the onset of World War II, the Vega factory became Lockheed's primary military facility, producing a quarter of the 12,000 B-17 bombers built during the war, and the P-38 Lightning – the "forked tail devil" that pressed the limits of propeller driven aircraft until jet engines were introduced in the later 1940s.

Of his work on the P-38, Brown wrote,

> **I was assigned to the Advanced Project Division at Lockheed, at the time when P-38's were being manufactured. They were having trouble because it made a high-pitched scream as it flew. There were a lot of other problems due to the vibration of the fuselage. I came up with the idea of a vibration damper for which a patent was drawn up by Lockheed's attorney. Since I was an employee, the patent**

**assigned to Lockheed. Shortly after that the screaming stopped and
the vibration of the fuselage was eliminated.**

That the Vega facility was already churning out more just than heavy bombers
and high-performance fighters is suggested by the nature of the facility itself.
Brown marveled that the location looked more like a Hollywood back lot than
an industrial facility. As Morgan noted:

> **Dr. Brown was amazed at the amount of effort that had been put
> into disguising the area from prying eyes. From the air, the plant itself
> looked like a normal suburb. There were houses, trees and streets – all
> of them *fake*. Dr. Brown told me that the thing that amazed him the
> most were the avenues of trees – really big trees, made entirely of
> chicken wire covered with papier-mâché bark. And the leaves were
> all feathers painted green. It wouldn't work today of course. But back
> then it was an important altered vision of California.**

Vega Aircraft was already the headquarters of Lockheed's most advanced
aviation research. The year after Brown arrived, work began on the P-80 Shooting
Star – the prototype for the first American jet fighters that flew just before the
end of the war.

But that's not what Townsend Brown was working on.

*The camouflaged parking lot at Vega Aircraft
in Burbank, California ca. 1943.*

48

Man On The Floor!

(1965)

*The Main Hall of Southern Seminary was built
in 1890 as the Hotel Buena Vista.*

In the summer of 1965, while Morgan was in Boston learning the first lessons of survival – and the lethal potential of a rolled-up magazine – Linda was getting ready for her final year in Southern Seminary's two-year program.

"I got a postcard from Vermont," she recorded in her journal. "All it said was 'Here I am and there you are. Morgan.'"

In Virginia, Linda found the pristine environs of the Southern Sem were losing their allure. A new dorm-mate shared her disenchantment.

"Tula blew in like a shaft of sunshine," Linda wrote. "What a wonderful sense of humor. She's a nut – but a funny nut. She may be the only one in this whole school who can understand what my thoughts and experiences have been, and I have the oddest feeling that she and I are going to become good friends. I need her point of view, and especially, I think, her companionship."

The first time Linda visited Tula in her dorm room, they had to wait for Tula's "three very conventional roommates to go to the library" before she could put her favorite record on. "When I visited her, I ran headlong into Bob Dylan's refrain, 'It's all over now, Baby Blue,' from the album *Bringing It All Back Home*."

The music "certainly brought it all back home back for me. I remembered listening to that song while Morgan showered. And later, cradled in his arms with my head resting on his chest, listening to his heart beating while Dylan whined in the background, *strike another match, go start anew…and it's all over now, Baby Blue*."

The Virginia mountains were unseasonably warm most of the autumn, but temperatures dropped by the weekend of the season's first big horse show. "It rained all day Friday and we worried that they would cancel the show," Linda said.

That Saturday afternoon, Linda was standing at the rail, watching as a classmate put her horse through its paces, not realizing that she was shivering in the cold. "Suddenly I felt a heavy, blue-and-grey cadet's coat falling on my shoulders. I turned around and thanked the cadet for it. He said his name was Phillip. We talked about horses and the rules. I thought about what a gentlemanly thing it was for him to give me his coat. 'Well, I have to,' he said. I'm a cadet!'"

"I think he was interested in me," Linda wrote in her journal, "or he wouldn't have come over and spent so much time with me. Ah, the discipline of the Virginia Military Institute. I admire them all, but I don't think I could be a military wife. I would rather not get involved."

Sunday morning, after a thrilling ride on her favorite horse, a bay mare named KoKoMo, Linda was shivering again. "I started feeling weak and then out of nowhere I developed a cough. I had been fine but all of the sudden I was feeling just awful."

A classmate named Pam walked with Linda back to the dorm and bought her a coke and some crackers, "and hovered over me. She said that it was probably the adrenaline leaving my body. 'God!' she said, 'What a ride'"

After the snack, Linda stumbled to her room and put herself to bed, skipping dinner. "All I want to do is sleep," she wrote.

The next day she wound up in a hospital, diagnosed with pneumonia.

"I was pretty sick. I'm pretty sure they were drugging me so I wouldn't cough myself into unconsciousness. Dad finally came up to talk to the doctors. He was not happy with them. He asked me what I wanted to do and I just said, 'I want to go home,' which to me at the time meant the dorm. So, at the end of my hospital stay I was afforded the luxury of returning to good old room #62, with permission to skip classes for as long as I wanted, with the instructions to just rest."

One afternoon the girl on phone duty knocked on Linda's door. She had a call.

"I knew it would be Morgan – and his 'sack full of quarters…'"

This time Morgan just said, "Can I come visit you?"

"When?"

"How about *now*?" He was calling from a phone in the lobby.

Men were not welcome upstairs in the Victorian mansion that served as Southern Seminary's main dormitory. But suddenly, there was Morgan, bounding up the big staircase amid squealing shouts of "Man on the floor! Man on the floor!"

"Tula came barreling out of her room and immediately introduced herself," Linda wrote in her journal, "and when she finally left, I could see one raised eyebrow that translated, 'Not bad, Brown...'"

"It all seemed so ridiculous. Here he was, sitting just a couple of arms lengths away from me. The door was open, of course; everything was entirely proper. So we laughed a lot."

A while passed before Linda thought to ask how Morgan knew she'd been sick.

"Oh, I talked with your parents," Morgan tossed off. "They have been really worried."

She didn't ask why Morgan had been talking to her parents during the several months when his only correspondence with her had been one sentence on a postcard.

Before leaving the dorm, Morgan hatched a plan.

"I'm not going to be able to come to Florida for a while," Morgan said. "I'm going to be stuck in New York at least through New Year's. If you're feeling better by then, why don't you come to New York for New Years?"

"I'll try," Linda said.

Morgan didn't say anything –he just gave Linda a long, hard, determined stare.

"I'll be there," Linda said.

*

After reading the first draft of this chapter in December 2006, Linda wrote back with a few notes.

"Dad must have pulled some strings. Morgan never would have just come bounding up those stairs without getting permission from the school first."

She also offered some thoughts about the changes she observed in Morgan's appearance and demeanor – his clean shave, the stylish clothes he was wearing and the sporty green MG he was driving.

"He did look really nice, but now I am realizing that he was under the influence of the world he was slipping into, which even he admitted could be pretty buttoned down. And the MG probably was O'Riley's."

The morning after Linda shared those fresh insights with me, another message came into my inbox, this time from O'Riley himself:

I wonder what it would have been like to get a glimpse of someone so special, and then have to stand aside, and let her walk by? Just a note from an old warhorse while we are speaking of that young girl: She may not have mentioned it to you but during that trip to the hospital she actually arrested and was brought back. Dr. Brown was going to "bring her home" to Florida but let her stay because that was her wish. She has never known that, by the way.

I forwarded O'Riley's message on to Linda,

"I never knew that!" she wrote back. "I knew that I had passed out, but nothing was ever said about 'arrested.' That means my heart stopped. No wonder Dad came up; no wonder he wanted me to come home; no wonder the school let me skip classes. Nobody outside a small group knew. Tula never knew. Hell, *I* never knew.

"But Morgan must have known. Why tell me about it now? Because it's probably supposed to be written about, I guess. Why else would O'Riley come forward with that bit of information after all these years? At the time, I guess, I needed.... *not to know*!

"If I had known how close I came to dying – that I had, in fact, actually died – I would have thrown my arms around Morgan, picked up my coat and walked out to that little green car and never looked back. Yes, I would have done that."

O'Riley explained it by drawing an analogy to Linda's days as an equestrienne:

When you ride a big course and fences loom in front of you, you *must* have a plan. You *must* look ahead, because where you look is where you end up. I believe that Dr. Brown's decision not to tell Linda about the incident at the hospital was a calculated choice on his part. He was looking toward the importance of the future and decidedly he was watching out for his own interests as well as his daughter's. Was it right for him to keep that as a secret? Probably only his daughter will be able to answer that. Secrets are dangerous things.

49

Structure of Space

(1943)

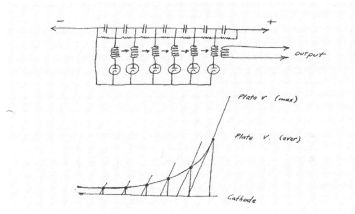

An illustration from Townsend Brown's Vega notebooks.

Other than that brief, autobiographical reference to the screaming wings of the P-38 fighter plane, virtually no documentation of Townsend Brown's activities from the time he left the until the end of World War II survives. Once Josephine sent that postcard to her family from the Will Rogers Museum in Oklahoma, the Browns vanished behind those fake palm trees and Hollywood-back-lot facades of the Vega facility in Burbank.

There is, however, a handwritten notebook in the family archive, rich with complex text and technical drawings that demonstrates the attention to detail and encyclopedic grasp of electronics and physics that inspired colleagues to call Townsend "Dr. Brown." The notebook is titled:

T. T. Brown

Vega Aircraft Corp

Burbank, Calif.

NOTES

This notebook may be the most important document in the entire archive.

The title of the very first entry – *Ultra-high Frequency Antenna (Multiple dipoles)* – is slightly misleading. Despite the reference to "frequency," Brown is not describing an ordinary antenna that generates radio waves. This antenna embodies his first discoveries, what he always called "stress in dielectrics[63]."

Returning to the observation of 'thrust' that Brown first observed twenty years earlier in the Coolidge tube, Brown describes an 'antenna' in which:

The effect is analogous to a nozzle of a fire hose.

The mechanical reaction is analogous to the "kick" of the hose nozzle.

This consideration now resolves itself into two objectives:

a) Production of highly directed (beamed) radiant energy;

b) The production of force or motion (reaction effect).

Both objectives will be borne in mind in the development of the method; both are equally important and useful.

Coming as it does on the heels of the revelation in Oklahoma, one might think that Brown would have turned his immediate attention to something more cosmic than a mere antenna.

But what he describes in the first half of the Vega notebook is just that: a cosmic antenna – a device capable of transmitting intelligence anywhere, instantly.

The key word is 'kick.'

*

If the first half of the Vega notebook describes a device capable of generating a 'kick,' then the second half addresses the *'what'* that is being kicked.

The second half of the notebook is entitled *Structure of Space*. It begins with a sidelong glance at one of the most accepted tenets of twentieth century science:

The failure of the Michelson-Morley experiment to detect a flow of ether does not necessarily indicate the non-existence of the ether. The results of the Theory of Relativity may be obtained with or without the ether.

For certain phenomena, it is desirable and almost necessary to assume the existence of an ether in order to evolve a satisfactory explanation. An example is the force of gravitation, particularly the electrogravitational effects; the phenomenon of the movement of a dielectric is such an example.

The idea that space is filled with a 'Luminiferous Aether'[64] reaches back at least as far as Sir Isaac Newton, who wrote in his 1704 treatise *Opticks* of an "Aethereal[65] Medium" capable of bearing light. In the mid-nineteenth century, James Clerk Maxwell described light as a wave-like portion of the electromagnetic spectrum, lending further strength to the idea of an ether: Just as sound waves travel through the medium of air, the idea of a 'light bearing' medium became one of the generally accepted principals of late nineteenth century physics. Maxwell proposed a variety of mechanical models for the ether.

There were problems, though, with Maxwell's models. The ether could be neither solid, liquid, nor gas, but nevertheless it had to be capable of carrying energy just as air carries sound waves. Maxwell's equations stipulated that electromagnetic waves travel at a fixed velocity – the speed of light. Thus, the ether would have to be fixed, or 'still' throughout the universe; otherwise, the speed of light would vary. On the other hand, the ether had to be fluid in order to fill all the nooks and crannies of space. And, in addition to being simultaneously both fixed and fluid, the ether could not display any mass or viscosity, lest it interfere with the orbits of the planets in space.

In 1887, two physicists, Albert Michelson and Edward Morley, thought that they would be able to detect the flow of the "aether wind" as the Earth orbits around the Sun. They built an elaborate and expensive apparatus to measure the earth's movement through the ether by splitting a beam of light at right angles and then observing the phase changes in the beams when they came back together.

The results from the first prototype of Michelson's 'Interferometer' were inconclusive. Seeking greater accuracy, Michelson joined forces with Morley and built a version in the basement of a stone building in Cleveland, Ohio, where it could be isolated from atmospheric effects like heat and vibration. It was mounted on a huge block of marble, which floated on a pool of mercury so that the marble could be easily rotated to measure the ether flow in infinite directions.

An 1887 article in the *American Journal of Science*, reported that the experiments were unable to detect any evidence of the "aether wind." Either because of the degree of precision – or in spite of it – the Michelson-Morley experiments have been remembered as "the most successful failure in all of scientific history."

In 1903 Frederick Trouton and H.R. Noble – using a different methodology – produced the same result as Michelson and Morley's.

The conclusion? There is no ether.

Not "we can't find it with these instruments" but "it doesn't exist."

Albert Einstein sidestepped the ether question in his 1905 paper on the photoelectric effect (for which he was awarded the Nobel Prize in 1921). Einstein redefined light as a 'particle exhibiting wave-like qualities.' Since particles would not need a medium to travel through in the way a wave would, the particle theory of light eliminated the need for an ether.

Still, opinions on the existence of an 'Aethereal Medium' wavered through the first decades of the new century. That experiments failed to find the ether, or that certain theories need not rely on its existence, doesn't necessarily mean it's not there.

Hendrik Lorentz, who won the Nobel Prize for physics the year after Einstein, wrote in 1911,

> **The theory of relativity can be carried out independently of what one thinks of the aether. Whether there is an aether or not, electromagnetic fields certainly exist, and so also does the energy of the electrical oscillations. If we do not like the name of 'aether.' we must use another word as a peg to hang all these things upon.**

In a 1920 lecture at the University of Leiden, even Einstein reconsidered his dismissal of the ether:

> **We may say that according to the general theory of relativity, space is endowed with physical qualities; in this sense, therefore, there exists an aether.**

Now here is Townsend Brown in 1943 – with no credentials to speak of, working under the cloak of a highly classified military facility saying almost the exact same thing in the opening lines of *Structure of Space*:

> **The ether would, then, have many interesting and hitherto unsuspected properties. It is the purpose of these notes to explore the subject qualitatively and to set forth some of the more important properties. Much of the work is based on facts derived from actual experiments which cannot be satisfactorily explained without the existence of an ether possessing substantially these qualities.**

Brown echoes Einstein's rumination on the 'physical qualities' of space. *Structure of Space* further explores how the *electrical* properties of space might offer insights into the nature of gravity. And he revisits the idea that gravity is 'a push not a pull' that he first expressed in the 1920s.

The pages of *Structure of Space* are dense with mathematical notations and symbols. Chief among these is "K" – the symbol for dielectric value, or the measure of "permittivity," or the "the ability of a material to resist the formation of an electric field within it." Another frequent symbol is "μ" – the lower case, Greek letter "mu," which in this case represents magnetic permeability of a material, or the extent to which it can be penetrated by a magnetic field.

Such symbols – and the equations they appear in – make the scientific case, but sometimes Brown could crystalize the essential properties of matter, energy and space using a simple analogy:

> **An evacuated glass globe, submerged to its crushing depth in the deep sea, would suddenly disintegrate and send out a wave motion**

possessing energy. The energy was contained not in the evacuated globe, but in the pressure of the water surrounding the globe.

It might appear that mankind lives in an aether 'sea' of tremendous pressure, an aether 'sea' of likewise unbelievable energy.

That may be as simple a passage as can be found in the pages of *Structure of Space*.

Another passage explores "Electro-gravitational equilibrium:"

It can be interpreted that pure space energy is essentially equivalent to electricity and that extra-galactic space is negatively charged. Any gravitational field will possess an electric field, the direction of which is from negative to positive. In this way, gravitational or space potential is inversely related to electrical potential. A freely insulated body assumes an electric charge which is related to the gravitational potential of the space in which it exists.

As an example, in the solar system, the electrical potential of the planets is of negative sign and that of the sun is positive. The more distant the planets are, the more negative.

In a sense, one may imagine the gravitational potential as inversely related to the electric potential.

Space, Townsend Brown is telling us, is an infinite sea of energy – acting as a dielectric and subject to the same negative-to-positive thrust that he first observed in the Coolidge Tube. What we call 'gravity' is just one manifestation of that energy – and it can be modulated with what we call 'electrical' energy.

*

The first time I sat down with it, it took me more than two weeks to grind through the verbiage *of Structure of Space*. I don't want to think about how many years it took to actually make sense of it.

It is only upon returning to it – 20 years after that first reading – that I finally realized that the Vega notebook embodies the pivotal element of this story – the piece that has been hiding in plain sight for as long as I've been falling down the rabbit hole.

We are now going to consider an alternative to 'radio communications.' For the sake of this story, I'll call this alternative 'gravitational communications[66].'

When we talk about radio communications, we're talking about sending a wave through the 'ether' – or whatever we want to call the medium that electromagnetic waves travel through. However, the waves are transmitted, it takes *time* for the signal to reach its destination.

Think of a child's jump rope. If you shake one end of the rope, the motion creates a wave, and moments later the wave reaches the other end of the rope. The longer the rope, the longer it takes for the 'signal' to reach the other end.

Instead of sending a wave *through* the rope, imagine that you just *tug* on one end of it. What happens to the other end? How long does it take for the other end of a taut rope to move after you tug? *It takes no time at all*; the opposite end of the rope will move at the very same instant that you pull on the first end.

Now imagine that the rope is the medium through which you are trying to communicate. Rather than sending a wave *through* the medium, you just *tug* on the medium itself. How long does it take for the signal to reach its destination?

It takes no time at all.

That is how 'gravitational communications' work.

In the two parts of the Vega notebook, Townsend Brown is describing both the rope, and the device that can tug on it.

50

Quantum Germans

(1944)

Artist's rendering of a Nazi flying saucer.

If Townsend Brown could envision devices that he might build around the ideas in the Vega notebook, then it stands to reason – especially in the middle of World War II – that others might be thinking along similar lines.

There are countless myths and legends about secret weapons that the Germans made during the war. Most of that intrigue stems from the expectation that the Germans were rushing headlong toward developing an atomic bomb. After all, the seminal discoveries in nuclear science occurred in Germany.

In December 1938, the German chemist Otto Hahn and his assistant Fritz Strassman were surprised when they discovered traces of barium in a test chamber after they had bombarded a sample of uranium with neutrons. Hahn wrote of his results to another colleague, Lise Meitner, a Jewish physicist living in exile in Sweden. Meitner discussed Hahn's experiments with her nephew, another German physicist, Otto Frisch. Meitner and Frisch arrived at the only plausible explanation: the barium in Hahn's apparatus was produced when the nuclei of uranium atoms split into smaller, lighter elements as a consequence of the neutron bombardment.

Frisch borrowed a term from cellular biology, calling Hahn and Strassman's discovery 'nuclear fission.'

Eight months later Albert Einstein wrote a letter[67] to Franklin Roosevelt, telling the President of the United States that with the energy released by splitting atoms, it was...

> **...conceivable that extremely powerful bombs of a new type may thus be constructed. A single bomb of this type, carried by boat and exploded in a port, might very well destroy the whole port together with some of the surrounding territory...**

Einstein – though still a pacifist after his own exile from Germany in 1933 – urged the president to accelerate the United States' research into this new kind of weapon. He inferred that the Germans were already on a similar path, noting that Germany had curtailed the sale of uranium from mines in Czechoslovakia. Einstein's warning to Roosevelt was clear: if the United States did not get with the program, surely the Germans would beat them to it.

Progress in the nascent realm of nuclear physics advanced rapidly from that point. In December 1942 Enrico Fermi, another European émigré, constructed an atomic pile – the first nuclear reactor – in a squash court underneath an abandoned football stadium at the University of Chicago. Soon after that, a cadre of scientists – many of them exiled from Hitler's Europe, including Frisch and Fermi – started to assemble atop a remote mesa near Los Alamos, New Mexico in what became known as the Manhattan Project.

The Allies suspicions were confirmed when Niels Bohr arrived at Los Alamos. A native Dane and one of the originators of quantum mechanics, Bohr escaped occupied Denmark before he would have been compelled to 'volunteer' for the German war effort.

According to Michael Bar-Zohar, writing in *The Hunt for German Scientists,*

> **Before leaving Denmark, Bohr had been in touch with German physicists, and he was certain that they were hard at work to make an A-bomb. But no one knew what was really happening in Germany, just how far the development in atomic energy had advanced. It was known, however, that a few weeks after the outbreak of the war, the leading atomic physicists had been banded into a 'Uranium Society,' the *Uran-Verein*, under the direction of Heisenberg. It was known that the Nazis had clamped down on the export of uranium from Czechoslovakia, and that they were working the heavy water factory at Rjukan, Norway to full capacity. It was presumed that Germany was making great strides in the race for the atom bomb.**

Werner Heisenberg – whose 'uncertainty principle' says you can't simultaneously know both the location and velocity of a subatomic particle – was the most renowned of all the physicists still living in Germany. He professed no allegiance with the Nazis, but considered himself a loyal German, and remained in his homeland to contribute what he could to her defense.

In 1944, the Director of the Manhattan Project, Brigadier General Leslie R. Groves, wanted to find out how close Germany was to building an atomic bomb. A new intelligence unit was formed to send teams into Germany. The new operation was called 'Alsos,' which is Greek for 'grove.' Because it combined expertise in physics with military commando skills, one Manhattan Project scientist likened Alsos to "Mata Hari with a physics degree."

When Alsos teams slipped into Europe in the fall of 1944, a surprising picture of German nuclear research began to emerge: German scientists were still having great difficulty in separating uranium isotopes. They had only built their first nuclear pile in August 1944 – a milestone that Enrico Fermi passed in America two years earlier. As Allied forces closed in on Germany, Bar-Zohar writes, "The terrifying specter of a German atomic attack evaporated."

Why was the pursuit of an atomic weapon in such disarray in the nation where nuclear fission was first discovered?

Many of the Fatherland's brightest lights had long since fled, taking their expertise across the Atlantic into the New Mexico desert. Much of the young talent that remained was fed into the Nazi war machine. Then there was the Nazi high command's disdain for eccentric, brainy types. As the Reich began to crumble, the military turned toward more readily deployable weaponry like the V-1 and V-2 rocket bombs.

The deeper reason why Germany was not farther along may have been more rooted in Nazi ideology: the Third Reich's wholesale dismissal of anything that wreaked of 'Jewish' physics.

Or maybe that's just the story we've been told.

What one writer[68] has called 'the Allied Legend' says that the defeat of Nazi Germany in the spring of 1945 abruptly interrupted Germany's atomic aspirations. What the legend doesn't say is what else the Germans might have been working on.

*

A few months after I started corresponding with Morgan, he introduced me to a colleague who had also worked closely over the years with Townsend Brown: 'O'Riley' - the diminutive Irishman with the near-lethal rolled-up magazine.

The email exchanges with my newest digital pen pal started about the time that I was learning about the cosmology that keeps the physics of relativity at arm's length from the physics of quantum mechanics. Sometimes the macrocosm doesn't dovetail neatly with the microcosm – a dilemma for those lettered experts who expect all the laws of physics to apply uniformly regardless of scale.

Newer theories try to reconcile the discrepancies. In the years while I was exploring this shaft of the rabbit hole, the physicist Brian Green breathed popular life into something called 'String Theory,' with books like *The Elegant Universe*[69] (2003) and *The Fabric of the Cosmos*[70] (2005).

A title like *The Fabric of the Cosmos* conjures concepts similar to those that Townsend Brown articulated in *Structure of Space* – most notably, that there is an energetic substance to the vacuum of space.

Long after Michelson and Morley, some physicists still concede the existence of 'the thing that is nothing' that occupies the otherwise empty space between the nucleus and the electron shell on the microcosmic scale, and between planets, stars, and galaxies on the macrocosmic scale: It is called by a variety of names like the 'Higgs Ocean' or the 'Dirac Sea;' A songwriter friend of mine calls it "The Infinite Field,"[71] and still others speak of the 'Zero Point.'

Whatever it is, just don't call it 'ether.'

In the midst of my own attempts to reconcile relativity, quantum mechanics, and the *Structure of Space*, I encountered a passage in Nick Cook's *The Hunt For Zero Point,* a book which had already become a recurring point of reference between Morgan, O'Riley and me because it includes the only recently published account of the mythos around Townsend Brown. Cook quotes Igor Witkowski,[72] a Polish researcher:

> **The Germans ignored Einstein and developed an approach to gravity based on quantum theory. Don't forget that Einstein physics, relativity physics, with its big-picture view of the universe, represented Jewish science to the Nazis. Germany was where quantum mechanics was born. The Germans were looking at gravity from a different perspective than everyone else. Maybe that gave them answers to things the pro-relativity scientists hadn't even thought of.**

In a message to O'Riley on Feb 18, 2005, I speculated that:

> **Theoretical Physics split off in two directions in the 1930s. One fork in the road followed the path of relativity; the other followed the path of quantum mechanics. Because the Germans dismissed relativity as 'Jewish physics,' their scientists followed the quantum path, which gave them a head start on things that their British and American counterparts were not attuned to – except, perhaps, for Townsend Brown and a few of his colleagues in the 'black' realm. Does that sound about right?**

Within a few minutes O'Riley replied:

Not just about right, dead on right. I feel like Henry Higgins: "By George, I think he's got it!" Don't know if you recognize that scene but the same amount of dancing around the den is occurring here. Thank you. I believe "You've got it!"

*

I'd got... what, exactly?

To answer that question, I returned to my correspondence with Morgan – and discovered that Morgan had referred me to passages in *The Hunt for Zero Point* more than a dozen times.

There are some curious parallels between the odyssey that Nick Cook relates and my own tumble down the rabbit hole.

For starters, Cook's journey began when an unknown somebody dropped a magazine article about anti-gravity research in the 1950s on his desk - much as my own quest began when an anonymous email showed up in my inbox just as I was finishing the Farnsworth bio and wondering what I would do for an encore.

More interestingly, Cook had his own shadowy source. In his opening acknowledgments, Cook identifies 'Dan Marckus' as one of four people "whose identities I have deliberately blurred." In Chapter 7, 'Marckus' first appears as "an eminent scientist attached to the physics department of one of Britain's best-known universities." Throughout the remainder of the book, 'Marckus' supplies Cook with quizzical data dumps and info bombs that guide Cook's further research and narrative.[73]

At one of their encounters at a country pub, Marckus comments on the path that led Cook to Germany, where he discovered that – contrary to "the Allied Legend" – some German scientists were exploring the other side of the relativity -v- quantum divide. Marcus told Cook,

When the Americans tripped over this other strain of physics and took it back home with them, they were astute enough to realize that their homegrown scientific talent couldn't handle it. The Nazis developed a unique approach to the science and engineering because their ideology, unrestrained as it was, supported a wholly different way of doing things. That's why the Americans recruited so many Germans after the war.

Cook's full title – *The Hunt For Zero Point: Inside the Classified World of Antigravity Technology* may be a perplexing mashup of several ideas, but it is not entirely off the mark. The title distills several threads of unorthodox science:

whether there is a link between electricity and gravity, and whether there is a seething cauldron of energy lurking in the quantum void.

If there is any validity to these unorthodoxies, then why they remain under wraps is revealed in something else that Morgan steered me toward, something that 'Marckus' said to Cook near the end of the book:

> **Release that energy slowly and you've got a safe, clean reactor that can go on pumping out power forever. Speed up the process ... and you've got a bomb – one that will make a thermo-nuke look like a child's firecracker.**

Maybe that explains why any viable research into 'zero-point energy' or 'anti-gravity' technology remains as much a secret now as the Manhattan Project was in the 1940s. Because, as 'Marckus' told Cook, "Things that appear impossible usually aren't, even when the physics *say* they are."

*

The Alsos missions ended in May 1945. The day after Germany's surrender on May 8th, Werner Heisenberg – the German equivalent of the Manhattan Project's enigmatic Dr. Robert Oppenheimer – was captured at his chalet in Bavaria.

By the time Heisenberg was captured, the Americans were already convinced that the Germans were far from producing any atomic weapons. The explanations for Heisenberg's failure vary. Some say that Heisenberg sandbagged the effort, not wanting such awesome power in Nazi hands. Others say he simply didn't grasp the demands of the actual physics. Heisenberg himself maintained that the hardships of the war itself forestalled any real progress.

The Alsos expedition was focused on finding a German bomb because the Americans were trying to build a bomb. Once they determined that the German bomb effort had fallen behind, they stopped asking questions. Nobody thought to ask Heisenberg or his colleagues just what else the 'quantum Germans' might have been working on.

While the Alsos teams scoured the German countryside, perhaps they should have thought to look skyward.

51

Foo Fighters

(1944)

Smokey Stover, the original 'Foo Fighter'

The unidentifiable flying objects known as 'foo fighters' started showing up in the skies over the Rhineland in the autumn of 1944.

As Allied bombers penetrated German airspace, the pilots and crews reported encounters with luminous orange and red 'balls of fire' that rose silently out of the darkened landscape. The fireballs never took any hostile action, but their ghostly appearance and eerie ability to follow the bombers' flight path made the crews reluctant to report what they'd seen.

They may have been named 'foo' after the French word for fire, which is 'feu.' Or the name was lifted from *Smokey Stover*[74] – a popular comic strip featuring a cartoon fireman with a habit of saying "Where there's foo, there's fire." Other variations had them being called 'Feurball,' 'Kugelblitz,' or simply 'Krautballs.' But in the decades since the war, 'foo fighters' is than name that has stuck[75].

In an article entitled *The Foo Fighter Mystery,* reporter Jo Chamberlain offered the first published account in the December 1945 issue of *American Legion* magazine. On the night of November 23, 1944, an Air Force intelligence officer identified as Lieutenant Fred Ringwald joined the crew of a Black Widow fighter-bomber of the 415th Night Fighter Squadron, taking off from Dijon, France, and flying a diversionary mission along the northern edge of the Black Forest. About

20 miles from Strasbourg, Ringwald directs the attention of the pilot, Lieutenant Edward Schlueter:

"I wonder what those lights are, over there in the hills."

"Probably stars," Schlueter said, knowing from experience that the size and character of lights are hard to estimate at night.

"No, I don't think so."

"Are you sure it's no reflection from us?"

"I'm positive."

Then Ringwald remembered there weren't any hills over there. Still, a row of eight or ten orange fireballs was moving toward them at terrific speed. Seeing the lights off his left wing, Schlueter radioed ground radar.

"Nobody up there but you," radar reported. "Are you crazy?"

Wary of enemy aircraft, Schlueter banked toward the lights, ready for action. The lights disappeared. Moments later they reappeared much farther off. Five minutes after that, they vanished altogether.

The puzzled airmen resumed their mission, destroying freight trains behind German lines. Returning to their base in Dijon, they agreed to do what any prudent aviator would do – keep their mouths shut about what they were certain they had seen.

In the remaining months of the war, there were dozens, maybe hundreds of similar encounters. Flight crews returning from their missions would speak under their breath of mystifying orange and red balls of light that floated up from the German countryside and mimicked the Allied planes' flight patterns before disappearing into the night. Details varied, but all concurred that the fireballs appeared to be under some kind of intelligent control.

In her *American Legion* article, Jo Chamberlain wrote of the final encounter, in May 1945 – the last week of the war in Europe.

> **The last time the foo-fighters appeared, the pilot turned into them at the earliest possible moment – and the lights disappeared. The pilot was sure that he felt prop wash, but when he checked with ground radar, there was no other airplane.**
>
> **The pilot continued on his way, then noticed lights far to the rear. The night was clear, and the pilot was approaching a huge cloud. Once in the cloud, he dropped down two thousand feet and made a 30-degree left turn. Just a few seconds later be emerged from the cloud – with his eye peeled to the rear. Sure enough, coming out of**

the cloud in the same relative position was the foo fighter, as though thumbing its nose at the pilot, then disappearing.

This was the last time the foo-fighters were seen in Germany.

*

The myth of the foo fighters is just the tip of an iceberg of speculation about Nazi secret weapons. It doesn't take a whole lot of effort – Google helps – to fill a bookshelf or a hard drive with theories about Nazi UFOs, Nazi flying saucers, even Nazi time machines with names like Schriever, Habermohl, Miethe and Beluzzo – names that mean little outside the annals of pseudo-science and pseudo-history.

Of equal interest is the speculation about Allied intelligence operations – where they went, who they recruited[76], what they learned and what was done with that information.

Questions abound: Did the Germans really develop exotic technologies that were recovered and brought to the U.S. (or other western nations) and hidden so well that they remain out of sight today? Would such exploits have been orchestrated by a government agency? Or could they have been safeguarded by an even more secret organization, one with tendrils into the intelligence establishment, but wielding even greater power and influence?

And what is the possibility that those technologies may have been based on the same discoveries that Townsend Brown made in the 1920s?

I am loathe to entertain conspiracy theories about government coverups and alien technologies. But even the most skeptical investigators are inclined to believe that something other than an apparition was darting about in the skies over Germany in the closing months of the War.

Andy Roberts,[77] veteran UFO researcher from the UK with a reputation for unraveling complex cases, supports the guileless reports of aerial lights:

> **Out of all this, some clear facts are apparent. Hundreds of aircrews saw and recorded what we now call 'foo fighters' during World War II. There must be many thousands of ex-aircrew who have stories to tell.**
>
> **I firmly believe that foo fighters were a real though non-solid phenomena, and I reject the hallucination/misperception hypothesis. These people's lives depended on being able to see and identify aerial objects very quickly. One mistake was their last. Some crews have admitted misperceiving Venus, etc., but realizing it in seconds, and certainly not a whole crew being fooled for any length of time.**

With the war ending in the spring of 1945, Townsend Brown needed to find out what the flight crews had seen. For himself – and for the Caroline Group.

52

Bombers And Parachutes

(1945)

*A Halifax bomber much like the one Townsend
Brown jumped out of in April 1945.*

On April 12, 1945, a news bulletin out of Washington shocked the world: Franklin Roosevelt – President since 1933 and only a few months into his unprecedented fourth term – was dead at the age of 63.

According to Morgan:

> **Brown was at home in California. Josephine was distraught over the death of FDR and turned to Townsend for consolation. The next day, Dr. Brown left on a mission, without a word – which was something that Josephine had become accustomed to. He was pulled away from his work in California because of reports coming from Europe about what the Germans had been developing.**

Those reports, Morgan said, were coming through channels within the Caroline Group, affirming the Group's reach and influence on both sides of the front lines.

I pressed for details.

> **Dr. Brown had information about a 'propulsion system' that the Germans were working on at the end of the war. I won't go into it specifically, but I think that you already know that it manifested itself by looking like... well... balls of light.**

The night after Franklin Roosevelt died Townsend Brown held Josephine in his arms. In the morning he slipped away.

Eight months later, their daughter was born.

*

In his 2001 exposé of the National Security Agency, *Body of Secrets,*[78] national security expert James Bamford writes about top-secret operations fanning out through the rubble of The Third Reich in the closing weeks of World War II. The ostensible purpose of the Target Intelligence Committee (TICOM) was to get its hands on a German cryptographic machine code-named 'The Fish.'

> **Although Bletchley Park had conquered the Enigma machine, the Germans had managed to go one better. They developed a new and even more secret cipher machine, the Geheimschreiber, or secret writer, which was reserved for the very-highest-level messages, including those to and from Hitler himself. Unlike Enigma, the Fish was capable of automatically encrypting at one end and decrypting at the other. TICOM's goal was to capture a working model intact and thus learn exactly how the Germans built such a complex, sophisticated encryption device.**

American intelligence during the war was orchestrated by the Office of Strategic Services (OSS), under the direction of General William O. 'Wild Bill' Donovan – who coordinated his operations with those established by William S. Stephenson in the U.S. and Britain. Shortly after Harry S Truman was sworn in to succeed Roosevelt, Donovan advised the new president that once the war ended, "the Soviet Union will become a menace more formidable to the United States than any yet known."

Consequently, as Bamford writes, Truman expanded TICOM's mission:

> **...to capture as many German code breakers and cipher machines as possible. With such information, Allied cryptologists could discover which of their cipher systems might have been broken, and thus were vulnerable to attack. At the same time, because the Germans had developed advanced systems to attack Soviet codes and ciphers, the West would gain an invaluable shortcut in finding ways to break Russian cipher systems. The key, however, was finding the men and machines before the Russians, who could then use the German successes to break American and British ciphers.**

TICOM became an umbrella for a wide range of intelligence efforts.[79] As TICOM military personnel scoured the German countryside in the spring and summer of 1945 looking for German cipher machines, other experts and specialists were operating on the periphery with their own agendas.

Of the chaotic days in Washington after Roosevelt died, Morgan told me:

> ...there were already powerful forces at work. There were some advisors around Roosevelt who were trying to lobby for 'better relations' with the Soviets. And Truman had been quoted as saying that he felt that the Soviets were "straight forward" – a statement that made many a blood stream boil over.
>
> Like Donovan, William Stephenson also knew that the Russians were going to be the next big threat to the free world, and from his position with the Group he mobilized forces, sometimes with – and often without – political approval. Stephenson operated that way. It was the trait for which the code name "Intrepid" was most apropos.
>
> Stephenson had already sent units – British, MI6 related units – into Germany, carrying their own 'laundry list' of things that were specifically of interest to the Group. The U.S. Army also had a system in place, but their guys were taking up space in the English countryside, waiting for the word to go. The moment that FDR died, the orders were given to saddle up. There is always a vacant moment during the change of power, and the Caroline Group took full advantage of the opportunity to send their units into action.

*

A few days after leaving Josephine in the Hollywood Hills, Townsend Brown found himself at a low altitude in the skies over Germany aboard a Halifax bomber with a parachute strapped to his back.

The Halifax was a heavy, four-engine bomber built by the Handley Page Aircraft Company in Britain with parts supplied by Stephenson ally Rootes Motors. More than six thousand Halifax bombers delivered a variety of explosives over the German countryside, but this one[80] was specially rigged to deliver spies.

The Halifax lumbered into German airspace just above the treetops, its sole passenger huddled near the open hatch, waiting for the order to jump. At the drop zone, flying at a mere three hundred feet, the bomb-bay doors opened to drop some supplies. Then the plane circled to six hundred feet – low enough to evade German radar and just barely high enough for a novice paratrooper to get his parachute open before hitting the ground.

Morgan wrote:

I close my eyes sometimes and wonder what it was like for Dr. Brown. He was not a trained military man. Oh, sure, he'd had his basic training in the Navy, was the top man at Great Lakes Station, but that was 15 years earlier. And nothing in that training would have prepared him to jump out of an airplane only 600 feet above the ground.

It took guts to jump out of that Halifax over what was then enemy territory, cold and dark. I have spent endless hours in the kind of quiet solitude that happens before jumping out into that darkness. It must have been a daunting challenge, both for him and his companions waiting on the ground; most of them just worried about keeping this mild- mannered man alive.

When I asked Morgan why this mild-mannered civilian was jumping out of an airplane into the crumbling anarchy of the Third Reich, he replied:

With your interest in 'foo-fighters' you are getting much closer to the main reason TTB wanted to be in Germany. Cipher machines were not the first thing on his particular laundry list.

Dr. Brown often said that if you want to see how nature utilizes his 'force fields,' that answer could be found in the plasma vortex sometimes called 'ball lightning.' So when reports of "balls of light that seemed to be under intelligent control" reached others in the military that were familiar with Brown's work, he was put immediately into the front of the search party.

Whether by luck or skill suddenly borne of necessity, Brown managed to get his feet on the ground in small clearing surrounded by trees.

A young Royal Navy Marine ran out of the woods and helped him gather up the parachute.

"I'm going to be your escort on this mission," the Marine said. "Just call me O'Riley."

53

Good For One Fare

1965/66

The daughter that was born to Townsend and Josephine Brown in December 1945 was almost twenty years old in the fall of 1965, when she nearly died from pneumonia. By the time she was fully recovered, Southern Sem was winding down for the Christmas break.

As her classmates dispersed, Linda obsessed on the promise she and Morgan made to meet in New York for New Year's Eve – but she hadn't heard from him since the day he was the "Man on the floor!" Absent any further word, Linda packed her bags and boarded a train, squirreling herself away in a private Pullman compartment for the overnight journey to Florida.

Her parents met her at the station in Miami. Linda noted in her journal that "Mother and Daddy had a big day with Mr. X from Nassau, escorting him around the lab. They were both already pretty tired, so we went straight home" to Homestead instead of spending some time in the city.

The next morning, Linda toured the backyard lab where her father was working on 'the Fan.' "I thought it was fantastic," Linda wrote. "The place looks great! Daddy's Inner Sanctum is bristling with new equipment. The air conditioning is wonderful!"

There was a lot riding on improving the fan, and the pressure was taking a toll on Townsend's health. "Daddy is not feeling well, and when he gets tired, he feels worse."

Linda made a decision:

I want to do more to help, but I won't be able to until I come back in January. That's right. I have decided to leave Sem at the end of this semester. Mother has asked me to do this. Daddy's health is not good, and finances are tight. The thousand dollars that I would have to come up with to finish the year is probably going to have to be used for medical expenses. Besides, I would rather be here, where I can be useful. Getting the Fan on the market will only help us in the long run.

After weakly protesting her decision, Townsend was grateful for Linda's help in the lab. The progress was steady, if slow:

I spent a few hours with him last night and watched it silently push the air. Dad tied a bright ribbon on the front – that's the only

way to tell what the output is. It makes no noise at all, so you really can't tell if it's even turned on without checking the ribbon!

Doctors were mystified by Townsend's shortness of breath and coughing spells. Linda hadn't heard from Morgan and didn't want to do anything that might further stress her father's health, so she didn't say anything to her parents about going to New York for the New Year.

Christmas Day came and went with still no word from Morgan. Linda wandered the grounds, every turn reminding her of the previous summer with Morgan She closed her eyes at a spot on the trail where Morgan had cradled her in his arms. "I could hear his voice and feel the warmth of him."

The following Monday Josephine took Townsend to a hospital for some tests. The results were inconclusive, and he was sent home with orders to rest.

Though she had still not heard from Morgan, Linda decided to engage in "the terrifying procedure of asking for Dad's permission to make the trip" to New York for New Year's.

She found her father in the lab and told him of the invitation. "He took his glasses off and looked out of the window for the longest time. I sensed that things were going to be OK when he put his glasses down gently on his desk – he only threw them down when he was mad."

Townsend put his glasses back on, turned to Linda and said, "If Morgan contacts you, I'll pay for your train ticket."

That same afternoon a letter arrived: "Meet me at Penn Station on the 30th," Morgan wrote.

Townsend bought a ticket for an overnight in the Pullman car and gave Linda $500 in travelers checks. That was "more money than I had ever seen in one place at one time, but if things didn't go well Daddy wanted me to have the means to leave the city if I decided I didn't want to be there."

*

Morgan had his own perspective on the pending rendezvous:

Linda got desperately sick in the fall of '65. Dr. Brown pulled me away from what I had been doing, saying that Linda needed to see me. That's how I became the "man on the floor." He had already promised me that Linda would be making the trip to New York. I think the little charade he put her through was his way of seeing if he still had her absolute loyalty. He needn't have tested her.

Dr. Brown had also told me – again before Linda knew – that we were going to have some time together a few months later in

Philadelphia. At the time, her future was unclear. She only knew that she was leaving school. That was a cruel situation, but it was just the first of many times when I have known more than I could disclose.

As Townsend and Josephine drove Linda to the train station, the highway was blocked by construction. "I was afraid I was going to miss the train," Linda recalled. Once on board and departed, every stop the train made added to her anxiety. Keeping her journal open en-route, Linda wrote, "The train has stopped again, and my impulse is to get out and push the damned thing. Changing locomotives is a pain. I'd better still be hooked to something that is headed for New York!"

The train was three hours late when it finally pulled into Penn Station. There was no sign of Morgan, but they had a backup plan: If he was not at the station, she was to take a cab to his apartment on East 7th Street. When she arrived, a roommate answered the intercom and buzzed her in.

When he finally showed up, Morgan grinned at Linda. "Get your stuff. We'll be spending the next two nights at The Statler."

When she recalls that weekend in New York, what Linda mostly remembers – other than those two nights at the Statler – is "endlessly walking around the city and taking the subway all over the place. I didn't know the city at all, so I had no idea where we were going."

The second night, they "ran into the writer Spaulding Gray,[81] who Morgan had somehow befriended; that man could talk at great length about just anything. We walked and talked with him, and I can remember thinking how much Morgan was acting like Daddy, going from one point to the next, to some special little place that had become his favorite, and then back down onto the subway again to another place, with long walks in between. I am sure that we ate, but I don't remember where. I liked what I saw of the city, and I could tell he loved it."

After they checked out of The Statler, Morgan and Linda returned to the apartment for a New Year's party. "There were quite a few people in the apartment, Linda said, "a couple of sleeping bags in a corner and several people cooking in the kitchen. I didn't know any of them. I remember lying there in this little nook, looking at the books Morgan had collected, and feeling wonderfully close to him, listening to his voice just in the next room, and drifting off to sleep."

Morgan darted out "to catch up with some friends."

When she awoke, "the cast of characters had changed. Morgan's friend Carlos had arrived while I was asleep. It had been several hours, but Morgan hadn't returned. Sometime before midnight I found Carlos in the kitchen reading comic books. At midnight, we watched the ball drop from Times Square on the little television. Carlos and I just sort of looked at each other and said 'Yippee!' He picked up another comic book and I went off to write in my journal."

It was nearly three in the morning before Morgan finally showed up, explaining that he'd been helping a friend find his girlfriend who'd gone missing. "We laughed quietly about my exciting New York adventure. He felt badly that he had left me alone. We whispered and giggled and made love."

As the sun rose over the city for the first time in the year 1966, Morgan and Linda caught the Staten Island Ferry so that Linda could meet up with a classmate and catch a ride back to Virginia. As the ferry approached the pier on Staten Island, Linda realized that she had no idea when she would see Morgan again. She felt a need welling up in her heart to leave him with something to remember her by.

Since she was twelve years old, Linda wore a dark blue, lapis lazuli ring with specks of gold her father had given her, "to help me remember that there are magical things in this world."

As the ferry docked, Linda slipped the ring from her finger and folded it into Morgan's hand, "To "keep you safe and to look over you," she whispered.

Morgan was at a loss.

I felt the urge to find something to give her in exchange, and it had to be equally special and magic. But I had nothing. I reached into my pocket, and all I found was a subway token. "Good for one fare," it read. I gave her that subway token, and with it a promise that she would always have that connection with me. All she would have to do is send me that coin and whatever I had was hers. She promised me that she would always keep that token. *Always.*

Nearly forty years later, when Morgan resurfaced after decades 'in the wind,' his first question was, "Does she still carry the token?"

54

Werewolves And Mud

(1945)

After his midget submarine mission to sink the *Tirpitz*, O'Riley was rewarded with a desk job at Farm Hall, the British intelligence headquarters near Cambridge. Still ranked "two points lower than pond scum," he was assigned to the office of Rear Admiral John Godfrey, the commander of the 30th Assault Unit. The '30th AU' had been formed by Godfrey's personal assistant – an intelligence expert named Ian Fleming[82] – and specialized in locating and retrieving technical intelligence from the Germans.

Their paths had crossed once prior to the night O'Riley helped Townsend Brown gather his parachute in a clearing behind enemy lines in Germany. At Farm Hall, O'Riley recalled:[83]

My duties at Farm Hall consisted mostly of typing and filing. I was told to blend into the walls. While I was learning my way around, a group of 'important Americans' blew through like a fresh breeze. Townsend Brown was one of them. He looked in my direction and nodded, but words were never exchanged. I am not sure, looking back on it now, that he ever really saw me. It's hard to see me in a room full of flag officers.

That's the way it was supposed to be. I ran messages and no one was supposed to notice me coming and going. It wasn't exciting enough for me, though. Strangely, at that age, I valued getting shot at more. So, I stayed quiet, and went through a process that got me dumped behind the lines.

O'Riley got his chance to dodge bullets in the late winter of 1944. As the Allies planned the invasion of Hitler's 'Fortress Europe' for the spring of that year, they began dropping commando teams organized under the code name of 'Operation Carpetbagger'[84] into France to survey the landscape. O'Riley got himself assigned to one of those commando teams.

Most of the agents involved in these missions were American; most of the crews that flew them into occupied territory were British and called their human cargo 'Joes.' In March of 1944, O'Riley and a partner dropped through the 'Joe hole' in the belly of a B-24 and parachuted into the Bergerac region of France. On the ground, O'Riley and his partner met up with French Resistance forces and worked their way east, blowing up bridges and railroads and sabotaging German installations. By the spring of the following year, as Allied forces stormed across the continent, O'Riley was working within the borders of Germany itself.

Of the night he rushed out of the woods to collect Townsend Brown, O'Riley recalled:

> **I had just blown up a train two days earlier. It was beautiful and I wanted to blow up some more stuff, so I was none too pleased when I learned I was going to be doing escort duty.**

> **The first time Townsend Brown spoke to me was as I half dragged, then dumped him into an old farm truck that we had standing by. As we turned out of the field and motored down the very quiet lane, there was no movement anywhere, except maybe a couple of cows watching our ragtag little convoy pass by. He started to laugh. I hadn't heard a sound out of him until that moment. But his laughter was contagious. He was so relieved to be on the ground again. I just started laughing too, and that pretty much set the tone of our experience together. He was an amazing man.**

The following morning, Brown and O'Riley climbed into a dusty, open jeep and drove into the ruins of the Third Reich, accompanied by a 'Caroline radioman' and a fourth soldier.

As Brown's escort and driver, O'Riley understood his instructions were "not to let this man out of my sight or permit him to fall into enemy hands – alive."

I asked O'Riley where in Germany he and Townsend were headed in the spring of 1945. More than sixty years after the fact, all O'Riley would say was, "Can't tell you where. Sorry."

*

In the climactic months of the war, British MI6 Special Operations Executive (SOE) and intelligence officers belonging to other 'obscure units'[85] units flooded the German countryside, determined to retrieve Nazi intelligence secrets.

A few weeks before he was assigned to escort Townsend Brown, O'Riley and a companion were working behind the lines with orders to infiltrate, take notes, and avoid any overt action that would reveal their presence to the enemy. But they were "looking for more than just the odd cipher unit." Most of what they found was reported to British intelligence headquarters at Whitehall, but anything that was truly 'sensitive' was reported directly to William Stephenson.

> **Most of the time I went to the right – to check out something that Stephenson was interested in, and that caused no small consternation in that big office. "Left!" they would repeat with all the ire they could**

**muster. "Damned Irish boatman!" I heard. "Wildly headstrong"
they wrote all over my charts. "Fuck 'em," I added.**

One night, O'Riley and his partner took refuge above the kitchen at a small
inn near a repair station for German tanks. A recon tour of the kitchen produced
only maggot-infested rations. They settled for a couple of beers and "retreated to
our little hole upstairs."

Later that evening, a German sergeant and four truck drivers showed up at the
inn to retrieve some armored vehicles. O'Riley had monitored their movements
earlier in the day.

**Taking notes, of course, always taking notes. That's all we were
supposed to be doing. My partner had other ideas, though. Knowing
that we were nearing the end of this scouting party we were on, he
thought that we should blow the repair facility as a parting gift.
We had just enough explosives left to get the job done. We agreed
between us that we'd blow it and disappear into the woods. Ha! Not
a bad day, we figured.**

From their hideaway above the kitchen, O'Riley and his partner eavesdropped
as the men talked about their families and what they hoped for when the war
was finally over. They were all just trying to keep their wits about them until the
shooting stopped. The sergeant talked about how much he missed his wife – they'd
been married just before the war, he had been with her only a month, but that was
long enough to produce a child he had never seen. O'Riley heard him "passing a
beer, boasting and weeping in the same breath."

Out of the night, a German officer drove up to the inn with three units of
military police. Even though O'Riley and his partner were well hidden...

**...they sent a chill over us. My partner reached for his sidearm but
no... they were not looking for us. We were about to witness what was
called a 'flying drumhead court martial' – a process Hitler himself
had imposed for dealing with suspected deserters which consisted of
an accusation in the field, perfunctory proceedings, a declaration of
guilt and a summary execution.**

**The officer in charge demanded of the sergeant, "What are you
men doing here instead of being at the front with your unit? There
are men dying up there and you cowardly bastards sit here drinking
and laughing!"**

**The sergeant tried to explain they had been sent to the rear
by their regimental commander, naming the renowned Panzer
Commander Colonel Hans Von Luck. "I was ordered to bring some**

armored vehicles that are being repaired here up to the front as quickly as possible," the sergeant explained. **"Work will be going on through the night. We will be able to get them back to the front in the morning."**

The officer demanded the sergeant produce his orders. The sergeant demanded to know who was asking: "I am a decorated platoon leader and not accustomed to being treated in such a manner."

The officer boomed "I AM CHIEF JUDGE ADVOCATE under the direct orders of Field Marshal Schoerner!"

The sergeant stammered, "My orders were word of mouth, directly from my commander!"

"THATS WHAT ALL DESERTERS SAY! In the name of the Fuhrer and by the authority given to me by the commander of Army Group Center, I sentence you to death by shooting on account of proven desertion."

The sergeant protested, "I am a war hero! I can show you my medals!" but it was no use arguing. As O'Riley and his partner watched from their hiding place, the military police "grabbed the man and dragged him out into the little garden and shot him."

While the military police looked on, the dead man's comrades were ordered to dig a shallow grave, into which the body was dumped. They were forbidden to add any kind of marker, because deserters were not allowed to have even a simple cross on their graves.

The next morning, O'Riley and his partner...

...blew the repair facility sky high – along with the officer who had ordered the execution. We let the rest of the dead sergeant's men go so that they could report back to Von Luck that he had lost a good man. And, oh, by the way, he wouldn't be getting his tanks back, either.

*

As their muddy jeep bounced over the ravaged countryside, O'Riley and Townsend Brown looked for secrets known only to Brown.

The weather was terrible the whole time we were there, and the roads – when we were on them – were muck. I wish I could give you specifics, but remember, units like ours did not officially exist. Aside from getting stuck in the mud my biggest fear was running into one of the young Werewolf patrols.

The 'Werewolves' were part of SS Commander Heinrich Himmler's last-ditch effort to preserve Nazi authority as the Third Reich descended into anarchy. They were rogue units of Nazi youth who resisted Allied occupation of the Fatherland with guerilla tactics – sniping, mining, random acts of sabotage and terrorism. One preferred tactic involved stringing decapitation wires across the roads; They were also known to poison food stocks and liquor supplies (which was particularly irksome for some Russians).

O'Riley knew the Werewolf patrols as...

> ...trigger-happy kids who were way too-well-armed. Their answer to a jeep full of Americans would have been to immediately open fire on us. I had seen just such an ambush happen to two other intelligence teams, so I was understandably edgy. Eisenhower[86] didn't want to get caught up in a never-ending war in those snowy mountains, but there were rumors of underground facilities, advanced weapons, and fresh SS-controlled troops sending the 'werewolves' out into the night and blending back into the population again by day.

> The rumor of those underground research facilities was actually quite true. We were pursuing an SS unit that was in possession of some technical stuff that Dr. Brown wanted. By the time we caught up to the town the SS unit had occupied, many of the townspeople had been hanged on the big trees that lined the main street – 60 or so, some women. White sheets were everywhere. The civilians had been hanged by Werewolves because they had put those sheets out when the army left town. We drove through sadly and Dr. Brown simply looked up at those bodies, hanging and turning in the wind and said quietly "...and this is the fruit..."

O'Riley knew that he alone was responsible for the safety and survival of the scientist seated beside him. "He'd made it perfectly clear to me that he had no intention of using the sidearm that had been issued to him," O'Riley said, "so... it was going to be up to me to avoid confrontations and track down the SS unit we were after."

O'Riley kept the mission on course despite the conditions:

> I remember one moment, as were bouncing along, Dr. Brown looked at me, and I looked at him, and we realized both of us were covered with mud – the result of me broad-sliding the jeep into a ditch and having to push it out.

> As we slithered through the mud, we saw displaced people of every description on the main roads. We avoided them as well as

we could by going across pastures. At one point we ran right up on a group of Panzer tanks that were dug in and skirted around them without as much as a how-de-do. All we wanted to do was get to that SS unit, report on them and then be there as soon as they were killed or captured.

O'Riley didn't know what the muddy scientist in the seat beside him was looking for. "Dr. Brown didn't volunteer the information and I didn't ask him, but from my work at the Admiralty I figured we were after some kind of submarine propulsion system."

*

Some tales are best told in the teller's own, unedited and unembellished words. In July 2004 O'Riley wrote:

> We had chanced upon a group of refugees walking along a very muddy road, wandering as many did during that terrible, cold spring. The mud was ankle deep. I had walked away from the vehicle and happened upon the body of a little girl who had been left behind. She was maybe two or three and had been wearing a cloth coat over a little pink dress. It was the flash of pink that had caught my attention.
>
> Now you have to understand. I had seen many things in my life up to that point and am able to say now, without reservation, that I was a murderous youth. To me, the world was only what it had appeared to be. All that mattered was survival. You could be smart, talented, gracious, lovely, warmhearted and it could all end in a flash as if it never existed to begin with. I held no illusions. There was nothing out there but life or death, and it was just pure luck where you ended up.
>
> I don't know why that little girl's body hit me so hard emotionally. She was just so innocent and so… abandoned. I think I pretty much had what might be considered a nervous breakdown right there. I can remember distinctly the feel of the water and mud seeping around my knees.
>
> I guess Dr. Brown saw me go down like that and came to investigate. He climbed out of the jeep, and standing in the ankle-deep mud beside me, he put his hand on my shoulder and said to me, "Join me for the rest of your life and you will be able to stop this in the future."
>
> I know that seems like an odd thing to hear, and out of context it might even seem ridiculous, but right then and right where I was,

with that little girl in that little pink dress lying in the mud in front of me, that statement made more sense than anything I had ever heard.

I just turned to him and said "Yes, Sir."

55

Pear Shaped

(1945)

Somewhere between Dresden and Berlin, as the jeep carrying Brown, O'Riley, the 'Caroline radioman' and a fourth soldier bounced over the muddy roads and slid through mucky meadows, Townsend confided the object of their mission: a secret rendezvous with a German scientist:

> **He told me he had a limited time to reach the area where a pick-up was going to happen. It wasn't going to be an exchange, just a simple handover of a German physicist. Today, the guy might be called a 'high voltage' expert: somebody who had been pressed into service of the SS for their own secret weapons work.**

> **I had been told more or less where we were going but, for most of the trip, had bought into the idea that we were chasing an SS unit. I didn't know until after the pink dress incident, that there was another layer of the mission, and that it involved William Stephenson.**

Townsend told O'Riley that the primary reason he was in Germany was to interview this scientist – to vet him and arrange to get him out of the country before the Russians got to him.

They expected to find their target in an abandoned farmhouse where the Germans were running a cipher unit. Their target would be wearing the uniform of a rank-and-file German soldier and carrying papers to match. Once the target's identity was verified, he would be ferried off to a location where other Caroline operatives could get him out of the country.

But before the handover was completed, O'Riley said, "Things went all pear-shaped."

Pieces of this story came to me over time, from different sources, and they don't fit cleanly together. First, O'Riley told me:

> **There were a lot of crews out there just before the end of the war, once it became obvious that the Russians were on the move and that Germany was finished. Technology was lying about like cotton in a field. You might even call those crews 'harvesters' because that's what they reminded me of. I had knowledge of the Mafia sending teams. And then the Americans of course, the British, the Canadians and the French. I even ran into a South African crew. There were black**

market privateers, and just plain dyed-in-the-wool bandits. Oh, it was interesting!

One of the American units operating in the area was a covert TICOM team under the direction of Lt. Commander Howard Campaigne,[87] who kept a tight reign over what he considered his province in hostile territory. Somewhere on those muddy roads, Brown and company crossed paths with Campaigne. According to O'Riley:

> The moment we ran into the patrol they took us into custody to check our papers. Our documentation listed us an 'intelligence unit,' which was enough to satisfy Campaigne that we weren't some kind German unit in disguise. Fortunately, prior communication had informed Campaigne that units such as ours were operating in his area, so he knew who we were – well, on one level at least.

Like it or not, Brown's errant foursome was part now of TICOM.

The narrative switches now, between O'Riley's first-hand account and details added by Morgan, who explained that Brown and his crew stumbled into Campaigne while his TICOM unit was in the middle of a delicate operation. Campaigne's unit had captured one valuable German installation, but according to Morgan:

> The German team leader wasn't stupid. He had been in charge of the cipher machine and knew how important it would be to the Americans. So even before the door burst open and he was faced with immediate surrender, he had previously arranged a better deal for himself. He informed the American commander that there was a second machine – a backup unit that was still in operation in the next town.

The location of the backup cipher unit was also Brown's destination – the farmhouse where he would find a high-value German scientist disguised as an ordinary soldier.

Whether by accident or design, Brown's team was included in the detachment that was sent to investigate the second unit. According to Morgan:

> Campaigne worked up a plan to send a small team to check out the report. Dr. Brown was folded into the group because he was familiar with the target machine. They took him so that he could identify what they were looking for. But 'cipher machines' were not the only things on *his* 'laundry list.' Most of these embedded scientists were rocketry specialists, others had a background in radar. The push was to find things the Germans had that we didn't.

One soldier that Campaigne did *not* include on the team was O'Riley:

> The fact that I was a Royal Marine became an irritation for him. Jerking me off the jeep was his way of taking over – like a cat or a dog marking their territory.
>
> My seat in the jeep was taken by a kid from Arkansas. Our Caroline radioman remained. This was a mix that was not supposed to be there. The kid from Arkansas had been the point man who knocked the door down on the first cipher unit the day before; his bell had been rung pretty hard, and he'd watched a buddy take a sniper's bullet in the head.
>
> Dr. Brown was supposed to meet and talk with his target, to decide if he was to come over to the American side, or perhaps be shifted to the English. Dr. Brown had first call on him. This was all supposed to be worth Dr. Brown's jumping into a very dark, cold night. The German scientist was carefully brought to the abandoned farmhouse, and all would have gone well if we hadn't run into Campaigne.

Morgan provided this detail:

> The leader of the second German cipher unit had been warned by the first. They were actually waiting, and the small team ran right into an ambush.

O'Riley again:

> Dr. Brown's team arrived at daybreak after driving through the night. All was quiet at this second farmhouse, but I am sure the Arkansas kid's back teeth were grinding. Dr. Brown walked right to the front door and simply knocked.
>
> A German soldier opened the door and stepped back. A man behind a table reached for something that he was going to hand to Dr. Brown, but the kid had stepped in by then and his senses went into overload. He drew and fired.

In the next instant a firefight erupted in the farmhouse, with German sentries adding fire from the periphery. When the shooting stopped, the German scientist – dressed as a common soldier – and three of the Americans including the radio operator were all dead.

And Townsend Brown lay bleeding from a bullet that had ripped through his shoulder and penetrated a lung before exiting out his back.

56

Eerily Quiet

(1945)

German Panzer Commander Colonel Hans Von Luck

When the smoke cleared in the farmhouse, the three Germans who survived the attack gathered up Townsend Brown and tied him to a chair.

In our correspondence, Morgan and O'Riley told me that the Group had an operative on the German side: the Panzer Commander Colonel Hans Von Luck, whose troops O'Riley encountered in the week before he was dispatched as Brown's escort. According to Morgan and O'Riley, Von Luck was in the vicinity, had some dominion over the cipher units – and now intervened on Townsend Brown's behalf.

Von Luck wanted to get Brown back in the hands of his own people. The officer in charge of the cipher unit, who wanted to recover the hardware and personnel TICOM had in its custody, proposed a trade and a diabolical plan to implement it.

The German officer noticed that the middle finger was missing from Townsend Brown's left hand[88]. Figuring that the German scientist – lying dead in a common soldier's uniform - wasn't going to need any of the fingers on either hand anymore, he severed the middle finger from the dead man's hand. He then took a knife to the semi-conscious Brown's left hand to make it look like it was Brown's finger he had just hacked off and handed the bloody, severed digit to the kid from Arkansas.

O'Riley picks up the story:

> **All 'Arkansas' saw was this badly wounded American with blood oozing out of his chest and hand. The kid found his way back to the American outpost, showed Campaigne the bloody finger, and conveyed what the German officer told him: that this American scientist would be returned "piece by piece" unless the prisoners in Campaigne's custody were released.**

But Campaigne placed a higher priority on maintaining TICOM's secrecy than he did on the life of the scientist who was now the bait in a high stakes gamble.

According to Morgan:

> **Campaigne wanted the scientist back, but it would simply be more convenient to have him dead. No information could be leaked out from this situation. For Campaigne, the only thing that needed to be done was overpower the second German facility. He'd write the entire thing off as a glitch, with the loss of some of his men and unfortunately a talented scientist.**

Back at the TICOM camp, O'Riley considered his removal from Brown's team…

> **… was of the big failures in my career – sending my scientist off and he being seriously wounded. I was certain I could have prevented that from happening. I thoroughly grilled 'Arkansas' about what had happened, and Dr. Brown's condition. The kid was not really helpful. All he could say was "I dunno, I think he's finished."**
>
> **A few minutes later there was a commotion as another jeep barreled into the middle of the TICOM command center, "with all flags flying…"**

Operating under the authority of the British Admiralty's Director of Naval Intelligence (DNI), the leader of that jeep's crew took command of the efforts to salvage whatever and whoever was left at the farmhouse.

> **This new figure pulled a lot of weight. Within a very few moments of this new arrival, Campaigne was told to "get your sorry ass in there and get those machines." Campaigne was already planning to do just that, but with this new input, was suddenly moving much faster.**

We don't know his rank or military position, but I was told the name of the man who pulled rank on Campaigne was Robert Sarbacher[89] – and his objective was to recover both the injured scientist *and* the cipher machines, alive and intact.

Before leaving, Sarbacher commandeered some additional muscle in the form of a young Royal Marine. He didn't let on to Campaigne that he already knew the Irish boatman.

Sarbacher swept past O'Riley, paused, turned back, and gave O'Riley a once-over.

"Who are you?" Sarbacher bellowed.

O'Riley replied with name, rank, and serial number.

"You are with me," Sarbacher said to O'Riley, with a withering gaze toward Campaigne.

We swept out the door, me following quickly behind and grabbing my gear, like Cinderella going to the ball. Based on what 'Arkansas' told me I figured this was strictly a mop up operation. I expected to collect Dr. Brown's body, along with our other men, our jeep with the 'Caroline' radio set. Though no one could have broken its code, it was a valuable piece to us. Plus, the fact that we needed to collect what was there as far as paperwork. Pick up the pieces and wipe off all the fingerprints, so to speak.

By the time Sarbacher and O'Riley arrived, the farmhouse yard was "eerily quiet." All the German soldiers who had been alive when Arkansas departed with the severed finger were found dead. Only Townsend Brown remained alive, tied to a chair, still bleeding from his chest and left hand. O'Riley:

Sarbacher went in ahead of me and went straight to a corner where he found Dr. Brown. That Dr. Brown was still alive came as a shock to me. Sarbacher just pointed, and then went off to do whatever it was that he was originally planning to do with the cipher gear and related paperwork. I tended to Dr. Brown while Sarbacher sent another team to collect our jeep and the other men we had lost. It was a Big Score for Campaigne, getting those cipher units – but he never saw the paperwork. I slowly faded to black along with Sarbacher once our chores were finished.

After triage in the field, Brown was evacuated to a U.S. military hospital near Farm Hall, the manor house outside of Cambridge that would become famous after the war as the destination for scientists active in the German pursuit of atomic weapons, among them Werner Heisenberg and Otto Hahn.

Within a few weeks, Townsend was recovered enough to flirt with the pretty

English nurses in their brown-and-white seersucker uniforms. One nurse made sure he always had fresh roses in a silver vase in his room.

*

Back in California, it was mid-June before Josephine Brown learned that her husband had been injured in April. O'Riley told me:

> **Josephine was never told about his experience in Germany. Dr. Brown may have told her, but I suspect that he did not. All she knew was that he had been injured and was recovering in England. She did not know the nature of his injury, nor where he was when he'd been injured. All she heard was that he had been fighting an infection.**

It was suggested that Josephine move out of the crowded Hollywood Hills to a location far from people who might be curious about her husband's condition. There were still whispers about the FBI and Townsend's abrupt departure from the Navy in the middle of the War. Rather than dodging her chatty circle of friends and bridge partners, it was easier to start a whole new story, to pack up the Wonderland bungalow and leave no forwarding address.

According to Morgan, The Caroline Group offered to provide "the house of her choice – anywhere except Washington D.C. or Ohio." She chose a house in Laguna Beach, on a bluff overlooking the Pacific Ocean. Once again, in the summer of 1945, she packed and unpacked her little green teapot.

The new home had a private flight of wooden stairs down to an isolated beach. The sun, the surf, and the exercise of climbing those stairs, she hoped, would help her husband heal.

In England, Townsend recovered slowly. The bullet that struck him had shattered, and one of the fragments nicked his lung. The lung healed, but scar tissue formed in it. Morgan said:

> **He also worried that others were getting hold of stuff that he needed, that things were falling into the wrong hands. Caroline Group colleagues were spread out all over and all of them knew the importance of what they were doing, but he had been injured and sent home. That just did not sit well with him. He was plagued by lingering feelings of having failed in his mission – even though nothing that went wrong was at all his fault.**

And, of course, it had rained most of the time Townsend was in England.

> **Because of that he was not doing well. Frankly I just think that he needed to be back with Josephine. She always had a way of bringing the sunshine to him, even when he couldn't see it.**

It was August before Townsend returned to the United States, to the new house in Laguna Beach. Years later, Brown told O'Riley that "he honestly felt that her attention to the location and her loving care saved his life."

Bedridden when he first arrived, Josephine brought him flowers and made sure he took all his medications. When he was ready, she guided his tentative steps down the wooden stairs the beach. "He complained," Morgan said, "but he did it."

Eleven-year-old Joseph was never told the truth about his father's injury, nor the circumstances that caused it. Josephine told Joseph – and anybody else in their new neighborhood who asked – that his father had been hurt in an auto accident.

As summer progressed into autumn, so did Josephine's pregnancy. Townsend's own strength improved enough that he could finally tend to *her* needs. When she joined him on the beach, he would scoop out a hollow in the sand so that Josephine could lie on her stomach and take the pressure off her back.

Their daughter arrived a few weeks premature on December 11, 1945.

"She was named Linda Ann Brown," Morgan said, "so that her initials would spell out her father's favorite place."

57

We Have Much To Decide

(1966)

After New Year's in New York with Morgan, Linda Ann Brown returned to Southern Sem only long enough to announce that she was dropping out. With the subway token safely tucked away, she boarded a train to Florida. In Homestead, she settled into a routine of working at her father's side in the place her initials spelled out.

In her journal, Linda wrote:

> **Daddy isn't even awake until nine o'clock. Then he putters around until noon, doing whatever strikes his fancy: maintenance on the house, running to the hardware store. At noon Mother fixes him lunch. Then he goes to the lab and works there until 4 o'clock – teatime – and everything stops for crackers and cheese and Earl Grey. After tea he takes a short nap, then goes back to puttering or sunbathing. After dinner he is back in the lab until two or three in the morning.**
>
> **Half of the time, he feels he does not have any worthwhile thoughts in the middle of the day unless he is on a beach somewhere. With the common distractions of the world – a dripping faucet for example – space propulsion and everything else connected to it goes out the window!**

On the surface, Townsend was still hard at work on the electrokinetic fan. Frequent visits with Mr. X from Nassau caused Linda to wonder what else might be going on:

> **'Nassau' being here is turning into a regular thing. Dad said at dinner that he'd been offered $100,000 cash if we would move the operation over there and cut the Homestead lab loose. Myself, I'd be packed already! Morgan has said that he can swim there if he has to – though I am getting the distinct impression from 'Nassau' that Morgan probably has a boat with his name on it waiting at the docks. I'm not sure I like that, but I'll not have a lot to say about that situation.**

In addition to the "Nassau" proposition, Linda was surprised to learn that her father was also thinking about returning to the Philadelphia area, to work again with Martin Decker, whom he had been working with when they lived at Ashlawn.

Martin Decker[90] ran a sprawling industrial compound on a hill in Bala Cynwyd, a lush suburb on the Main Line, the spine of Philadelphia high society. Townsend had moved his family to Philadelphia before Linda's junior year in high school in order to use Decker's facilities to work on his projects. At the beginning of that arrangement, Brown exchanged several patents for stock in Electrokinetics, Inc., a new company Decker created to develop and market The Fan. When that deal went south, Decker informed Brown he could "paper your privy" with his worthless stock. Linda learned of all this months later, after her parents had closed up and left Ashlawn.

Given their past history, Linda was surprised that her father would give Decker a second thought. They drove together to Philadelphia where Townsend "met with some people." Along the way Linda learned that her father had sued Decker for fraud, suggesting that Decker was trying to resolve their dispute by offering to fund the operation in Homestead or move it back to the compound in Philadelphia.

*

Linda heard little from Morgan after stepping off the Staten Island Ferry with the subway token. From one of the few letters she received, she knew that he'd wrapped up his work-study program in New York and resumed his Russian studies major in Ohio.

"He mentioned a book his class was reading," Linda recalled, "Lermontov's A Hero of Our Times[91]. They were reading it in Russian and translating as they read. I think that he made a point to tell me that so I could put two and two together regarding his future plans."

Linda knew she had made the right decision. "Dad was not well, and I made the right move leaving school and joining the project," she wrote. "Something important was brewing between Dad and Nassau, and somehow Morgan was even then becoming a part of that inner circle."

As the winter of 1966 warmed into spring, Linda noted in her journal:

> **Daddy says that we have much to decide: Nassau on one side and Decker on the other. I love the way that he says that: We have much to decide – the royal 'we' again. Mother sniffs. She likes it here in Florida but has already started to pack little things off the walls again.**
>
> **Before you even realize it's happening, Daddy will say, "I think perhaps we should move to..." And Mom will say, "I think that's a**

good idea, Dear, I'll start packing." Dad never seems to notice she's half packed already.

For the first time, living at home as an adult, I am seeing things I never saw before: Where does Mother get her patience? How does she deal with Daddy? He is an all- encompassing force when he enters the room – always quiet, but also quietly demanding of all her attention. If she is reading and he comes in from the lab, she knows that she might as well put the book down because he is going to want to talk, and she can't ignore him.

Josephine may have held the strongest hand in the deliberations. She missed the life she'd enjoyed on the Main Line and hoped "that the lifestyle could be pasted back together."

Linda, too, thought of rekindling old friendships – and "voted for Philadelphia mostly because of Morgan."

At the very least, summer in Philadelphia would offer refuge from the heat, humidity and bugs in south Florida.

58

Mileage, Folks!

(1966)

After weeks of no contact, on March 19, 1966, Linda got a letter from Morgan:

> **Linda Kid,**
>
> **Next to the last day of school. Have done very poorly this quarter. I might drop out. Don't want to be tied down.**
>
> **Probably will work in NYC post office until I have enough money to go to Germany and get a BMW, then travel in the USA most of the summer, maybe Mexico too. Don't know for sure where I am going to be.**
>
> **Have you found out where you will be this spring yet?**
>
> **Can't think of too much else, I'm pretty thoroughly hassled right now.**
>
> **Will write as soon as I know what's going to happen.**
>
> **Love Always,**
>
> **Morgan**

Morgan had always been a straight-A student. Linda could not fathom how he could have done so poorly that he was considering dropping out. The vagueness seemed so unlike Morgan.

This being the mid 1960s, with an unpopular war raging in the jungles of Vietnam, Linda worried that without a student deferment, Morgan could be drafted into the military. She didn't comprehend that Morgan had already been recruited into a very different kind of army.

The only certainty for Linda was knowing that she was where she needed to be – at her father's side and taking some of the burden off her mother – regardless of whether the next move went north to Philadelphia or east to the Bahamas.

On long walks with her father...

> **...we rarely talked about what was actually going on in his lab. We talked about space propulsion or communications. As interesting as it was, 'the Fan' was always a stepchild of his interest. I don't remember any of our conversations including it. He'd occasionally worry about technical details like reducing the ozone output, but his actual interest was next to nothing. An 'ashtray product,' he called it.**

When Townsend made several trips to Nassau, Linda declined the invitation to join him. "My heart just isn't into being there without Morgan."

The appearance of two new characters tilted the discussion toward Philadelphia.

'Puscheck and Spirito' were a package deal: like Amos n' Andy or Laurel & Hardy: Puscheck and Spirito – except these guys didn't do much comedy. Linda described Puscheck as "a nice man with a round, jovial face and a receding hairline." The weather had been "cold and miserable in Philadelphia, so he was grabbing all the sun that he could in Florida." Spirito was "darker in both countenance and attitude, but I managed to get a smile out of him. It wasn't easy."

When Puscheck and Spirito arrived in Homestead Townsend was already meeting with Stephenson and Peter Graham, the attorney who had pulled Townsend and Morgan away from the lunch table at the Graycliffe Hotel during their previous trip to Nassau. Graham had initiated an offer of $100,000 for the move to Nassau, but the attention was now turning toward Philadelphia.

The die was cast when Martin Decker arrived in Homestead and flew with Brown to meet Stephenson in Nassau.

"Decker seems very amiable at the moment," Linda journaled, noting also that her father referred to Puscheck and Spirito as "our men at Decker."

In the first week of April, Townsend made another a trip to Philadelphia, where he leased an apartment near the center of the city. "Not just an apartment," Linda noted, "but the penthouse on the 26th floor" of the magnificent Drake Hotel. "It has two terraces and overlooks the river and all of the city." There was access to a swimming pool and parking for the Cadillac – which would soon be motoring up the coast.

Linda still had no further word from Morgan. Desperate for some sort of contact, she called the only phone number she had for him, at his family's farm near Valley Forge.

"I just took a shot," Linda said. "Whoever answered said, 'He's not here right now, but I'll give him a message.'" – which meant that Morgan was, indeed, somewhere near current destination.

Townsend, Josephine and Linda stuffed the trunk of the Cadillac convertible, put the top down, and headed north out of southern Florida at oh-dark-thirty on Thursday, April 21, 1966. As always, the 'El Nido' teapot – safely packed in a leather hatbox – was the last thing Josephine packed, so that it could be the first thing she unpacked as soon as she started setting up housekeeping at their new location.

As they drove north, Townsend kept finding places of interest. The first stop was Alexander Springs, "for a dip."

On Friday, April 22, Linda wrote:

Daddy is still asleep. Mother is drinking the coffee that she just made. I am showered and dressed and now WAITING. In a word: *mileage*, folks. We need mileage today! Rise and shine!

It was several more days before the Cadillac pulled into the Drake. The minute she'd set her bag down, Linda picked up the phone and dialed Morgan's number.

This time, Morgan answered: "I'll be on the next train."

59

You Have The Green Light

(1966)

Morgan told Linda he would meet her at 'the lion' – a statue at the center of the small park named for David Rittenhouse, a scientist, astronomer and esteemed citizen of Philadelphia in the Colonial era. The park was part William Penn original vision of recreating England in a vibrant 'green Country Towne' at the confluence of the Delaware and Schuylkill rivers.

Linda arrived thirty minutes early. "It had rained that morning, and the trees were just beginning to show their buds. There was still a slight chill air. But I was just sitting there, watching for Morgan."

As she waited, "A black guy came up to me and tried to start a conversation. He was sorta shabby, and I got the sense that maybe he was 'on' something, so I was getting uncomfortable but was trying to maintain my cool."

Morgan finally appeared, but instead of greeting Linda, he addressed the vagrant. "Alfie! When did you get in from New York, man?" For ten minutes, Morgan chatted with Alfie about Greenwich Village and a mutual friend who'd been busted for something. When she tired of watching her romantic movie jump its sprockets, Linda rose from the bench where she'd been sitting and started walking away.

Morgan followed, taking her by the arm and saying softly, "Let's walk, Linda."

They walked in silence at first, out of Rittenhouse Square into the streets of Philadelphia. "I was just too wound up," Linda said. "I had waited too long and imagined too much. I just didn't know what was in store for us."

As they walked the narrow streets of the old city center, it occurred to Linda that this was the first time since those first tentative days at Ashlawn that she and Morgan might be able to spend more than a few fleeting days together. "That scared me a little," she said. "We walked back to the Drake, and visited with my parents, who were as pleased to see him as I was."

While she and Josephine were in the kitchen making tea, Linda tried to eavesdrop on Townsend and Morgan conversing quietly in the adjoining room. She heard her father ask Morgan about his classes, and what he had in mind for the coming summer. And she heard Morgan say, "I've decided to go in that direction."

Morgan stayed with the Browns until his brother picked him up around 9:00.

As he was leaving, Morgan noticed Linda's travel bag was still sitting by the door, where she'd left it when she sped off to meet him. Morgan slipped his arm around Linda's waist.

"Don't unpack," he said. "Talk it over with your parents. If it's alright with them, I will be back in the morning, and we'll go out to the farm. We need some time together."

He kissed her and was out the door.

*

The next morning, Morgan's brother drove Morgan and Linda from Philadelphia to Valley Forge, dropping them off at a white clapboard farmhouse that would for a time be the center of their private world.

The old farmhouse reflected a style that Linda recalled as "spare – Pennsylvania Dutch or Shaker." Extra chairs in the kitchen were hung on the wall. The thick oak floor planks were polished but still creaky. The refrigerator was stocked with food and Pepsi-Colas for Linda. "The place was immaculate. He said he had even paid for a cleaning lady!"

And Morgan had gone shopping, just to find blue sheets and a blue-and-white quilt that reminded them both of the Bahamas. He placed an arrangement of roses and daisies in a big stone jug by the bed. Linda and Morgan spent the afternoon "enjoying each other…and those Nassau blue sheets…"

As the sun set on their first day, Linda and Morgan walked across the yard to the big barn. "That's when he said that we were not going to have very much time together," Linda said. "He told me that he was waiting for travel orders, and that he would be "meeting some people" and then going to some sort of training camp. I had already figured that it had to have something to do with the FBI or the CIA."

"What kind of training?" Linda asked.

Morgan rattled off a list of commando skills: "Martial arts…. handguns… rifles… other useful stuff," he said, grinning.

"Don't you already have a black belt?" Linda asked.

"Baby, it's different when your life depends on it."

Linda felt "a chill running up and down my spine."

That evening, "when we were rid of all the things that were between us – clothes, attitudes – their intimacy took on a deeper dimension.

Linda was touched to hear how much a role she played in the choices he was weighing.

"If I stay," Morgan said, "then we should get married. This is Philadelphia – not the Bahamas. I would want us to make that kind of commitment."

Linda wondered, "What happened to the guy who said 'I don't think marriage will work for me'? The guy who said he just doesn't want the big house and mortgage, the guy who said he doesn't want to have to stay in one place except for two weeks every year?"

"A person can change his mind. I have already looked for a place for us to live and I know I can get a good job at the University language department..."

Linda had to break the long pause that followed: "But...?"

Morgan played with her hair, then pulled her closer.

"But," Morgan said, "I don't think that's where I need to be, Linda. I can be. I want to be. I don't want to lose you."

"But...that's not what's really in your heart, is it? You still see those stones falling away from your boots, don't you?

*

Morgan and Linda played house at the farm for almost two weeks.

"I just moved in," Linda recalled, "and we settled into a routine. We made love a lot. We talked a lot. Morgan worked on a tractor and did some repair work around the big red barn. We painted the porch of the farmhouse. We fixed dinner together and got positively domestic."

But the elephant in the room loomed so large, Linda wrote, "you can smell the peanuts on its breath..."

In their idyll, they tried to imagine the path to all of their dreams. After all, Linda's parents had found a way to share their lives despite whatever separations intervened over the years.

But Josephine had married Townsend *before* he was drawn into whatever intrigue now beckoned to Morgan.

In the morning of the last day of their 'American Gothic,' Morgan and Linda drove around in the upscale village of Bryn Mawr, admiring the houses on the tree-lined streets. Morgan stopped in front of a little brick house. Roses grew wild among otherwise well-tended flower beds.

Morgan turned to Linda. "We can have this house, if we want it."

"I think he had the keys," Linda recalled. "I just wanted the day to freeze right there. I was wrapped up in the daydreams of a young girl. I wanted a baby with Morgan, I wanted a home – something I'd never really had. But there was just something that kept me from jumping out excitedly and saying 'Oh, show me!'"

With the silence that can only pass between soul mates whose destinies do not run parallel in the current timeline, Linda said nothing. Morgan drove on.

The next morning, Linda and Morgan took a train back into the city, their walk from the station to the Drake cloaked in silence. A block from the hotel, they stopped at a traffic light.

Linda gazed at Morgan for another moment, and then noticed over his shoulder that the light had changed.

"You have the green light, Morgan."

Linda turned and walked away, her eyes focused on the revolving door of the Drake Hotel.

*

Later that spring, Morgan had another encounter at the base of the Rittenhouse Lion – with Townsend Brown.

He recounted the meeting in an email I received in June of 2005:

> **That's when Dr. Brown hit me with the whole deal.**
>
> **Sitting at Rittenhouse Square, watching children play on a stupid goat statue, their nannies watching their every move. He told me then that there was every possibility that his developments were going to come to some kind of fruition. That not only would his saucers fly – as I already knew they would – but that time travel was a distinct possibility. And that's what my life would be in the future.**
>
> **He left me alone with that. To join up or not. "If you join," he said, "you will remember this conversation. If you decide not to, this meeting will just be a shadow in your mind."**
>
> **If I had insisted, I could have married Linda and settled down there in Bryn Mawr, getting a job at the University – which was being offered to me through the Caroline Group. I could have gone either way.**
>
> **As I walked away from that meeting, I recalled our earlier conversation, late one night at his lab in Homestead, when he'd asked me what I would do if I could travel back in time. When I said I would try to save my little sister, he'd said "there are rules" to prevent that kind of thing – adding that he thought that time travel would be possible "in your lifetime."**
>
> **Leaving him at the square, I was struck with a fresh insight into what Dr. Brown was really telling me: if time travel is possible "in**

the future," then it has always been possible. What does time even mean in a universe when you can travel through it as freely as we travel through space?

60

No Need For Formalities

(2004 / 2005)

It took a year and a half – dozens of snail mail letters and hundreds of email messages – before Morgan was comfortable enough to share such revelations with me.[92]

I never doubted his sincerity, but I often wondered about Morgan's motives. Why had he gone into hiding? Why ask about the subway token and then emerge from the sagebrush after so many years?

Morgan's first letter, addressing the swarm of questions I'd sent to the lady with the honey-dipped voice in Texas, arrived in my mailbox on March 15, 2004. Per the exchanges with Linda and Miss Honey Dipped, I'd addressed my letter to "Mr. Paperman." Morgan's first words in reply were:

No need for formalities. I go by different names. 'Reverend' when it suits me though that is out of date. Paperman works well for now. Only hoping that I can live up to it.

This is not the first time a character based on 'Morgan' has appeared in print.

"Enter the Reverend" is the title of a chapter in *Fist Full of Kings*[93] – the autobiography of Louisiana casino executive John Brotherton published in 2001. In the mid-90s Brotherton took a trip to Belize to explore business opportunities in Central America. From Belize City, the plan was to fly with a colleague named Duke to nearby Ambergris Cay in a small plane operated by a friend of Duke's.

"He's a spook," Duke told Brotherton of the pilot. "Or something like that, and a good one. I've heard people say he's the best. To me, he's a complete puzzle. I've never known what to make of him. Five minutes with him and I'm totally confused."

Brotherton asked, "What's his name?"

"I have no idea. He wants you to call him the Reverend. His real name is a mystery."

"Sounds like an odd sort of bird. You think he's what the British would call 'daft'?"

"He's brilliant, really. He loves esoterica. He's always talking about ancient cults and rites – Egyptian stuff like Osiris, Asian gods, deities like Shiva the Destroyer. He reads the Kabala, the Koran, and some Tibetan book. He even likes James Joyce. I don't know what to call it, but I wouldn't call it 'daft.'"

Across the tarmac, Brotherton and Duke saw "what's left of a Cessna" – a battered single-engine airplane with bullet holes in the tail. Beside the plane stood its owner and pilot: the Reverend.

"He looked pretty old, in his seventies, I guessed," Brotherton wrote. "He also looked like he had both seen and been through it all. He walked toward us with a limp, with a cane in his right hand but using it to help him walk. It looked to me like a sheath for some kind of blade, and I wondered whether his limp was put on.

"He was about five foot ten, completely bald. His eyes were kind, but I had the feeling that he could look right through me.

Duke introduced Brotherton. "Pleased to meet you, Mr. Reverend, sir."

"No need for formalities," the Reverend laughed. "Just plain Reverend will do."

*

Other instances of 'Morgan' appearing in tales of espionage and intrigue can be found in the bibliography at the end of this volume. Those exploits occurred in the years when the man I'm calling Morgan was presumed dead; they came to my attention in the spring of 2004, just as Morgan was re-entering Linda Brown's life and became a commanding presence in mine.

As was his custom throughout our correspondence, Morgan dodged direct questions why he had staged his demise. In one exchange, instead of telling me about his fake death, he dipped into telling me about his nearly real one.

Other things were happening in 1987. I was pretty sick at the time – I'd been diagnosed with multiple myeloma, a bone marrow malignancy that is nearly 100% fatal, so I was visiting old friends and settling old scores.

Despite all of his preparations, Morgan didn't die. In an email on June 30, 2004, he wrote a message that alluded to his experience with Townsend Brown, William Stephenson and the Caroline Group:

I knew I was dealing with something enormously powerful. I knew that Dr. Brown had some strong, intuitive influences. But in the physical world, I hadn't made that last leap yet. I knew in the back of my head that I was dealing with something way beyond my normal understanding. Like most humans I just retreated into my comfort zone. A strictly need-to-know basis worked with the information I was being given. The actual source of that information, I just didn't need to know. I didn't actually want to know because then I would

have to recognize what was really going on. And I wasn't ready for that. I truly didn't want to make that leap.

I knew that at some point I was going to have to check myself into a hospital. I was also certain I would not make it out alive. The night before I did, as I was falling asleep, I had a vision. It was a strange, complicated, encounter. I could see Dr. Brown and a gathering of other individuals. At the end of this encounter, I came away with these words in my head: "You are healed – you have work yet to do." That's when I realized that I was dealing with another dimension.

I checked myself in to a hospital the next day, and even with that vision still vivid in my mind, I waited to die. But I wasn't getting worse. I was getting better. Two weeks later I was released.

Several months later, Linda got the word that "We've lost Morgan."

*

From the first moments of his re-appearance, when he called himself 'Norman Paperman,' Morgan liked to quote Jimmy Buffett. In addition to *Don't Stop The Carnival,* he was particularly enamored of Buffet's 1996 release *Banana Wind.* Several times during our correspondence he implored me to pay heed to the lyrics of one track from that album, *Only Time Will Tell.* "Listen for the sound of time," he said. And he would sometimes refer to Linda as 'Desdemona' - borrowing from the title of another track, *Desdemona's Building A Rocket Ship.*

In March of 2005, Linda and I made plans for her to come to my home near Nashville to work with me on this book. Before she left California, Morgan wrote:

She will bring you something that has special meaning to me. You may, or may not recognize it. I want you to keep it until the book is done. Then I will reclaim it and you and I will enjoy the company of some good people on a warm island where the necker berries grow. Take care of Desdemona for me.

Linda arrived on a chilly day in late March. The Vernal Equinox had passed, but the trees around my house were still winter bare. As she walked up the brick walkway toward my front door, I noticed that Linda was carrying a white cane. I recognized it immediately as the cane that 'the Reverend' carried on Ambergris Cay in Belize, as Brotherton had described in *Fist Full of Kings.*

This 'thump stick,' as Morgan called it, sits above my desk as I type this sentence.

The cane is a yard long. Its shaft consists of a stack of carved ivory cylinders, each about three inches high and one inch in diameter and adorned with carved figures of Asian monks - or space aliens. Morgan later confirmed my guess that the carvings were Tibetan. The bottom of the staff is a rubber-tipped wooden dowel. The handle is made from an animal horn, riveted through an ebony piece to the ivory cylinders. Since it is made of solid ivory, this cane is heavy, and that handle could have done plenty of damage if swung toward an adversary.

*

Once Linda settled in, I asked her how the drive east had been.

I knew she'd rented a car for the trip, since her own daily driver was a vintage Mercury Cougar with a zillion miles under its wheels. (When I'd asked Linda why she hadn't ever gotten herself a newer car, she brushed the question off: "When your father has promised you a ride in a flying saucer, cars don't hold a whole lot of fascination."). When Linda retrieved the rental, the agent behind the desk pointed to the lot and said, "It's the red one over there."

"Oh, I'm sorry," Linda said to the agent, "I don't drive red cars. It's just not my color."

"Trust me," the agent said firmly as she handed her the keys. "It is for this trip."

Two days later Linda arrived at my doorstep in a sporty, red Pontiac coupe. But as she described her journey, I noticed her 'I'm not sure how much I can tell you' giggle. She was reluctant to tell me that Morgan – and a handful of his most able-bodied cohorts – did most of the driving.

The expedition started from the parking lot of a Wal-Mart with instructions to…

…just to head east. When I left that parking lot, I had two choices: Left would take me to Interstate 40 and east through northern Arizona and New Mexico. Right would take me toward I-10, closer to the border with Mexico. As I left the parking lot, a sign said, "right turn only." So I headed for the southern route.

A hundred miles west of Alamogordo, New Mexico, a small convoy of black Hummers and SUVs converged on the little red Pontiac and guided Linda to a stop by the side of the road. The passenger-side door of a Hummer flew open, and out jumped Morgan, who walked up to Linda's car and slipped into the driver's seat. "We're in the wind," he said.

Morgan drove for a couple of hours to Holloman Air Force Base. "He just held up some kind of badge and flew through the gate without even stopping," Linda recounted. Once inside the base, Morgan ushered Linda aboard a black helicopter. Eighteen hours later, with a few stops along the way, the chopper landed in an empty field a few miles from my house where a Hummer picked them up. After waiting a few minutes at the end of the road, the red rental car drove up behind them. Linda got out of the Hummer, got back in the red rental, and drove the short distance to my house, where our visit began with the delivery of Morgan's thump stick.

*

Linda and I spent two days poring through our notes. Despite being his daughter, and having lived and worked closely with him, Linda found some of the things we were learning as mystifying as I did. It felt to both of us like we were assembling a thousand-piece jigsaw puzzle without the benefit of a picture on the box top.

Before she left, it occurred to me that I wanted to give something to Morgan in return for his gift of the thump stick. In a keepsake box on top of the dresser in my bedroom, I found a brass pin that had belonged to my father[94] – a decades-old fleur-de-lis badge from the Boy Scouts of America. This exchange felt appropriate: in 1958 when I was seven years old, Harvey Schatzkin died at age thirty-seven of multiple myeloma, the disease Morgan told me he had survived at about the same age.

I gave the pin to Linda and asked her to pass it on to Morgan.

A few weeks later, Morgan wrote:

> **Your dad's badge is pinned securely under my collar. I tell myself with a little voice that someday I will be able to take it off and trade it for my thump stick and take a long walk on the beach with you. I can almost see that too. We just have to keep going, you and I. Just keep going.**

61

Will You Please Come With Us?

(1945)

Recovering on Laguna Beach, 1946

Townsend healed steadily in the sanctuary that Josephine created at their seaside villa in Laguna Beach. Josephine relished the time, not only with her husband but with her nearly 12-year-old son Joseph and baby daughter Linda.

She was not surprised when Townsend started talking about moving again – to Hawaii. And with his mother, who had been a widow since L.K. Brown passed away in 1943.

The rationale he floated at the time was to protect his family from the holocaust he was sure would come in the wake of Hiroshima and Nagasaki. Hawaii, surrounded two thousand miles of ocean, was the most isolated location he could think of that was also a territory[95] of the United States. A more likely explanation is that the Caroline Group wanted to set Brown up with a secure laboratory near the Pearl Harbor naval base, where he could continue his own experiments and incorporate some of the technology that had been secured in Germany.

Josephine entertained the proposition, but once Linda was born, she insisted that they stay put until their daughter was at least two years old. Townsend reluctantly agreed. Still regaining his strength, he wasn't ready to contend with the challenge of packing up and moving his mother.

*

Meanwhile, amid the rubble of eastern Europe, O'Riley and Sarbacher were in pursuit of a German physicist named Richard (or Rickard) Miethe, who had unusual expertise in handling extremely high voltages. O'Riley told:

Dr. Sarbacher and I worked together in the chaos at the end of the war. Dr. Brown had been safely taken to England so I turned my attention then to what you might call the 'pure reconnaissance' mission of the Caroline Group.

We had learned of a physicist who had been captured by the Russians, and Sarbacher was determined to go after him.

At one point I found myself standing in the middle of a muddy quagmire, a road filled with refugees. Entire families trekking along with stray German soldiers that hadn't given up. Typhoid had been mentioned. The German prisoner of war camps had been emptied out, and some of the more despicable guards from those days were wandering among the populace. There were white flags and sheets flying everywhere.

This was madness – and we were looking for just one man.

Sarbacher and O'Riley's mission stalled when they learned that Miethe was being held in a prison camp in Soviet Georgia. "Some of the paperwork gave us clues about where he had been stashed and where he was going to be moved," O'Riley said. "But we still had Dr. Brown's laundry list to work on." They spent the remainder of 1945 "networking the area," before resuming their quest.

Among the prisoners the Russians rounded up with Richard Miethe was the aforementioned Caroline operative, Colonel Hans Von Luck. In his autobiography, Von Luck describes his capture by Russian troops on April 27, 1945, and the arduous trek to a coal mining camp in the Caucasus Mountains of Georgia the following October. Von Luck and his fellow captives were put on a three-day march, with new prisoners joining the column until more than ten thousand weary souls poured into a crowded camp. Von Luck described conditions as "catastrophic." Prisoners subsisted on a diet of a "thin soup, cooked from unhusked oats or fish meal, which was normally used for pig swill."

Weak and sickened prisoners were sent home; those healthy enough for work were loaded into cattle trucks with wooden bunks along the sides and a hole in the middle of the floor for calls of nature. The doors of their transports were closely guarded and opened just three times a day when the bowls of watery soup were passed in.

For more than a month, the convoy of human cargo lumbered east into Russia. Only from the position of the sun could the prisoners tell that they were traveling east and south, toward the Caucasus Mountains – not east and north, toward Siberia. "We never left the truck," Von Luck wrote, until they arrived in the town of Tbilisi, deep in Soviet Georgia, where Colonel Hans Von Luck the proud Prussian aristocrat and former commander of a tank division, began his new career as a common coal miner.

After several months in the mines, Von Luck was re-assigned to a road crew, where he became adept at the Russian art of 'Kultura' – a quasi-legal, look-the-other-way system of barter where those in authority appropriated the communal resources of the State for their personal use.

While setting cobblestones into a muddy roadbed, Von Luck chanced upon a Russian officer he had befriended earlier in his captivity. Surprised at the sight of Von Luck working as a laborer, his Russian friend reassigned him to a brigade that was building houses for officers. To that crew, Von Luckbrought with him a handful of farmers, clerks and Miethe – disguised as a civilian "too weak for mine work" – who was assigned such light duty as "holding up a plumb line."

In the spring of 1946, Sarbacher and O'Riley resumed their mission. They knew the conditions Miethe and Von Luck were living in and were determined to "steal Miethe away before he dies on us."

Sarbacher and O'Riley hitched a ride as 'shipping agents' on a supply convoy, spending weeks "groaning along in a 6x6 2.5-ton Studer," – the Russian nickname for the Studebaker trucks the U.S. had supplied as part of an extensive lend-lease program during the war.

Top speed, downhill with a tailwind and smooth road was maybe 45 mph, but usually just 30. Trucks in our convoy were mostly loaded with bolts of flannel. Lucky for us, when the lend-lease program ended, these babies were already in the pipeline and on their way – with us aboard. It was a matter of timing. I would have taken horses, but Sarbacher did not love horses and was sure that our scientist was no horseman. He had some lung problems, which was a genuine concern."

We found our scientist building houses. Some of the other German prisoners had taken care of him, somehow sensing that this was a man of unusual qualities. When we found him, he was holding a string line while the others in his crew were making the concrete.

Sarbacher walked up to the frail man holding the plumb line and said, "Sir, will you please come with us?"

The Russians didn't know that this prisoner was actually a physicist known for his pioneering work with unusual electrical phenomena.

He, like Von Luck, had been shuffled around, getting odd breaks that even they didn't understand. The Russians had no idea who Sarbacher represented or how far we had come. To the supervisors at that camp, we were just delivering copper fittings, some canned goods, and a whole shit-load of flannel cloth – in trucks, which is what they really needed.

Once the object of their mission was secure, Sarbacher walked over to the prisoner in charge of the work detail. After a long pause, Sarbacher looked Hans Von Luck squarely in the eye, said "Thank you, Sir," and walked away – leaving Von Luck behind in the muck.

62

The Browns of Ka Lae Hau

(1947)

Josephine, Linda and their little grass shack in the Wainiha Valley on the north shore of Kauai.

The decade after World War II witnessed a rapid consolidation of America's military, intelligence and security interests. The benign neglect of the 1920s and '30s – when men of honor were not supposed to read each other's mail, when stand-in networks were organized by men like Eldridge Johnson and William Stephenson – gave way to the web of alphabet-soup agencies that future president Dwight D. Eisenhower would decry as the "military industrial complex."

As early as 1943, Colonel William 'Wild Bill' Donovan – Stephenson's counterpart in the United States – lobbied President Roosevelt to make a permanent institution out of the Office of Strategic Services (OSS), which was the American component of Stephenson's espionage network during the war.

With his attention now turning toward America's new adversary in the Soviet Union, Donovan advocated for the creation of a centralized, civilian agency, under direct control of the President to coordinate all the country's intelligence operations. After the war it fell to Roosevelt's successor, Harry Truman – who did not even know about the Manhattan Project until it was up to him to drop The Bomb on Japan – to enact Donovan's proposals.

Harboring reservations about the potential mischief such an agency as Donovan proposed could get into, Truman started off on a different path. In his first year in the Oval Office, he dissolved the OSS. Donovan retired from the military to practice law in New York.

Truman's attitude started changing as the Soviet Union asserted its dominion over the nations the Red Army had marched through on its way to Berlin. In Poland, liberation from the Nazis morphed into another kind of occupation – from fascist to communist. That pattern repeated itself in Romania, Hungary, Czechoslovakia, East Germany and elsewhere as the Stalinists spread their Dictatorship of the Proletariat.[96]

In 1947, Truman's economic advisor, the financier Bernard Baruch, described the growing tension between the former allies as a 'cold war.' When that phrase was repeated in a series of essays by Walter Lippmann, it became a permanent fixture in the postwar lexicon and made a full convert of Harry Truman, who signed the National Security Act in July of 1947. The Act's sweeping reforms included separating the Air Force out of the Army, creating a huge new Department of Defense,[97] and established the National Security Council (NSC).

Like a bureaucratic phoenix born out of the ashes of Donovan's old OSS, the 1947 Act also consolidated all of the country's military and civilian espionage operations into a new Central Intelligence Agency. In lieu of Donovan, Admiral Roscoe H. Hillenkoetter was named the first Director of Central Intelligence (DCI).

*

While these bureaucratic intrigues unfolded, Townsend Brown wasn't just lazing on Laguna Beach, pondering how to spirit his family away to the remote safety of a cluster of islands far over the horizon. In the two years Josephine had insisted on before they could move, Brown opened a new laboratory in the Los Angeles area with at least two other colleagues. Beau Kitselman was a mathematician who Brown worked with at the Vega Aircraft facility after leaving the Navy. Bradford Shank was among the technicians who worked with Enrico Fermi when the first atomic pile was activated in 1942. Shank accompanied Fermi to Los Alamos and was part of the team that developed the 'gadget' that was first detonated at Alamogordo on July 16, 1945.

Shank had misgivings about that blast – dubbed 'Trinity' from a poem by seventeenth-century poet John Donne – and passed on the opportunity to witness that July morning when the sun rose twice. Shortly after Trinity, Shank flew with like-minded colleagues from New Mexico to Washington D.C. – in a DC-3 dubbed 'The Peace Plane' – to implore President Truman not to drop an atomic bomb on the civilian population of Japan. Albert Einstein joined the delegation, urging Truman to demonstrate the bomb over an unpopulated area instead.

After the war, Shank continued his anti-nuclear activism, and had a hand in the production of a documentary film entitled *Where Will You Hide?* He left Los Alamos for Los Angeles and went to work with Townsend Brown in 1946.

Kitselman and Shank are the only specific names we have, but the laboratory in Los Angeles employed as many as fifteen other people, working directly under Dr. Brown and integrating his theories with things that the Caroline Group found in Germany.

Linda Brown, barely a toddler at the time, learned later that her father "bought ten acres of land at Dana Point," in southern California, "on land that was at the very highest elevation overlooking the ocean below. He had plans drawn up and I remember seeing a very professional drawing of the 'Townsend Brown Foundation Radiation Laboratory' but that never actually happened. Things were very fluid before they switched to Hawaii – or simply went underground in California once we were safely in Hawaii."

On Linda's first birthday in December 1946, Townsend's mother Mame, widowed and living alone in Zanesville, was visiting with friends from the days when she and Lewis spent their winters in Pasadena. Townsend used the visit to broach the subject of moving to Hawaii with his mother. In the meantime, Linda recalled, her father was "spending time at the Los Angeles Public Library, looking for the most obscure and safe place where he could stash his family – and leave us."

Not-quite 2-year-old Linda and Josephine aboard
the Lurline enroute to Hawaii.

The Brown family made the passage to the Hawaiian Islands aboard the passenger/freighter *Lurline* in November 1947. After a few days in Honolulu, the family crossed the Ka' ie 'ie Waho Channel to the neighbor island of Kauai, the north-and-western most of the major islands of the archipelago. From the harbor at Nawilliwili Bay on the southeast corner of the island, the family wended their way north toward Wainiha, a valley situated between the picturesque Hanalei Bay and the rugged cliffs of the Na Pali coast.

An article in Kauai's *Garden Island* newspaper in August 1948 invited readers to *Meet the Townsend Browns of Ka-Lae-Hau*,[98] who had come to Hawaii "on a mission for the Townsend Brown Foundation" to establish a Biological Research Department.

The Browns told the newspaper they had been "dreaming for years of coming to the Hawaiian Islands," and chose Kauai on the advice of friends. Like most newcomers, they dreamed of finding "the MGM version" of island life: "A palm-fringed valley covered with wild orchids, a babbling brook running through the center to a waterfall which drops off into a cool crystal pool, and a large grass shack that could be converted into a villa."

Their quest led them to village of Haena, at the end of the road along Kauai's north shore – as remote a location as they would ever find within the territorial limits of the United States, but still near a road that could return them to civilization.

At the Hotel Hale Hoomaha, they asked the owner, Ivy Ishimoto, if she knew of a 'verdant valley' they could rent. According to the *Garden Island*:

> **Ivy suggested some property in the Wainiha Valley that she owned. There was an old shack on the lot, but she was sure that it would not suit Townsend and Josephine. At their insistence, she finally consented to show it to them. Lo and behold! There was the MGM set they had been dreaming of – all but the orchids and the grass hut. Mrs. Ishimoto was quite amazed when they chortled with glee and said they would take it.**

The seventeen-acre property rented for a dollar per acre – per year! "The best rental bargain" she'd ever known, Josephine told her friends.

The grounds were overgrown, and the only dwelling was a run-down tar-paper shack, but the Browns...

> **...attacked the ravages of time and the elements, awakening their newly acquired, sleepy valley with a barrage of hammers, brooms, mops, axes, rakes, DDT and plenty of pioneering spirit needed for the ordeal ahead, dampened but never depressed by the winter downpours that greeted them.**

Even 76-year-old Mame pitched in, swinging "a mean paint brush and hammer as they set about rejuvenating the old shack" while the family slept in surplus army tents near a stream that emptied into a fresh-water pool they used as a natural refrigerator.

In the old shack, bamboo columns were freshly lacquered and walls splashed with finger-painted murals. For the floors, Townsend carried in buckets of white sand from a nearby beach which they raked into a smooth, hard surface. Mame provided the crowning touch: a plush Persian rug which had once adorned the hardwood floors of her home in Zanesville that she'd had shipped across the ocean.

In much the same way that Josephine could make any place her home by unpacking her green teapot, Mame made this old cabin a home by unrolling priceless Persian carpets across the sandy floor.

A visitor protested, "You can't put those Orientals down in that sand!"

"It worked for the Bedouins," Mame replied, "it can work for me."

Once one of the noblest ladies of Zanesville Ohio, "Grandma became a real tutu," Linda said. "She just put on her mumu and went native."

*

Townsend purchased an old tractor, plowed up a field and began experiments with 'electroculture' – investigating the effect of electricity on plants. A document in the family archives shows that he was working as a consultant for the Grove Farm, one the island's largest sugar plantations, conducting…

…biological studies on the growth and flowering of sugar cane. Development of electroculture methods. Biological effects of radiations – including the use of high voltages, etc. and the natural variations in growth produced by sidereal radiation (changes in the gravitational component).

(That last note reminds us that his interest in 'sidereal radiation' was never far from the center of this thoughts. Note also yet another reference to 'high voltages.')

The family was settled in, but as Linda recalls, Townsend "wasn't home much."

The 1948 *Garden Island* profile says, "Mr. Brown is now in Los Angeles moving the Foundation offices to larger quarters" – confirming Linda's recollection that for most of the time the family was camped out on Kauai, her father simply "was not there."

"He was there to get us set up," Linda said, "to put in the gardens, to get things started, to make sure the house was right, but when that article mentions that he's getting equipment in '48, he did not come back. We would occasionally get a phone call."

Linda has tried to reconstruct her father's travels with evidence as slim as a couple of photographs, likely taken with the same camera and possibly from the same roll of film. In the first photo, we see Townsend Brown, posing with his two children. He has one arm around his son, he holds Linda's hand in the other. He is wearing a flower lei – a traditional Hawaiian symbol of arrival or departure. "1948" is handwritten on the back.

In the second photo, we see Townsend in the company of two gentleman, posing in front of the rainbow fountains that squirted into a pool at the foot of the Washington Monument until the mid 1950s. We have a positive ID on the two gentlemen standing beside Dr. Brown.

Their names are Puscheck and Spirito.

(l) One of the few photos of Townsend with his two children, Linda and Joseph; (r) Townsend and the two mystery men, Puscheck and Spirito.

63
Missing Files and Moles
(1948)

Much of what we know about Townsend Brown's activities in the 1940s and 50s is gleaned from the roughly one-hundred-page file that the FBI compiled during those decades. Just why the FBI was following Brown, interviewing his neighbors, family, friends and colleagues is not clear from the file.

Reading that file is where I first learned the real meaning of the word 'redacted.' In a redacted document, words, sentences, paragraphs – often entire pages – are covered by thick strokes of black ink. Forget what the dictionary says. 'Redacted' means "the *documents* have been declassified, but their *contents* have not."

I spent countless hours digging through the treasures of the National Archives and Records Administration, at both the primary facility in downtown Washington DC (where the originals of the Declaration of Independence, the Constitution and the Bill of Rights are displayed) and the enormous annex in College Park, Maryland. I made one such expedition in the spring of 2005 to dig up Brown's FBI file.

I first learned of the FBI file from Andrew Bolland, who operated the website where I made my first contact with the family. Andrew gave me his heavily reacted five-year-old copy of the file. In December 2004, I filed a FOIA request with the FBI, hoping a more recent edition would be less redacted.

I got no response from the Bureau for nearly six months. On June 9, 2005, Mr. David M. Hardy, Section Chief of the RIDS Records Management Division, wrote:

> **A search of the Central Records System at FBI Headquarters has revealed two files which may be pertinent to your request.**
>
> **One file which may be pertinent to your request was destroyed January 18, 1990.**[99]
>
> **The second file, 6548896, which may pertain to your subject has been permanently transferred to NARA. You may wish to correspond directly with NARA, 8690 Adelphi Road, College Park, Maryland.**

In July 2006, I flew to D.C., rented a car, and drove through some of the densest urban traffic in the country to NARA College Park, where I spoke with Patrick Osborne, a military archivist who had helped me with several previous requests.

Patrick sifted through his resources, finally informing me that the file I sought was not in fact stored at College Park and advised me to look for it at the primary NARA facility on Pennsylvania Avenue, a few blocks from the U.S Capitol.

Rather than fight even more traffic and non-existent parking, I took the Metro downtown, where another archivist, Mr. Byron, took my request and disappeared into the stacks. Thirty minutes later he reappeared.

"The file is not here. Have you tried College Park?"

"Umm.... College Park told me to come here."

Patrick Osborne was surprised to see me when I showed back up at his desk in College Park. He took my info again and disappeared into the corridors of the archive.

"This is very unusual," Patrick said when he returned. "That file is not here."

Patrick told me he had a contact at the FBI Records Section; he called Darlene Norman and asked her to trace the file.

Another hour later, Patrick approached me looking chagrined.

"That file was never transferred to the National Archives."

"Well then, where is it?"

"Darlene Norman has informed me that the file you are looking for was destroyed on February 15, 2002." Patrick then rattled off the protocols under which such documents are reduced to piles of ash.

I cut him off. "Let me get this straight. The FBI told me in June 2005, that the file is in the possession of the National Archives. Now you're telling me that the FBI actually destroyed the file in February 2002 – three years earlier?"

"Yes, that is correct."

Now, *that's* some redaction.

*

A short obituary in the Thursday, December 23, 1948 edition of the *Zanesville News*, noted the passing of Mary Townsend Brown:

> **Mrs. Mary T. Brown, 76, former resident of Zanesville and widow of Lewis K. Brown, died Wednesday in St. Joseph hospital in Santa Ana, Calif. She was stricken while visiting friends in that city.**
>
> **Mrs. Brown left Zanesville two years ago to join her son Townsend Brown and his family in Hawaii where she has since resided.**

From Andrew Bolland's copy of the file, we know the FBI's take on Mame's passing. Citing an interview with a family friend from Culver City, the report says:

BROWN is an only son whom she has never thought of as dishonest, although he was very badly spoiled as a boy and is, in her opinion, a very selfish man. She recalled that on the night BROWN's mother died at a sanitarium in Santa Ana, California, BROWN was aware of her imminent passing but rather than stay with his then destitute mother in her last hours he took an airliner to Hawaii with the comment that he could not do anything for her anyway. [redacted] said this thoroughly disgusted BROWN's two second cousins who live in Los Angeles and [3 full lines redacted].

Mame's remains lie interred at the Rose Hills Memorial Park in Whittier, California – half a continent away from her husband Lewis in Ohio.

*

For four years, the United States was the only nation on Earth with a nuclear arsenal.

The Cold War became more ominous on August 29, 1949, when the Soviet Union detonated its first atomic bomb, a device that U.S. intelligence dubbed "Joe 1."

Despite General Leslie Groves' preoccupation with security, Russia's bomb was built with secrets stolen from The Manhattan Project. As far back as July 1945 – when Truman and British Prime Minister Winston Churchill met with Soviet Premier Josef Stalin at Potsdam – knowledge of the American bomb had already leaked. When the Trinity test proved successful, Truman received a cable from New Mexico: "It's a boy." He told Stalin that the U.S. now had a powerful new weapon that would end the war in the Pacific. This was not news to Stalin. He knew about the bomb before anybody told Truman.

It has been well documented that one of the physicists at Los Alamos – a German émigré turned British citizen named Klaus Fuchs[100] – was quietly feeding the critical details of uranium and plutonium bomb engineering to researchers in Russia. That information accelerated Igor Kurchatov – the Soviet Union's Oppenheimer – along the tricky path to vaporizing large tracts of the Kazakhstan desert – years before Western intelligence expected that to happen.

Russian interest in Western secrets did not stop at acquiring the technology to build atomic bombs. In fact, the entire Western defense establishment in the 1940s and '50s was riddled with Soviet spies.

Before joining the Manhattan Project, Klaus Fuchs' work in Britain drew him into a circle of Communist sympathizers, many of whom came from the ranks of the British upper middle class – graduates of Oxford and Cambridge who were critical of the British class system even as they benefited from it.

In 1947, Fuchs was one of the members of the CPC – the Combined Policy Committee – which coordinated efforts to share atomic secrets between the 'ABC' countries – America, Britain, and Canada.

The British representative on the CPC, Donald Maclean, turned out to be part of the most notorious spy ring in British post-war history. Maclean's name is often mentioned along with two others in what became known as the 'Philby-Burgess-Maclean affair.' Philby was Harold 'Kim' Philby; Burgess was Guy Burgess. Along with two others in a conspiracy called the 'Cambridge Five'[101] – these men served in the highest ranks of the British intelligence services MI5 (which handles domestic espionage like the American FBI) and MI6 (which handles foreign espionage, like the CIA).

From their trusted positions, they conveyed valuable Western intel to the Soviet Union. Philby was so highly placed – and so far above suspicion – that when the Brits first learned of the moles in their midst, Philby got himself assigned to direct the investigation.

By the time Philby's treachery came to light in the 1960s, it had already had a profound impact on the life of Townsend Brown.

64

Pearl Harbor

(1950)

Townsend Brown's Naval records indicate that 'scientific equipment' was shipped to the Atlantic Fleet Schools in Norfolk, VA in the summer of 1942. In our correspondence, Morgan would only refer to that equipment as 'stuff' – writing in March 2005:

> **I can tell you that the 'stuff' being moved from the University of Pennsylvania to the Atlantic Fleet Radar School was Dr. Brown's own development – backed by both the Navy and the Caroline Group. Later the 'stuff' was shipped to California, where it continued its development under the darkest of conditions. Some of these developments ended up in front of some Admirals in Pearl Harbor. Some did not.**

Again, much of what we know of Townsend Brown's activities while his family was tucked away on Kauai comes from the FBI file. The section that covers this period includes a sentence that is fully redacted except for the last two words: Pearl Harbor.

An unidentified informant tells the Bureau's interviewer:

> **BROWN was escorted to the Electronics Office by [redacted] and [redacted] (both of whom have since left Pearl Harbor Navy Yard), and the Electronics Office was told to give BROWN a place to work. As far as [redacted] recalls, a Form 57 – Application for Federal Employment – was never completed by BROWN.**
>
> **[Redacted] stated that for about three weeks BROWN worked in seclusion, and upon instructions from the Electronics Office had an open job order for him, with which he could order any type of apparatus which he required in connection with his experiments. [Redacted] stated that after approximately three weeks, during which no one but BROWN was allowed access to the room, it was decided to allow [redacted] and a few others to be "in on Brown's experiments."**
>
> **[Redacted] stated he immediately recognized BROWN's experiments as a fundamental phenomenon which could probably not be recognized as such by a physicist or Persons remembering their high school physics.**

One of the people who escorted BROWN was Beau Kitselman, Brown's colleague from the Vega Aircraft facility and later the author of *Hello Stupid,* the 1962 pamphlet considered a thinly veiled account of Brown's experience demonstrating novel concepts to a skeptical audience. Calling Townsend 'B.', Kitselman wrote:

> **B. and I were separated for some years after the war, but we kept in touch. When I was teaching calculus to a group of Navy men at Barbers Point, my students built and operated a 'gravitator' and we all became very enthusiastic. The FAWTUPAC [Fleet All Weather Training Unit Pacific] Commander took an interest, B. was sent for, and finally no less a personage than CINCPAC [Commander-in-Chief Pacific] Admiral Radford witnessed a demonstration.**

Sometime in the spring of 1950[102], Brown's preparations were far enough along to show to the Navy. Several accounts of "The Pearl Harbor Demonstration" have found their way into the record.

For example, the FBI file reported:

> **During BROWN's employment at Pearl Harbor Navy Yard, he caused to be constructed a gadget resembling a toy model carnival ride.**

In *The Hunt For Zero Point*, Nick Cook wrote:

> **His demonstration supposedly failed to impress the Navy, but there is no official record of the reaction. One account is that [the Navy] "refused funding for further research because of the negative opinion of other scientists" – although in none of the accounts found in the FBI files is there anything that says that other scientists were present for the demonstration. The FBI cites only "Navy and Marine officers."**

Cook conveys another version of the story from Josh Reynolds, a family friend who worked with Townsend Brown while he lived on Catalina Island in the 1970s. Reynolds told Cook what Brown told him: that his lab at Pearl Harbor was broken into and his notebooks were stolen, but they were returned a couple of days later with a declaration that the Navy was uninterested in whatever they contained. Whoever witnessed the demonstration was convinced that what they'd witnessed was common "ionic wind" – not some previously unobserved phenomenon of physics.

In the pages of "Hello Stupid," Beau Kitselman offers this account:

> **B. was well treated by his Navy acquaintances, but the demonstrations were still rather primitive, and no scientists appeared.**

We all thought the millennium was at hand, but it wasn't. Actually, this sort of thing had been going on for years. Even though B. was more of a shrinking violet than a bold promoter, every now and then his friends would try to get somebody interested.

In the spring of 2004, Morgan offered this account in one of his very first letters to me:

> **Dr. Brown had been working steadfastly on his two main developments since leaving the Navy.**
>
> **At one point his major benefactor (the Caroline Group) decided that it was time to introduce his two creations to the military and move them from one shade of black to another. A horizontal shift in frame though still highly classified. He was lent a lab to put the finishing touches on two units: One was 'the set' and the other was described by the FBI as a "toy carnival ride."**

'The set' is the communications system disclosed in the Vega notes and *Structure of Space*; the "toy carnival ride" was a propulsion system based on Brown's first Gravitator patents. Morgan continued:

> **After the demonstration it was discovered that *there had been a mole in the works* and important information regarding both developments was already being circulated. Dr. Brown was furious and appalled. He charged the Navy with gross security negligence and near treason. For their part most of the military involved were busy covering their own asses or figuring how they could turn this situation to their advantage.**

Morgan identified the 'mole' as a...

> **...Russian born American citizen with a long history at Pearl. He was there when the base was attacked in 1941 and helped haul the injured to a hospital. Despite a poor medical history, he still worked at the base as a janitor – which gave him way too much access to information, some of it right off the Admirals' desks.**
>
> **There were allegations that this 'janitor' also enjoyed a compromising relationship with one of the senior officers on the base. With all of his access, he successfully planted a very sophisticated kind of electronic 'bug' – which revealed upon its discovery that everything taking place at that facility was being closely monitored by the Soviet Union.**

The Navy suspected that there was a spy in their midst and brought in their own counter-espionage operative – Rear Admiral Stephen E. Jones – to try to flush him out. But before he could finish his investigation, Jones was transferred. He left his findings and warnings with his superiors, but nobody followed up in time to prevent the breach of Townsend Brown's demonstration.

Instead, that listening device was only detected because...

...the Caroline Group had access to one of the latest detection devices developed by the Services Electronic Research Lab – a British electronics firm that was formed under the direction of the MI5.

Several days after the compromised demonstration, Admiral Radford convened an emergency meeting.

It was basically "What the hell do we do now?' – or what we call a 'WTFN situation.' The officers involved were already working diligently to save face in the political arena. Whatever reports the demonstration might have generated were already being silenced. "Good reason to hush this incident up," the officers figured.

Despite his mounting irritation, Dr. Brown tried to offer a calm assessment of the situation – until one of the officers brushed the whole thing off as a matter of little consequence.

"Why should we even be concerned?" the officer said, dismissing what he'd witnessed with, "It's nothing but a toy carnival ride!"

"That was not the vocabulary that Dr. Brown would have ever used to describe his propulsion system," Morgan said. "I think that you can understand how, after all of the hard work and the hardship he had endured, that did it."

Townsend Brown let the bile rise until he was surprised to hear his own voice shouting as he pounded a fist on Admiral Radford's desk and bellowed, "What has happened here is tantamount to treason!"

"Needless to say," Morgan concludes, "he didn't win any friends that day."

65

Mortally Wounded
(1950)

That "toy carnival ride" crack gave Brown the cover he needed for the road ahead. According to Morgan:

> The officer that made the comment was not astute enough to realize that he had opened a useful door. Dr. Brown quickly picked up on that gem to lay the cornerstone for a prolonged disinformation campaign. The horse was already out of the barn. Now the deal was to make it look like a worthless nag. If the disinformation was complete enough, then maybe even the experts would discredit it before they even looked at it – as some American scientists had already done.

This, Morgan told me, marks the beginning of Townsend Brown's "mortally wounded prairie chicken" routine:

> Prairie chickens have a trick to distract predators from their nest: they limp away from the nest as if injured; then, at a safe distance, they recover and fly away.

> Dr. Brown's object was to demystify the information that had been compromised. He even managed to have a dysfunctional gravitational radio inspected by those who would report that there was "nothing technically valuable about it."

> Once it had been discredited, the Caroline Group took 'the set' into safekeeping, but Dr. Brown felt that simply making things disappear was not going to work in this case.

> He agreed that 'the set' should go under and stay there. Then he developed a disinformation campaign which would allow him to take a version of the propulsion system into the 'light.'

The plan revolved around promoting a version of the system based on fluid dielectrics, a version like the Fan that could move air utilizing the common phenomenon of 'ion wind' – *not* the version based on solid dielectrics like the Gravitator.

> Once the plan was agreed upon things happened quickly. He was relieved of his position as a consultant to Pearl and just as quickly the FBI was flashing messages that he was operating "in the twilight zone." He demonstrated his propulsion system everywhere and to

everyone who would come to see it. He held press conferences. He approached investors.

This was the pivotal moment for Townsend Brown's whole family. Everything that happened in all their lives from that moment onward was colored by what happened at Pearl Harbor. Everything we think we know about Townsend Brown today, every story that has been told, every myth that has been perpetrated, is colored by his own effort to discredit himself that started in the wake of the security breach at Pearl Harbor.

*

As all of this came to light in the first weeks of my correspondence with Morgan in the spring of 2004, I wanted to learn more about the mole who'd planted the bug at Pearl Harbor. Who was he working for?

For once, Morgan answered directly:

You asked about the mole responsible for the Pearl Harbor fiasco. Your assumption is correct: He worked for Harold Adrian Russell Philby.

The questions remain: what was seen or heard that should not have been, what was conveyed to the Soviet Union, was that invisible audience more receptive than the one in the United States?

Everything about these events is opaque. Scouring the available records reveals nothing. "Everything has been weeded," Morgan says, and then, using another expression that the spy trade uses when records are completely wiped: "It's all been sheep dipped."

But after scouring through the FBI files, I found two words that were not redacted that maybe should have been:

BROWN said he went to Pearl Harbor, where he demonstrated his propulsion principal in a *model boat* to a group of Naval and Marine officers who, he said, were so impressed that they caused his discovery to be classified as a secret.

The words "model boat" harken back to the pages of *Popular Science* magazine in 1929[103], and the proposal for an electrically propelled vessel that was submitted to the Naval Research Labs in 1933[104] – a concept that has not been seen nor heard of since.

After Pearl Harbor, Townsend Brown went into the second half of his life associated with flying saucers and ships that disappear into the fifth dimension.[105]

Before that, Morgan assured me, "The Navy got what they wanted."

66

Flying Saucers
(1947)

Civilian pilot Keneth Arnold with an artist's rendering of the UFOs he observed near Mt. Rainier, Washington in 1947.

A few months before Townsend Brown sailed his family to Hawaii, a businessman by the name of Kenneth Arnold was piloting his CallAir A-2 over the Cascade mountains in Washington State when he observed "a formation of very bright objects" through the cockpit window.

For this sighting, Kenneth Arnold has found an enduring place in the annals of UFO mythology for having been the first to describe 'flying saucers.' Except he never really called them that.

Arnold owned and operated the Great Western Fire Control Supply Company, selling and installing firefighting equipment over five sparsely populated western states since 1940. His lightweight aircraft was designed for taking off and landing in high altitudes in outlying areas with no actual airstrips. In an average month Arnold spent from forty to one hundred hours in the air, making hundreds of take-offs and landings "from cow pastures and mountain meadows" with no more mishap than a flat tire. The kind of flying Kenneth Arnold required, as he himself put it, "a great deal of practice and judgment."

On June 24, 1947, Arnold was airborne north of the Columbia River between Washington and Oregon, scouting for the wreckage of a C-46 military transport plane that had disappeared near Mount Rainier the previous winter. As he leveled off at 9,200 feet, just above the treetops west of Mt Rainier, in a crystal-clear sky, a bright flash reflected off his cockpit window.

Arnold scanned the skies around him until he observed a chain of nine peculiar looking aircraft flying from north to south at approximately 9,500 feet. At first, he thought he might be seeing one of the new jet aircraft he'd heard about. Then he realized that these aircraft had no tails, no rudders or ailerons. "When the sun reflected from one or two of these units," Arnold reported, "they appeared completely round. They were also moving very fast."

After landing in Pendleton, Oregon, Arnold told some of his pilot friends what he'd seen. None of them doubted his story. A veteran of the war in Europe said that he had been briefed that he might see flying objects before going into aerial combat over Germany and assured Arnold that he wasn't "dreaming or going crazy."

Arnold's first instinct was to report his story to the FBI in Pendleton. Finding their office closed, he talked instead to Bill Bequette, a reporter for the *East Oregonian* newspaper. Bequette's story appeared under the fold on the first page of the next day's paper:

Boise Flyer Maintains He Saw 'Em

Kenneth Arnold Sticks To Story of Seeing Nine *Mysterious Objects* Flying At Speed of 1200 Miles An Hour Over Mountains

Kenneth Arnold, a six-foot, 200-pound flying Boise, Idaho, businessman, was about the only person today who believed he saw nine mysterious objects – as big as four-engined airplanes – whizzing over western Washington at 1200 miles an hour.

Army and civilian air experts either expressed polite incredulity or scoffed openly at Mr. Arnold's story, but the 32-year-old one-time Minot, N.D. football star, clung to his story of shiny, flat objects racing over the Cascade mountains with a peculiar weaving motion "like the tail of a Chinese kite."

A CAA inspector in Portland, quoted by the Associated Press, said: "I rather doubt that anything would be traveling that fast."

When first sighted, Arnold thought the objects were snow geese.

"But geese don't fly that high – and, anyway, what would geese be going south for this time of the year?"

Near the end of the story, Bequette quoted Arnold describing what he saw as "saucer-like." But nowhere in the article does the expression "flying saucer" appear.

One version of the story misquoted Arnold as having seen something that "looked like a saucer would if you skipped it across the water." Later in the summer of 1947, as Arnold's report was echoed by reports of other, similar sightings, the phrase 'saucer-like' morphed into 'flying saucers.' Whether or not that expression ever formed on his own lips, Arnold's contribution to the lexicon was secure.

Three years later, the growing fascination with 'flying saucers' became a key component of Townsend Brown's 'mortally wounded prairie chicken' charade.

*

In the summer of 1950, Josephine packed her teapot in the hut in Wainiha Valley. When she unpacked it, she was living in a cottage near Waikiki Beach in Honolulu that was part of an apartment hotel complex called the San Souci.

Linda Brown was not quite five years old, but she remembers "a large hotel on the beach, at the base of Diamond Head. We could walk along the seawall to the Royal Hawaiian Hotel. I'm fairly certain this was the time that Dad was at Pearl, because this was near the end of our Hawaiian adventure. We stayed there long enough for me to graduate from first grade. I made my first girlfriends there. Dad must have been around, but I have no actual memory of him at San Souci."

Townsend returned to his family in the wake of 'Pearl Harbor' – after the mole was discovered, after his experiments had been compromised, and after he'd begun orchestrating the subversion of his life's work.

Linda says, "Dad spelled it all out to Mom. The next few years were going to be some kind of living hell. He would completely understand if she wanted to stay in Hawaii."

Josephine decided to stay with her "rare force of nature."

67

Hot Air

(1951)

The method of controlling the flight of the saucer is illustrated
by the following simple diagrams showing the charge variations
necessary to accomplish all directions of flight.

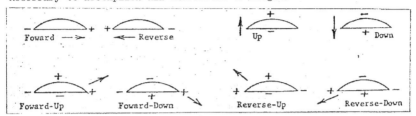

Since the saucer always moves toward its positive pole, the control
of the saucer is accomplished simply by varying the orientation of
the positive charge. Control, therefore, is gained by switching
charges rather than by control surface. Since the saucer is traveling
on the incline of a continually moving wave which it generates to
modify the earth's gravitational field, no mechanical propulsion is
necessary.

In the fall of 1951, the Brown family flew from Honolulu to San Francisco,
where Linda remembers seeing her first television, a coin operated model in the
lobby of the hotel where they stayed. Joseph, now nineteen years old to Linda's
seven – was captivated by the flickering grey images of professional wrestling,
featuring such stars as Gorgeous George, and kept feeding quarters into the set in
the lobby until Josephine finally relented and rented a set for their room.

"Joe didn't really have much use for a seven-year-old sister," Linda recalls,
"but I was good for one thing: He would watch very carefully all of the wrestling
moves on the TV, and then try them all out on me!"

The family stayed briefly in San Francisco, where Linda encountered such
modern marvels as cable cars. Then they drove down the coast to Los Angeles,
enjoying along the way the many natural wonders of the Golden State, like snow
in the mountains and their first earthquake.

In Los Angeles, Townsend reconstituted the Townsend Brown Foundation at
306 N. Vermont Avenue in Los Angeles. He teamed up once again with Bradford
Shank, the Manhattan Project veteran who had been part of the operations before
Brown spirited his family away to Hawaii in 1947.

Besides Brown and Shank, a third individual named Mason Rose signed on
as the principal promoter of the enterprise. Rose compiled a 'white paper' that

explained the Biefeld-Brown effect as it was applied to Brown's tethered saucers, which the Foundation demonstrated from their facility on Vermont Avenue. The document describes how the saucers are levitated and propelled, and suggests the course of further research:

> Through the utilization of the Biefeld–Brown effect, the flying saucer can generate an electrogravitational field of its own which acts against the earth's field.
>
> This field acts like a wave, with the negative pole at the top of the wave and the positive pole at the bottom. The saucer travels like a surfboard on the incline of a wave that is kept continually moving by the saucer's electrogravitational generator.
>
> Since the orientation of the field can be controlled, the saucer can thus travel on its own continuously generated wave in any desired angle or direction of flight. Control is gained by switching charges rather than by control surfaces.

This is the clearest description yet of how an electrically generated, synthetic gravitational field can lift, propel and control a flying vessel. With this explanation, the Townsend Brown Foundation invited visitors to see a demonstration of their flying saucers and began soliciting private funds for the venture.

*

Marilyn Monroe and Interplanetary Saucers – two icons of the 1950s on the cover of LIFE.

The cover of the April 7, 1952, edition of *LIFE* magazine provided Mason Rose with a headline that would expand the reach of the enterprise. Just above the bare left shoulder of a saucy Marilyn Monroe, the headline reads:

There Is A Case for Interplanetary Saucers

Inside, the accompanying story took its lead from an August 1951 UFO sighting called the Lubbock Lights, in which a V-shaped formation of lights were "considered by the Air Force the most unexplainable phenomena yet observed."

The article began with Kenneth Arnold's encounter with "saucer-like things... flying like geese in a diagonal chainlike line" in the summer of 1947 and went on with a "Top Ten List" of subsequent incidents.

Such popular media coverage supplied Mason Rose with a perfect cover for injecting Townsend Brown into the public fascination with UFOs, space aliens and cover-up conspiracy theories. After the *LIFE* story hit newsstands, Rose invited the Los Angeles press core to see some flying saucers for themselves. The demonstration was so impressive that on April 8, 1952, the *Los Angeles Times* ran an article above the fold on the front page of the second section with the headline…

Flying Saucers Explained

Beneath a photo of Shank, Brown, and Rose, the article describes:

Two metal-plexiglass disks, suspended from a central pylon, swung through slow circles in a darkened room yesterday as spokesmen for a new university sought to convince newsmen that they have solved the flying saucer mystery.

"We have hesitated to divulge our findings," said Mason Rose, president of the University for Social Research," because they read too much like science fiction."

Substance of the alleged discovery, credited to inventor Townsend Brown, is that saucers operate in a field of 'electro-gravity' that acts like a wave with the negative pole at the top and the positive pole at the bottom.

"The saucer travels like a surfboard on the incline of a wave that is kept continually moving by the saucers electrogravitational generator," explained Bradford Shank, third spokesman for the group claiming knowledge "almost too sensational, too spectacular."

The *Times* stopped short of dismissing the demonstration as a crackpot scheme, but does cast some aspersions on the trio's credentials. One reporter asked Shank,

"Do you have a degree in this field?"

"No, Shank replied, "I'm free of those encumbrances. That's why I find it so easy to talk in these new terms."

The *Canyon Crier*, a weekly circulated primarily through the Hollywood Hills offered a more skeptical account. Along with its reporter, the *Crier* sent along a Cal Tech physicist, Dr. Stanley Frankel. *The Crier's* April 10, 1952, edition offered its own take on what appeared two days earlier in the *Times:*

Hill Scientist & Crier Investigate Secret Behind The Whirling Disks

Bug-eyed at the recent article in LIFE magazine about the possibility of extra-terrestrial visitors hovering mysteriously over the earth in bright flying saucers, we accepted with somewhat quaking enthusiasm an invitation to attend a flying saucer demonstration last week at 306 N. Vermont Ave., right here on earth.

We marched into a handsome suite of offices which read "Townsend Brown Foundation" and were escorted with some 20 other members of the press to seats in a room with two aluminum saucers.

In one corner, a sinister looking device with two arms stood. Struck us as maybe an extra-terrestrial personality for a moment, but Dr. Frankel pointed out its Model T-type condensers and murmured calmly that it seemed like a harmless balance device.

Just as we were beginning to find the suspense unnerving, a husky, dynamic looking chap stepped up to the blackboard and introduced himself as Dr. Mason Rose, who turned out to be president of a "University of Social Research."

"With proper development," said Dr. Mason Rose, piercing us with an intent look, "the discoveries of the Townsend Brown Foundation can be applied so that man will be able to travel in space possibly within ten years."

How much money was needed, asked a reporter.

Dr. Mason Rose said he thought about a half-billion would do it, and even as little as two and half to three million could build a gravity-free laboratory right now!

We clutched the fifty-cent piece in our pocket and settled back thoughtfully.

The article continues in this tongue-in-cheek manner, explaining how the Biefeld-Brown effect could "propel an object with no machinery or no moving parts." As the demonstration proceeded, Dr. Frankel, became "even more bemused" – especially with Bradford Shank "a scientist who was unfettered in his thinking by any degree." Finally,

A man in a blue suit got up next. Turned out to be Townsend Brown himself, who invited us affably into the other room. "Come see them fly with your own eyes," he said simply.

We went next door into a room which was bare except for a pole with two arms about seven feet high from which hung two metal disks with plastic rings around them, suspended by electric wires.

We felt a chill. Here we were – in on the very first public demonstration of what makes flying saucers fly. A historic moment. "What hath Brown wrought," we cackled nervously.

Shank said we would now see the disks propelled by electrogravitational force, just as they believed the observed flying saucers in the heavens to be propelled. "Don't come within one foot of the disks!" He warned earnestly. "They're loaded with 100,000 volts of electricity."

As the lights gradually dimmed, an unearthly green glow started to emanate from the disks. "The corona effect," breathed Shank.

"Smell the ozone," sniffed our physicist from Cal Tech.

Our scientist companion, Dr. Frankel, suddenly pushed out a hand after a disk had passed. "Quite a little electric wind observable," said he politely.

Mr. Shank said that, uh, he'd never observed electric wind before.

Dr. Frankel thrust his hand out behind a disk as it flew past again. "Definite electric wind," he smiled courteously, and snatched his hand back, whispering reassuringly to us, "I'm afraid these gentlemen played hooky from their high school physics classes...."

Frankel then asked Shank,

"Have you ever tried your demonstration in a vacuum?"

"Oh no," replied Mr. Shank. "Too expensive. Take a hundred thousand dollars."

Dr. Frankel leaned toward us. "Last I heard, vacuum pumps were selling for a couple hundred dollars...."

The lights went on. The disks stopped whirling. We snatched a sandwich courteously provided by the Townsend Brown Foundation and went down into the street.

"Electric wind," said Dr. Frankel. "It's a regular demonstration in every high school lab in the country. The corona discharge heats the air and the resultant wind propels the object."

You mean hot air?" we asked incredulously.

"Hot air," smiled Dr. Frankel.

Dr. Frankel was exactly right. He had witnessed the *fluid* dielectric version of Townsend Brown's inventions – not the *solid* dielectric version that had been compromised at Pearl Harbor.

The wounded prairie chicken was playing its part perfectly.

*

The charade was working on the FBI, too.

Townsend Brown was still on the FBI's radar, though the file had been relatively dormant since being opened in the wake of his discharge from the Navy in 1942. At the time, the Bureau concluded that despite such defects of character as being an "impractical dreamer" who "traveled with a group which did considerable drinking" and running around "with other women while married" that there was "no information of a derogatory nature with respect to Subject's Americanism" and the case was closed.

Now the file was reopened to investigate the possibility of fraud. A synopsis from May 29, 1953, reported:

> Two wealthy Los Angeles men concede loss of more than $60,000 invested in Townsend Brown Foundation for scientific research. Support withdrawn when promised efforts failed to materialize and investors' suspicions aroused that principals lack sincerity. Investment broker refused to participate in raising one and one-half million dollars for Townsend Brown Foundation experiments because "the people looked like a bunch of gyps and the spiel was too good." A financier refused to invest when he realized he was being high-pressured, although claims and predictions made to him were never investigated. Another prospective investor admittedly lacked enough electronics knowledge to evaluate claims made by BROWN and [redacted] but reasoned that if true, financing would have been readily gained from the government or other responsible institutional type source.

The synopsis describes the "luxurious, aesthetic offices of the Foundation, engraved stationery," and titles of "Doctor" that were all designed "to entice wary, credulous persons." The names are all blacked out, but one of the promoters, presumably Mason Rose, is described as...

...too glib. A real huckster. An engineer who consulted for months with the subjects left them because of their unscientific, un-business-like, selfish attitudes.

The file has this to say about the Foundation's business practices:

Foundation bills for equipment, supplies, and services settled to the detriment of creditors in 1952 despite sufficient funds supplied by investors.

and concludes:

An attorney visitor to the Foundation headquarters believes subjects are either frauds or security risks. His reasoning – they discuss their business openly with strangers who might invest yet claim discoveries of secret and vastly important military significance.

The rest of the one-hundred-plus pages of the FBI's report goes into considerable detail about specific instances where the Foundation entertained prospective investors and offered insights into its perilous finances.

By the end of 1952, Townsend Brown's work in Los Angeles – such as it was – was done.

In January 1953 – despite an apparent lack of funds – the family boarded the luxurious Santa Fe Super Chief and headed east. When Josephine unpacked her little green teapot, it was only a few miles from its original location in Zanesville – where another chapter was added to the tale of failure and insolvency.

At seven, Linda was old enough to have strong memories of the ride aboard the gleaming, diesel-powered train:

Dad had taken the last Pullman compartment on the train, so the observation car was right behind us. He got me to walk all the way to the front of the train and persuaded the engineer to let me up in the engine room so that I could see what was really pulling the train. I had been totally freaked out by all of the sights and sounds and was nervous about the train leaving before we were even on board. He showed me the engine and I can remember him telling me, "When you don't understand something, Sweetie, just go to the front and you will find out what is the real thing. You can always find out about things that scare you by just going and taking a good hard look." Frankly I have hated enormous engines ever since but guess it was a good lesson.

313

Los Angeles Times

C C   TUESDAY MORNING, APRIL 8, 1952   Times

LIGHT ON MYSTERY—Watching two model flying saucers hanging from pivoting arm are trio of the new University for Social Research: Researchers Bradford Shank, left, and Townsend Brown, and Mason Rose, president. They present a novel theory.
Times photo

Flying Saucers 'Explained' by Men of New Research University Here

Two metal-plexiglass d i s k s, suspended from a central pylon, swung through slow circles in a darkened room yesterday as spokesmen for a new university sought to convince newsmen they have solved the flying saucer mystery.

"We have hesitated to divulge our findings," said Mason Rose, president of the University for Social Research, "because they read too much like science fiction . . ."

Substance of the alleged discovery, credited to inventor Townsend Brown, is that saucers operate in a field of "electrogravity" that "acts like a wave with the negative pole at the top and the positive pole at the bottom."

Travel Like Surfboard

"The saucer travels like a surfboard on the incline of a wave that is kept continually moving by the saucer's electrogravitational generator," e x p l a i n e d Bradford Shank, third spokesman for the group claiming knowledge "almost too sensational, too spectacular."

All three men are convinced that flying saucers are real, "controlled by an intelligence rather than a pilot" and capable of speeds up to that of light—186,000 miles a second.

Their research is new and novel, they insist, and "it is dis-

tinctly improbable it has been duplicated anywhere in the world," experiments coupling electricity and gravitation that apparently go even beyond Einstein's unified field theory.

Asked about official government study of their findings, Rose said details had been given to "some Navy admirals" but as yet there was no censorship. He talked guardedly about military "interest" in the work but declined to mention specific agencies.

He spoke too about the early trials and tribulations of Marconi, Edison and the Wright brothers.

The three men said space travel will be possible within 10 years.

At one point Shank was asked if he had a degree.

'Superior Intelligence'

"No," he acknowledged, "I'm free of those encumbrances. That's why I find it so easy to talk in these new terms."

To all dead-end questions there was the answer: "A superior intelligence thousands of years ahead of ours would have many answers we don't know about."

For more than four years Brown has been attempting to predict the ups and downs of the stock market with electronic apparatus he installed in the basement of a building on S Spring St. His equipment, he said, registers small variations in sidereal or cosmic rays which bombard the earth from outer space.

These rays, in some yet unexplained manner, are suspected of influencing human psychology. Brown declined to say how his stock market "barometer" has worked.

Rain, Holiday Snarl Traffic

It looked like the day before Christmas in the downtown area yesterday as slowly moving traffic was backed up solid from Temple to 12th Sts. and crowds crammed the sidewalks.

The really big crush was at noon.

Contributing factors: (1) rain-slickened streets, which always slows traffic; (2) pre-Easter shopping; (3) youngsters out of school for Easter vacation.

Throughout the city, of course, there was the customary epidemic of minor collisions, most of them resulting in locked bumpers—and tempers.

The hardest lessons fell on Joseph Brown. For starters, Townsend didn't really have any place for the family to stay, nor sufficient funds to secure a suitable rental. He made it look like he was returning to Zanesville in order to impose upon the goodwill of his remaining family.

The February 8, 1953, edition of the Zanesville *Times Recorder* carried a photo of a smiling Josephine and Linda, standing beside a forlorn looking Townsend:

> **The Townsend Browns have returned to Zanesville to make their home, bringing back a name once prominent in Zanesville affairs. Townsend Brown – pictured above with his wife, the former Josephine Beale, and their seven-year-old daughter, Linda Ann – is the grandson of the contractor who built the Schultz opera house, the courthouse, the Clarendon, the county infirmary, and many more local buildings. The Browns are living at Sharongate on the South River road, home of Mr. Brown's aunt, Miss Sybil Burton.**
>
> **Mr. Brown came home to the refuge of Sharongate to do writing on his electronics research carried on through the Townsend Brown Foundation, a family trust. He has done experimental work on the west coast and in the Hawaiian Islands and his entire life has been spent in electronics research.**
>
> **The Browns have a son, Joseph, who has just entered Ohio University at Athens. He is a graduate of the University of Hawaii high school. Linda is a pupil in the second grade at Duncan Falls School.**

Joseph Brown was living on the campus of Ohio University. Instead of attending classes fulltime, Joseph Brown – two generations removed from the Townsend and Brown family fortunes – was working his way through his freshman year with a job in the school cafeteria.

Linda recalled, "During this period a rift developed between Joseph and my dad which was never healed. Being back in his hometown again, Joseph was also surrounded by cousins from both sides of his family, and I am sure he picked up on their pinched attitude toward Dad, how much of a failure he must have been. 'After all,' they'd say, 'look at all the money his parents had.' And now, because of his father's silly flying saucer pipe dreams, the enormous fortune that Joseph should have stood to inherit was long gone. Joseph developed a bitter attitude that remained always just beneath the surface."

Her memories of Joseph fade after they moved back to Zanesville and Joseph went off to school, at least until years later when he began to make his own life and would occasionally visit his parents on Catalina. "There was twelve years difference in our ages anyway," Linda laments. "Joe was usually at college, then joined the Air Force and was stationed in Europe. So, it was like growing up an only child."

Townsend, Josephine and Linda at Sharongate, where they lived for a time Aunt Sybil Burton.

68

Good Morning, Sweetie Peach

(1966)

Mornings in the penthouse at the Drake Hotel often began with Townsend greeting Linda at the breakfast table with "Good morning, Sweetie Peach, did you sleep well?"

But her first night back, after two weeks in the idyllic embrace of Morgan's family farm – after Morgan took the green light and walked out of her life – Linda did not sleep well at all. "I pretty much cried all night," she wrote, certain that she had just made the biggest mistake of her life:

> **I am feeling really displaced. If I had said "Don't go…" we would probably have set a date by now. What would I be doing? Starting my new life as a bride? Living somewhere on the Main Line? The last time we were together he drove me past that little brick house in Bryn Mawr. He said, "This could be ours." I have never really had a home, and there it was, with roses starting to bloom for the summer. A substantial little house in a lovely town. I looked at him, tall and strong. I could see our children.**
>
> **It was all I could do not to reach for the phone, to call him, to ask him to look at that house in Bryn Mawr with me again.**

Her father knew exactly what had happened. The next day he came home from the lab with a package under his arm.

"Here, this is yours," he said, handing the package to Linda.

When she opened it, Linda found a neatly folded, starched, white lab coat, just like the one her father always wore, with a security badge already sewn over the pocket.

"I really need you, Sweetie," Townsend said. "Please come to work with me."

The Homestead lab had been relocated to Martin Decker's sprawling compound in Bala Cynwyd, where Linda's co-workers included the ubiquitous Puscheck and Spirito. Linda had heard stories about how clever they were, and worried they had taken her place.

"It's OK," Josephine assured her, "it's taken the two of them to replace the one of you!"

The next day, after Josephine laid out a breakfast of fresh strawberries, Linda and her father took the walnut-paneled elevator to the lobby. A doorman tipped his cap as they went through the Drake's big revolving brass doors and crossed the street to the garage where the Cadillac convertible was retrieved by a valet. Linda slid into the driver's seat and steered across the Schuylkill River into the suburbs. "We were fortunate because we are going out when everyone else is coming into their jobs in the city."

The Decker compound occupied a hilltop about seven miles away. At the gated entrance, Townsend "always signed in with his long, elegant signature." Linda signed in after her father, just jotting "ditto, ditto, ditto" under all the other entries on the form. "Then we put on our lab coats. No one got anywhere on the complex without the badges sewn into those lab coats."

That badge, Linda learned later, was actually a dosimeter – a device made to measure doses of radiation in the air.

"Everyone admitted to 'the hill' is required to wear one of those specially issued white lab coats," she noted, "and no one is allowed past the front gate without one of those badges. Now that I know about those little radiation tags, it makes me nervous about what else this place is up to."

A stand of pear trees lined the sidewalk in front of Dr. Brown's lab. Building #4 was "big, modern and all ours," Linda recorded. Their space was "large and airy but not cold. It's a far cry from Homestead. It's full of equipment, but Daddy still grumbles about the lack of proper small tools – things like sharp knives, or extra plugs, or even pliers that actually meet at the tips!"

Surrounded by stands of pine and oak trees, the location was "isolated in the middle of the city. Yesterday I watched a rabbit hop right up to our door and peer in."

It did not occur to Linda that she was the one in the rabbit hole.

Martin Decker was rarely seen, but there was one ominous reminder of his looming presence: "Mr. Decker keeps a gorgeously plumed peacock – in *a cage* – by the wall of our building," Linda noted, unable to fathom why the colorful creature was caged up when "there is plenty of room here for him to roam safely and happily."

Asked why the bird was so confined, a guard could only say, "Mr. Decker's orders."

Seeing "that poor bird, its cramped quarters wearing down its plumage," became a metaphor for Dr. Brown's commitment to Decker at the behest of his Nassau colleagues.

"I think," Townsend whispered to Linda, "we are in very big trouble."

*

The ostensible reason for returning to Philadelphia was to make a commercially viable product from the loudspeaker variation of the electrokinetic Fan. By mid-May, Linda had settled into a daily routine, helping fabricate a "theater-sized loudspeaker that took up a whole side of the building." Puscheck and Spirito – Nassau's "men at Decker" – showed her "how things needed to be soldered," and she worked "all day long, every day, all summer," stringing delicate filaments with the thickness of a human hair into the enormous framework.

All summer long, they played the soundtracks from *Camelot* and *The Sound of Music* to demonstrate the system's sonic qualities. Not only was the output crystal clear, but the dynamics also remained consistent no matter where a listener stood: with your nose right in front of the speaker or standing sixty feet away, level and tone always sounded like the speaker was ten feet away.

Linda's other job was looking after her father: Every day, they would work through the morning and well past noon, "until sometime after one, when the hunger pains would make me complain. Then Dad would finally be forced to stop what he was doing to feed his daughter and, yes, by the way, to eat something himself."

One item at a time, they punched through improvements in the design and output. When an annoying background hiss was eliminated, Linda wrote

One bug squashed and she is running smoothly now. It's marvelous music anyway – *The Sound of Music* with Julie Andrews. That was the first music that anybody ever heard from the loudspeaker – in 1962! It's been four years already. Damn, where did all the time go? My mind flashed on everything that had gone on between me and Morgan since then, and my heart aches suddenly.

It looks like I'll be here for a while, but this is strictly a labor of love. I get no official paycheck, but Dad has made sure that I always have money in my pocket. I have no expenses at home, so why shouldn't I spend my time at the Lab? If I was working somewhere else, could I contribute more? I don't think so, and my future is hanging by every thread of wire that I string.

Everyone involved was delighted with the progress – until mid-June, when Spirito ran an endurance test on the honeycomb design of the speaker matrix. In less than 48 hours, the apparatus started to fall apart.

"In one single day we felt that the world had suddenly ended," Linda noted, "as if we had been on the wrong track and some giant power had slammed us into a stone wall. Daddy was floored!"

Townsend "just threw his glasses down on his desk and walked out to the shade of the trees outside. Everybody knew enough to leave him alone."

An hour later he returned, saying, "You know, I've been thinking…"

Linda ran for a pad and pencil, as Puscheck and Spirito gathered around his big desk. Soon Spirito was on the phone dictating the specifications for some material to be machined overnight and delivered in the morning.

"Tomorrow we start all over," Linda wrote, "with a brand new design. It's the most amazing thing when you see that process unfold."

*

As usual, Linda and her father were the last to leave the lab the day the honeycomb was re-assembled.

When they got home, Townsend fell asleep on the bed. Josephine, needing to get out of the penthouse, took Linda out for dinner.

"It was a rare moment for us," Linda said. After talking about what had happened in the lab, Linda realized that "Mom was treating me as a grown woman, not the girl who was her daughter. We talked about our hopes for the future."

Then Josephine asked about Morgan.

"How long will he be in Virginia?"

"I don't know. At least until September."

"And then what?"

"I don't know."

"It's a strange world we live in," Josephine said "and sometimes I think it's better just to go along with everybody else. Knowing too much can be painful."

69

Summer In The City

(1966)

SS-478, the USS Cutlass

One Sunday in the middle of June Linda awoke to the ringing of the telephone and her mother calling out playfully, "There's a Mr. Morgan calling for a Miss Brown!"

It had been weeks since their parting at the green light. Now Morgan was calling from a payphone at a bus station with only a moment to talk.

"I just wanted to remind you... I love you."

The line went dead. Minutes later, Morgan boarded the bus that would take him to Camp Peary – 'The Farm' – where he would begin training alongside other recruits for the United States' intelligence and security services.

*

Sensing the void that her devotion to work and family still left a hole in Linda's life, Townsend suggested she invite Tula, her high-spirited former classmate at Southern Seminary, to visit during the summer. Tula had graduated that spring and had the summer to herself before starting a job in October. She arrived at the Drake late in June.

Through the month of June, Linda noted, work at the lab was "moving forward steadily." She was building Plexiglas frames for the speaker components as fast as she could. Her daily lunch excursions with her father had stopped, though.

"Mother has packed us a lunch because Dad will not stop to go out anymore. I am eating as I am writing, so if this page smells of ham and cheese."

She made some observations about her mysterious co-workers:

> Daddy and Mr. Spirito have left for New Jersey to check out some sheet metal plates. The lab is quiet now except for Nick (Puscheck) re-crating the honeycomb grid panels He is a funny, boyish-looking man who stutters when he is pressured. I remember how charming he was in Florida the first time he came down to visit, as one of "Nassau's men at Decker." He and Mr. Spirito acted then as if they had known each other for years, maybe went to school together. It's hard for me to believe that you could get that close just working together for a long time. But how would I know? This is my first real job."

Of the actual work, she wrote:

> I'm getting a great sense of satisfaction with this project, because everywhere I look I can see things that I have accomplished. All the painting, wiring, gluing, and now making the actual frames for this enormous model. I am a large contributor, and it is a really nice feeling.
>
> It has helped me to keep my chin up, and I have used all this work to keep my mind off of Morgan.

After working past the point of exhaustion "into some kind of altered state" Linda noted their progress:

> It's a wonderful, massive thing. We have all worked really hard. I know that I strung 20 wire frames, glued all of the Plexiglass frames together, insulated each, painted the entire frame system black and grey, learned how to solder and put the pieces together, learned how to handle a little blow torch and shrink tubing.
>
> I take as much pride in it as I know Daddy does, and I have caught Tom and Nick looking over their shoulders at it, too. It gives me a marvelous feeling."

Even with the system running at a fraction of its capacity, the performance steadily improved. As word spread around the hillside that "Building #4 is making music," people started to wander into the lab to hear the acoustic marvel. Linda recalled one man "who has been visiting us every lunch time, sitting dead center and smiling with a grin that lights up his entire face!"

"Go Fan! GO!" she wrote as her father turned up the volume on the Naval anthem, *Anchors Aweigh*. "Daddy is cranking her up again, it is the loudest that it has ever been, and the music is going right down into my bones."

With the last bugs ironed out, the apparatus was ready for testing:

The loudspeaker is really stepping out! It is doing what so many people told us was impossible! They told us we couldn't possibly make a loudspeaker with nothing more than metal plates and grids. They said it would never work without a diaphragm! Well, LISTEN UP FOLKS! A new age is here!"

*

When the phone rang in the penthouse on a Saturday morning in July, Linda didn't bother to answer it. She waved her mother off as Josephine tried to hand her the phone.

"Oh," Josephine said, "I think you should take this one."

Reluctantly putting the phone to her ear, Linda was stunned to hear Morgan's voice.

He said he was a twenty-four-hour furlough with Carlos – the friend Linda spent much of her New Year's Eve with – and he wanted to spend as much of that time as he could with her.

"Well, Tula is here with us for the summer," Linda said, trying to quickly sort out the possibilities and permutations.

"That's *great*," Morgan boomed through the handset. "Grab the train… quick! We'll meet you both at the Paoli station. Be *quick*!"

Tula, who could only hear half the conversation, was gesturing and making faces, trying to get some idea who was on the line. Suddenly Linda hung up the phone and started barking orders.

"We are leaving. Now. Jeans! *Now!*"

Quickly doing the math in her head, Linda turned to Josephine and said, "we should be home by midnight."

Not wasting a moment for explanation, Linda and Tula were down the elevator and out the revolving door in front of the Drake in less than two minutes, Tula pulling curlers out of her hair as they ran.

Morgan was waiting for her when she stepped off the train. This time, he picked her up and whirled her around in his arms, like he had learned his lesson from the last time. "He wasn't going to waste any time ignoring me," Linda said.

Carlos introduced himself to Tula, and as they shook hands, Tula raised an eyebrow in Linda's direction, as if to say, "OK, this is going to be fun!" And off they all went "on the best double date ever."

Their coach for the day was a battered Volkswagen with a balky clutch. The first stop was the observation tower at Valley Forge Park, where Morgan and Linda ran to the very top, "out of sheer joy." The next stop was back to the farm, where they waded in the cool waters of an old swimming hole and lunched on peanut butter sandwiches.

"It was all very peaceful, warm, and unhurried," Linda recalled.

That evening, when the old VW pulled up in front of the Drake, Linda was surprised to see a small parking space right in front. Linda couldn't imagine how anybody was ever going to parallel park the thing.

"Relax," Carlos said, "I have a plan."

He steered the VW straight into the empty parking space, driving it very carefully onto the curb. Everybody piled out of the car – "like clowns in the circus" – then the two secret-agents-in-training grabbed hold of the rear bumper – and lifted the old Beetle. It took a couple of hefts, but soon the car was parked perfectly parallel to the curb.

Upstairs, Linda checked in with Josephine. Her father was not home. He was spending another Saturday night at the lab.

The foursome then walked to a nearby restaurant where they all spent the remainder of the evening lingering over a "wonderful dinner." From the restaurant, they walked toward Rittenhouse Square. Tula and Carlos peeled off for a nearby jazz club, making good on her promise to "keep Carlos busy" and give Morgan and Linda some time alone.

Linda and Morgan found a bench beside "*our* lion." In the street-lit darkness beside the lion, they kissed. Morgan buried his face in Linda's neck and whispered, "God, I have missed you…"

"Do you have any idea where you will be going next?" Linda asked.

"No," Morgan said. "Not because I am hiding something, because I just don't know."

Morgan covered Linda's hand with his own.

Looking into Morgan's eyes, Linda repeated a line that Morgan had once teased her with.

"What we have together is 90% biological…" she started to say.

"Yes," Morgan said, finishing the thought. "But the other 10% is pure *magic*."

*

The line about the "10% magic" is actually something that Morgan quoted to me early in our correspondence. Later, he offered his usual veiled references to what the Caroline Group might have been doing in Philadelphia during this period besides developing Dr. Brown's electrokinetic loudspeaker. He inferred that the dosimeter badges sewn into those lab coats might be our only clue to what else was going on during those weekends and nights that Dr. Brown was spending at the lab when Linda *wasn't* there.

In addition to the dosimeters, Morgan hinted at one other clue, and with his encouragement, during one of my visits to the National Archives in Maryland, I found the logbooks for a diesel electric submarine, SS-478 – the USS *Cutlass*.

On Saturday June 11, 1966, the *Cutlass* slipped from her moorings in Norfolk Virginia, and began steaming north. four days later, the *Cutlass* was "moored starboard side to the west face" of a pier at the Philadelphia Naval Yard.

By Sunday, July 1, the *Cutlass* was in dry dock, "resting on keel blocks and receiving miscellaneous service from the pier." The *Cutlass* remained so disposed through July and August, finally coming "off the blocks" on September 7, 1966. She remained moored pier side until October 31, receiving, in the unvarnished Naval vernacular, still more "miscellaneous service from the pier."

The *Cutlass* conducted sea trials out of Philadelphia during the month of November before returning to her permanent berth in Norfolk on November 24.

With Morgan's prompt, we can note here only that the *Cutlass* was first moored and then dry docked in Philadelphia during the same period of time that Townsend Brown and "Nassau's men at Decker" were also anchored in Philadelphia and working – so far as anybody knew – on a wall-sized, electrokinetic loudspeaker at the Martin Decker compound nearby.

And remember that after the fiasco at Pearl Harbor, "The Navy got what they wanted."

70

Flying Saucers In the Bible

(1966)

*Engraved illustration of the "chariot vision" of the Biblical book of
Ezekiel, chapter 1, made by Matthaeus (Matthäus) Merian (1593-1650)*

I met Tula in October 2004.

Linda and I were on our research trip to the Zanesville are. Tula lived not far
away and joined us on a deck overlooking Buckeye Lake – the same lake where
Townsend Brown, sailing with Josephine on their first date almost eighty years
earlier – told his future wife that someday great ships would "just sail away" from
the Earth" as easily as their boat pushed away from the dock.

Tula had a vivid recollection of the time she spent with the Browns at The
Drake in the summer of 1966. The story that follows[106] is reconstructed from our
hours-long conversation that night.

*

After a sumptuous dinner of Josephine's "killer spaghetti" at the Drake
penthouse, Linda and Josephine cleaned up the kitchen while Townsend and
Tula settled into the living room to continue discussing a recent UFO sighting
in Virginia.

"Do you think these things are real?" Tula asked, as she took a seat in the
overstuffed chair next to Townsend.

"Yes Tula. I do," he said. "And I think that they have been observed here on Earth for a very long time. The Bible even mentions them – events that are described as flaming chariots and pillars of clouds or columns of light in the night sky."

"But that doesn't mean they are flying saucers, does it?"

"What else could they be?" Townsend asked, "unless you really believe in flaming chariots and pillars of fire?"

"Can you give me a for instance?" Tula asked.

"Sure, let's see, there must be a Bible around here somewhere."

"You're kidding me," Tula said. "You've got a Bible?"

"It's here somewhere," Townsend said as he scanned the bookshelves, finally pulling a well-thumbed volume off the shelf.

"Genesis is probably a good place to start," he said, smiling at his own pun. "These stories could not possibly have been invented out of whole cloth. They must have had some basis in, well, something. Maybe they happened just the way they're told in these chapters and verses. Or, maybe, what really happened was so foreign to the authors' experience that they had to reduce it to terms that they could understand."

"What do you mean?"

"Look at it this way: we're living in a world that is technologically very advanced by the standards of the people who wrote the Bible. Most of the world we live in now has evolved over just the past two or three hundred years. We've had electricity, which we take so much for granted, for only the past hundred and fifty years. Before that, the world was not all that much different from the world of the Bible. Machines that move under their own power and machines that can fly are commonplace to us. It's a short leap for us to flying saucers, or at least to flying things that might come from another world. But to the ancients, all such technologies were completely foreign to their experience."

"You're kind of jumping ahead there, aren't you? We don't have any proof yet that we're being visited by space aliens. That's all pure speculation."

"That's true," Townsend replied. "We don't have any solid proof, even today, that our planet is being visited by emissaries from other worlds. But before Columbus showed up in their waters, the natives of this hemisphere had no way of knowing that there was a whole other civilization just across the water, or how advanced that civilization was. Who's to say that, despite our apparent advances today that there isn't another civilization just across some unseen horizon, and that their civilization is as advanced by our standards as the fifteenth- and sixteenth- century Europeans were advanced by the standards of the natives of North America?"

"OK. But how do you get from that to flying saucers in the Bible?"

"Just by reading what the Good Book says, and then layering what we know now over what we read." Townsend stopped flipping pages in the Old Testament, in the book of Exodus.

"Try this. Exodus, chapter 13, verse 21. It's talking about the Hebrews wandering around in the desert after their escape from Pharaoh's Egypt."

> **And Jehovah was going ahead of them in the daytime in a pillar of cloud to lead them by the way, and in the nighttime in a pillar of fire to give them light to go in the daytime and the nighttime.**

"What does that sound like to you, Tula?" Dr. Brown asked.

"I don't really know, but they must have thought that it was something solid and tube shaped or they wouldn't have called it a pillar."

"Ah, Tula, you're catching on. Not all of what appears in the sky is disc or saucer shaped. The sighting in Virginia a few days ago was shaped like a *triangle*. And many other sightings are of things that even *we* don't know how to describe, so when I say 'flying saucer' to you I just mean the whole class of strange things."

"I still don't see how you get from a 'pillar of fire' to a flying saucer?"

Townsend admitted he was using the term 'flying saucer' to cover a multitude of inexplicable phenomena. "Nowadays, rockets launching things into outer space are almost commonplace. And if you saw a rocket taking off for the first time, and you had no idea what it really was, how would you describe it to somebody?"

"As a pillar of fire and smoke?"

"Exactly. You know from your own experience that machines can fly, so it's much easier to make the mental leap to something that flies but is just slightly outside your experience. To these ancient tribes wandering in the desert, 'clouds' and 'fire' were about the extent of their grasp of technology. So that's the sort of terminology that they would use to describe something which might be entirely more plausible to us. And that's hardly the only example."

Townsend flipped some more pages, stopping in the Second Book of Kings. "Ever heard of the prophet Elijah?"

"The Old Testament prophet?"

"Yes, who predicted the eventual arrival of both Moses and Jesus. Do you know how he left the Earth?"

"Let me guess. In a chariot of fire?"

"Exactly right. Let me read this to you, from Second Kings, chapter 2, verse 11. It's just another day in the desert. Elijah and his son Elisha are out for a stroll when…

… it came to pass that as they were walking along, speaking as they walked, why, look! A fiery war chariot and fiery horses, and they proceeded to make a separation between them both, and Elijah went ascending in the windstorm to heavens."

"You think Elijah was abducted by a UFO?"

"Now Tula," he gently chided, "don't get sarcastic. We're just trying to look at ancient stories through a contemporary lens. Based on what the ancient Hebrews knew, it shouldn't be surprising that what we call a 'UFO' they might have called 'a chariot of fire.' We have the advantage of at least being familiar with flying objects, identified or otherwise."

"OK, I see your point. But you're taking on some pretty powerful myths here."

"Oh, that's just the beginning. That's just the Old Testament."

"You mean there are flying saucers in the New Testament, too?"

"Well, flying somethings. Like the one that carried Jesus to his final reward."

"Jesus was abducted by a UFO, too?"

"Appears that way," Townsend said, now flipping through the Scriptures to find the New Testament. "Assuming you buy the theory for the first two examples. Here it is. Acts. Chapter 1, verse 9. A couple of days after Mary Magdalene found the empty tomb, and the resurrected Jesus has completed his teachings:

And after he had said these things, while they were looking on, he was lifted up and a cloud caught him up from their vision."

"Another cloud…?"

"I'm afraid so. Except, what kind of cloud do you know of that can lead a tribe of wanderers around in the desert by day or night, or carry a prophet off into the heavens? Certainly not any strato-cirrus or cumuli-nimbus that I know of."

"I'm still not convinced these clouds and chariots were flying saucers from another planet or something."

"Look, Tula, I'm not sure either. I just know that there are numerous ancient myths that can be seen in different light when viewed from a modern perspective. You're entirely right, we don't know what UFOs are. We don't know if they're visitors from another planet, phantoms from another dimension, creatures from a parallel universe, or just super-secret military aircraft that the government isn't telling us about."

"Or maybe they're something the Russians have developed that we're way behind on?"

"That's entirely possible too. I'm just saying…"

"That there are more things in heaven and earth…"

"You got it, Horatio."

71

Mostly Absent

(1953)

While the Browns lived with Aunt Sybil at Sharongate in the first months of 1953, Townsend found work as a consultant to the Clevite-Brush Corporation in Cleveland.

Clevite-Brush was formed in 1952 from the merger of Cleveland Graphite Bronze Corp. and the Brush Development Company; its principal business involved audio technologies like piezoelectric pickups. Brush Development was descended from Brush Labs, the company formed in 1919 by electrical pioneer Charles Francis Brush,[107] who wrote the 1911 paper about the *Kinetic Theory of Gravitation*[108] which supplied some of the inspiration for Brown's own ideas about gravity being "a push, not a pull."

That this engagement with Clevite-Brush is another chapter in the 'wounded prairie chicken' charade is apparent in a letter that Townsend wrote to Josephine on stationery from the Hotel Allerton in Cleveland:

> **August 12, 1953**
>
> **Dearest,**
>
> **Yesterday was a really bad day for me. It took an enormous amount of self-control to keep from flying to pieces. In the first place, everything went wrong at the laboratory. Nothing worked as it should have – and I was repeatedly tempted to throw the whole thing in the air. I was down to $2 in cash and a $53 hotel bill. I went back to the hotel exhausted and tried to sleep. Then there was a knock at the door and the credit manager said I would have to pay in full – that I had already exceeded my credit limit. I asked him to wait until today, so he finally agreed.**
>
> **Today Woody[109] phoned me that $75 had been deposited at Riggs – so now I have paid the hotel bill and have a little pocket money.**
>
> **Woody says that the interest in Washington – due largely to the newspaper and magazine articles about Einstein connecting gravitation and electromagnetism is steadily increasing. Two prospects for funds have appeared which they are now working on.**
>
> **I think something will come in soon which we can use to pay Sybil – and return Joe's loan at least. We are really working against time.**

> **Today things at the lab worked better. I am sure they must be influenced by my emotional state. I want you to keep level, too. Don't get upset about anything. After all, they are trivial matters compared to the one big one. We have ridden out storms before. Something always happens and we keep a steady course.**
>
> **Remember, you still have me.**
>
> **Lovingly,**
>
> **T.**

Josephine recognized in the last paragraph of that letter a code known only to her and Townsend, an encouragement to see through their temporary hardships and keep an eye toward the eventual outcome.

*

Linda Brown recalls that her father was mostly absent while she and Josephine lived at Sharongate. The FBI files indicate that much of that absence was spent in the Washington, DC area. On March 21, 1955, Assistant U.S. Attorney Lloyd F. Dunn submitted a summary of the FBI's investigations. Dunn draws a thumbnail sketch of Brown's life, paying particular attention to his claims that "his Sidereal Radiation Recorder could predict the movements of the stock market" and questioning whether such a claim could be construed as fraud. The report then goes in to Brown's...

> **...electrogravitational theory, the electro-culture of plants and animals, an explanation of flying saucers, and the claim that through his experiment it was possible to maintain communications through mountains and under water. Demonstrations that were given in support of these theories were of the simple high school physics experiment type. It is not clear the exact time that the scheme here under consideration began, but apparently it started sometime around the 1940s.**

Once again, the dismissal of a 'high school physics' experiment discounts all the verbiage that comes before. Mr. Dunn's summary then offers this revelation:

> **Information at the present time indicates that T. TOWNSEND BROWN has ceased efforts to promote his 'electro-gravitational' theory and has entered into the business of operating a laundry in Washington D.C. with his wife, mother-in-law, and father-in-law. There is no information that he is engaging in any promotional activity at this time.**

That would be the Embassy Laundry in Washington, which, as Morgan explained, was the final chapter in the Saga of the Wounded Prairie Chicken:

The years clicked off. The nagging from the FBI continued, his family fortune dwindled away, there were occasional bad credit instances and a few bounced checks, the sad letters written home to a near starving family. Eventually one of this country's finest scientific minds was busying itself washing soiled clothing for customers. He made a point of declaring to any bystander that he was "finished with science forever." Feathers settled into the dust and the mole's employers finally dismissed the whole situation.

Which, a long last, permitted the wounded prairie chicken to return to the nest.

72

Winterhaven:
A New Age of Speed and Power
(1953)

Shortly after attorney Lloyd Dunn summarized the Townsend Brown's FBI file, an informant from Columbus, Ohio sent a letter on to the Cincinnati field office with word of a new proposal that was beginning to circulate. The informant's name is redacted in the letter that we found in the file:

The Cincinnati Office reports advice from [redacted] in Columbus, Ohio, that by personal letter dated January 10, 1953, BROWN announced to [redacted] formation of a project called 'Winterhaven' by the Townsend Brown Foundation, 306 North Vermont Avenue, Los Angeles in a letter that reads:

Dear [redacted]:

Enclosed herewith is an outline of the project we are preparing to submit for a Government research and development contract. This is Registered Copy No. 21 assigned to you.[110] Kindly treat this as confidential material. The estimated cost of the project may run approximately one million dollars.

The costs of organizing are to be shared by the various subcontractors, under a special fund established for this purpose here in Washington by the Foundation.

I hope to be able, in the near future, to come to Columbus and bring you up to date on all these matters. It is possible that I can be there toward the end of this month, if this is convenient for you.

Kindest personal regards with all good wishes for 1953. Sincerely,

Townsend

The *Project Winterhaven* proposal starts with an elaborate organization chart: layers of private enterprise and academia, all operating under the supervision of the Townsend Brown Foundation. It recounts the history of the theory, beginning with Einstein's General Theory of Relativity and his quest for the Unified Field Theory that would unify the forces of electromagnetism and gravitation. It recaps Brown's own story, his encounter with Dr. Biefeld at Denison, the affidavit Biefeld submitted verifying the theory in 1936, and the "strange new effect as manifest in electrical capacitors," which is then called "the Biefeld-Brown effect" – the first published use of that nomenclature and the origin of its use to this day.

Project Winterhaven proposes to gather, test, and implement all that has gone before:

> **For the last several years, accumulating evidence along both theoretical and experimental lines confirms the suspicion that a relationship exists between the Electrodynamic field and the Gravitational field.**
>
> **It is the purpose of Project Winterhaven to compile and study this evidence and to perform certain definitive experiments to confirm or deny the relationship. If the results confirm the evidence, it is the further purpose of the Project to examine the physical nature of the 'electrogravitic couple' and to develop practical applications.**

On the topic of propulsion, *Project Winterhaven* envisions:

> **A new age of speed and power and revolutionary new methods of transportation. Theoretical considerations would predict sustained speeds far beyond those of jet propulsion or rocket drive, eventually approaching the speed of light.**
>
> **It now appears that materials are available to conduct experiments which will be conclusive in proving or disproving the hypothesis that a gravitational field can be effectively controlled by manipulating the electromagnetic field.**

On the subject of communications:

> **No person would have believed that the obscure phenomenon witnessed by Prof. Hertz[111] would lay the groundwork for worldwide radio communications, radar, television and the countless electromagnetic devices which today we take so much for granted. But we have become acutely aware of the limitations caused by the curvature of the earth, shaded areas behind mountains and large buildings, where satisfactory reception is virtually impossible.**
>
> **If the basic experiments set forth in Project Winterhaven prove the controllability of the gravitational wave, a fundamentally new system of communication will become available. Theory indicates that the gravitational wave may be one of the most penetrating forms of radiant energy. Employed as a means of communication it may solve many of the difficulties inherent in present day radio[112] and, at the same time provide countless additional channels for communication.**

Development of the electro-gravitational communication system can provide a secret, untouchable channel for classified military communications. Message transmissions could be put through without breaking military radio silence. Due to the high penetrability of the gravitational wave, communications could be maintained between submerged submarines, between submarines and shore installations or between underground installations without the use of external wires.

That is a detailed description of exactly what Morgan will observe ten years later – when he ventures into Dr. Brown's study at Ashlawn and says, "and nobody else would be able to hear it, huh?"

The remainder of *Project Winterhaven* lists a number of avenues of research that would be conducted to test the hypothesis of the 'electrogravitic couple,' and presents a number of appendices from various institutions and companies expressing interest in the project.

Photocopies of *Project Winterhaven* have been circulating since it was first introduced. Most of those copies bear the notation Registered Copy No. 36,[113] which is the copy from the Brown family archives that Andrew Bolland shared with several people from the website where I first learned of Brown in the summer of 2002. One of those copies found its way into the hands of aviation journalist Nick Cook, who described[114] *Winterhaven* as "a systematic approach for the establishment of a U.S. antigravity program – echoing the origins of the U.S. atomic bomb project a decade earlier."

When I got my own hands on a Copy No. 36, I asked Morgan if *Winterhaven* was a serious attempt to obtain government funding – or yet another layer in the web of deception that Townsend Brown spun around himself after the Pearl Harbor demonstration.

Morgan answered my direct question with another riddle: "Beware of 'either/or' thinking. It can be an enemy and can limit your sight." I took that to mean that for the answer lies in either a combination of those two possibilities, or something else altogether.

But then, that too an is 'either/or' proposition.

*

In early 1954, Josephine packed up her green teapot once more, finally leaving Sharongate and Zanesville to join Townsend in Washington.

"We moved to Washington, D.C.," Linda recalls, "where I stayed with my grandparents[115] for a period of time. Mom and Dad were living somewhere else."

"Somewhere else" was the elegant Georgetown home of a man known as Jacques Bergier[116]. The house was only a few blocks away from the Beale's home on Greenwich Parkway, but it was truly a world away. Bergier's three-story townhouse, filled with priceless antiques, oriental rugs and works of art "was not an appropriate place for a child," Morgan told me, adding, "Dr. Brown did not want to mix his family with this particular group. Such men sometimes have longstanding enemies."

Born in Russia in 1912, Yakov Mikhailovich Berger was the son of a Jewish grocer and his wife, a former revolutionary. During World War II, Yakov Berger gained some renown as Jacques Bergier, resistance fighter and spy. In 1944, when the allies were trying to locate the source of Germany's V-1 and V-2 rockets, Bergier's intelligence network pinpointed the Nazi facilities at Peenemunde, leading to the site's ultimate destruction.

O'Riley told me Bergier was...

...the storehouse where most of us got our explosives, listening devices and forged papers. History has treated him as a shadowy character, but I knew him as bold and brave and able to fit in anywhere. He was Russian by birth and descended from a long line of 'seers' and 'witches.' He used to read constantly when he wasn't helping to blow up a bridge. He carried the Russian sadness with him even after moving away from his boyhood home and into the Saar region of France.

He and Sarbacher worked together on many projects.

*

Eight-year-old Linda was not at all happy with the arrangement and decided that she was "going to walk to Mom and Dad's laundry. I started out late in the afternoon and I remember that I was still walking when it got dark."

As she tried to get her bearings in the fading light, a black Cadillac pulled up against the curb beside her. The window rolled down and the driver asked, "Are you lost?"

Linda didn't answer but "it was pretty obvious that I was."

"You need to call your parents, little girl."

"They are not home. And I don't know their number."

The driver never suggested Linda get in the car; he kept pace with her along the curb. After a few minutes, he pointed to a flight of stone steps and said, "See those stairs? That's the police department. Go in there and ask them to help you."

The driver stopped the car and led Linda up the steps, telling the officers that this little girl had run away from home. Then he turned around and left, and after some time Townsend and Josephine arrived to collect their daughter.

"I didn't have my Mom and Dad's phone number," Linda recalled. "I don't know how they would have contacted my parents. I just know that someone behind the desk said something like 'Sit down there and don't you move.' And then my parents showed up."

A few months later, when the family had moved to yet another location in rural Virginia, the same Cadillac pulled into their driveway, and Linda recognized the man behind the wheel – who was introduced to her as Robert Sarbacher.

73

Like Fish In Water
(1954)

Leesburg Virginia, a picturesque village situated near a bend in the Potomac River about thirty-five miles northwest of Washington, D.C., boasts a proud heritage from America's Revolutionary and Civil Wars. During the Cold War, the town became known as a haven for 'spooks' – operatives working in America's burgeoning alphabet soup of intelligence agencies like the CIA and the new kid on the block, the NSA.

The CIA was established in 1947 to oversee the gathering of 'HUMINT'-information collected through human agents that infiltrated America's foreign adversaries. The NSA was created five years later to establish dominion over the rapidly expanding field of 'SIGINT' – signals intelligence, information gathered through various electronic means. Since so many of the messages the Agency intercepted were sent in ever-more-complicated forms of code, much of its resources were devoted to the science of cryptology. Its operations were so secretive that the acronym "NSA" was jokingly translated to mean "No Such Agency."

Today's laptops and hand-held computers can trace their origins to the earliest efforts in cryptology. Starting with Alan Turing's 'bombe[117]' – the enormous electro-mechanical apparatus that cracked the code of Nazi Germany's 'Enigma' machine – nearly all the advances in digital computing in the 20th century grew out of the need to crack increasingly complex international cyphers.

And right in the middle of all this, who should show up but Townsend Brown, who moved his family to Leesburg in the fall of 1954.

*

The first place Josephine unpacked her teapot in Leesburg was an historic fieldstone cottage just a block from the town center.

One rainy morning shortly after their arrival, Linda answered a knock at the door, where a slight, wiry woman in her early thirties stood in the rain wearing a beige leather trench coat. A scarf over the visitor's head revealed red curls so tight that not even the drenching rain could straighten them. Josephine recognized Helen Towt, a family friend from Zanesville. Like Townsend Brown, Helen had served in the Naval Reserve during the War, where she formed a network of connections that brought her to the Brown's threshold, where she became "the girl who came for lunch and stayed for three years."

Helen hung up her drenched coat and scarf and started helping Josephine unpack boxes.

"She was like an older sister to me," Linda recalled. "She was a very intelligent, funny, and lovely woman. I adored her."

Helen introduced Linda and Josephine to a card game called Russian Bank.[118] "We didn't have a TV then, so we read a lot and played that game constantly," Linda recalled. Russian Bank is a fast, intuitive game that "teaches players to instantly assess what is on the board; at some point you have to stop *thinking* and trust your that your eyes have absorbed it all. Helen said that it trained you to trust in your instincts to the point you nearly become a mind reader."

Given the game's emphasis on concentration, intuition and instinct, it's no wonder that it was a favorite around the spook haven of Leesburg.

Weekdays during the first months in Leesburg, Townsend lived in a tiny apartment – "not big enough to turn around in" – near Dupont Circle in downtown Washington. For the weekends, he often came home to Leesburg in a black Cadillac driven by the man Linda would eventually come to know as Robert Sarbacher.

*

In the spring of 1955, Linda "spent two weeks with my cousins in Zanesville, and when I came home, we moved out to Montressor."

Montressor – French for 'my treasure' - was a sprawling antebellum estate six miles from the Leesburg town center. The large white clapboard house with its expansive porch was well hidden from the nearby county road, nestled among fields large enough to land a helicopter – or anything else that could take off and land without a runway.

The mistress of Montressor was a woman with a French accent that Linda remembers only as Mrs. Stanford. "When Dr. Sarbacher drove Dad in for the weekend, Mrs. Stanford and Sarbacher greeted each other warmly in French. They seemed to know one another."

Josephine unpacked her teapot in a spacious apartment above the old carriage house that seemed designed to Townsend's own specifications. To an opening between the kitchen and living room, "Dad added a faux brick wall and a striped awning so that when you stood in the kitchen it looked a bistro. It was all very artistic and we loved it."

Another Townsend touch was an enormous pantry. "That was Dad's thing. He liked shelves stacked with canned goods and supplies. He did the same thing in Catalina, and Hawaii, too – shelves painted avocado green. You could always tell where Dad lived – if it didn't move, he had it painted green."

The apartment had three bedrooms – one for Townsend and Josephine, one for Linda, and one for Helen, who was by then a fixture in the Brown household.

Townsend was home often enough that Linda recalls many long and wide-ranging talks with him, often on the subject of recent UFO sightings that been reported in the news.

Linda wanted to know "Why don't the aliens just land on the White House lawn?"

"Why should they sweetie? They already know all they need to know about us from a distance. Besides, getting too close to humans *at this time* would only hurt everyone involved."

Linda understood what her father meant from a conversation she'd had with a classmate who'd said that "if he saw a flying saucer, he'd shoot it down."

It seemed to Linda that most of the people considered UFO sightings as some kind of hoax, and anybody who took the sightings seriously was some kind of nut case.

"Most people," Townsend said, "are like fish, swimming in a comfortable patch of water. They have learned the rules of their environment. Then suddenly a strange shape appears above them, the water near the surface churning behind it. They dart away to whatever safety they can find. Some look up to get a better look. But the thing above them is far beyond their comprehension. And then the object is gone, and they go back to the world they understand. A fish can have absolutely no concept of sails or land or cars or TV sets, or space or universes. We, Sweetie, are still fish in water. What we call 'flying saucers' are the hulls above us. Don't be upset with your classmates, there are just some things fish are never supposed to know."

On another occasion, Linda was riding a plump Welsh mountain pony from the Montressor stable, when she saw her parents watching from across the meadow. She galloped over to give her Dad a hug. Josephine smiled and left, to give father and daughter time together. Linda saw sweat on her mount and knew she shouldn't leave him standing. "I have to cool him off before I can put him up."

"Well then, let's walk."

"We were down in the big pasture in front of the barn. It was quite a walk back up to the stable," Linda recounted, trying to remember, how, as they walked and talked "we started talking about Albert Einstein" – who had died that week,[119] – "and I wondered why he was so darned important."

Townsend proceeded to introduce his ten-year-ole daughter to Einstein, relativity, and the connection to his own work. It was Einstein who had first proposed a connection between electricity and gravity, the mathematical concept he called the 'Unified Field Theory' – for which Townsend Brown believed he had found the physical proof in his flying capacitors.

Linda was puzzled by Einstein's statement that nothing could travel faster than the speed of light.

Her father took his cue from the chubby pony they were walking across the pasture. As Linda turned the pony loose, her father asked, "Linda, how fast do you think that fat pony can run?"

"I dunno, maybe twenty miles an hour?"

"Well then," Townsend explained, "for that pony, twenty miles an hour is the equivalent of the speed of light. That's as fast as that pony is ever going to go."

Linda looked at her father, still perplexed.

"But remember," he said, "that the Creator has a whole stable full of racehorses, that *never* go *slower* than the speed of light."

"That was my introduction to particle physics," Linda reflected decades later. "He was trying to teach me the difference between electrogravitation (the racehorse) and electrokinetics (the pony). He had made the point that not all is known and there is a helluva lot more out there, not yet recognized. By thinking of fat ponies and thoroughbreds, I got the concept."

74

Not A Dream

(1955)

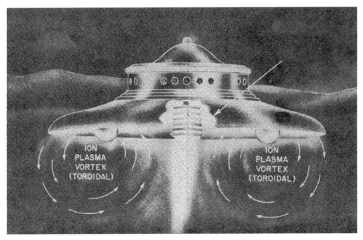

Artist's rendering of an Electro Hydro Dynamic
(EHD) flying... umm.... saucer.

Linda often wondered why the family was living at Montressor while her father was living in a tiny apartment near Dupont Circle. "It was a drive from the Leesburg town center. Mom had a job in town. So did Helen. So going back and forth to Montressor was a real imposition on them. Sure, it was good for me because of the horses. But still, other than maybe Mrs. Stanford's connections with Sarbacher, I don't know why Dad wanted us living all the way out there. We could have found a place in town."

The answer lies in what Morgan told me had happened after Pearl Harbor:

> **The Caroline Group quickly took 'the set' into safekeeping but Dr. Brown felt that simply making things disappear was not going to work in this case. He agreed that 'the set' should go under – and stay there. Then he developed a plan – a disinformation campaign – which would allow him to take a version of the propulsion system 'into the light.'**

By the summer of 1955, that disinformation campaign – the 'mortally wounded prairie chicken' – had run its course.

*

During the spring and summer of 1955, the Browns were often visited by Helen's sister, Bobbie Williams, her husband Tom, and their son Chip, who was about Linda's age. The Williamses would come out to Montressor from their home in Washington, to relax in the country and partake of Josephine's 'killer spaghetti' dinners. Tom Williams was also a commercial artist and had drawn some illustrations for a proposal that Townsend Brown was writing.

One weekend when the Williams family were due to visit, Linda Brown had a dream...

Linda is in the backyard, playing with a plastic toy horse Helen had given her for Christmas.

Out of the corner of her eye Linda sees three circular vessels descending slowly and silently toward the field. She watches as the tall wild grass swirls and flattens in the force-field under the shiny metallic ships as they settle toward the ground.

Linda drops her playthings and runs up the stairs to the apartment, screaming for her mother and father. Her father meets her at the top of the stairs and then, to her terrified surprise, he starts walking down the stairs and toward the field where the shiny craft have landed.

Crying and pulling on his arm, Linda yells, "No! Don't go out there! Please! Don't go!"

Her father keeps on walking, turning to Linda and assuring her, "Everything will be alright."

Still hiding behind her father, Linda notices something familiar about the ships. They look just like the illustrations Tom Williams drew for her father's proposal.

Three figures from the ships are standing in the field, walking toward them. They are wearing a metallic, pale blue suit with a circular insignia. Though none wear any kind of headgear, she can't really see their facial features.

The leader of the trio – his reddish hair and beard looking to Linda "like a Renaissance painting of Jesus" – stops in front of her father.

Her father asks a question – something about a radio – and the visitor replies, "It can communicate instantly over many millions of miles."

The dream shifts, as dreams do, and...

The visitors are all upstairs in the apartment. Her father is examining the box they are going to leave behind.

Calmer now, Linda studies their faces, then asks the leader why the other two appear so pale compared to him.

"They have different fluid in their system when they are traveling far from home," the red-haired visitor explains. "When they return, the fluid will be drained, and then replaced with their natural blood."

All Linda could say was, "Oh...."

The next morning, Linda didn't say anything to anybody about her dream, though she remembers it vividly to this day. Later that afternoon, the Williams family arrived for their Sunday spaghetti dinner. While the adults sipped sunset cocktails, Linda took Chip aside and told him of her dream.

At dinner, Townsend told Bobbie and Tom about a strange dream he'd had the night before: Three circular flying craft descending silently into the field behind their garage apartment; three humanoid visitors; a discussion of instant contact over vast distances; some sort of box being left behind.

Linda and Chip could only gaze across the table at each other. Could Linda and her father have had the exact same dream?

When I posed that question to Morgan on April 18, 2004, he replied:

Just before Dr. Brown's trip to Paris, 'the set' was brought back to him. It was not a dream.

75

Paris

(1955)

The morning after Townsend described his strange dream, Robert Sarbacher drove up to the garage at Montressor in his black Cadillac, gathered up Townsend and his leather travel bag, and drove away.

On the 15th of July 1955, Dr. Brown's passport was stamped on arrival at the Orly Airport in Paris. The passport was stamped again on departure from Orly, on July 21. This was the first of two trips to Europe that Dr. Brown made in a nine-month period; the second begins with his arrival at Orly on the 5th of March 1956 and ends with his departure from Southampton, England aboard the French liner *Liberté* on March 29.

Accounts of these trips that have appeared in books and articles about Townsend Brown say that he experimented with his 'tethered saucer' apparatus in a vacuum chamber, demonstrating the Biefeld-Brown effect absent the presence of any electronic wind. These stories are often cited in support of the notion that somebody is hiding gravity-defying flying machines in underground hangars in the Nevada desert.

Morgan inferred that there were other aspects to the Paris visits that were a more direct consequence of whatever Townsend and Linda experienced two nights before his departure: The vacuum chamber tests were a decoy for the return of 'the set' and the Caroline Group's role in preserving its secrecy. Morgan wrote[120]:

> **You know that 'the set' was made available to the military for that demonstration at Pearl. When the shit hit the fan, acting on Dr. Browns request, it was withdrawn – by the Caroline Group. They did not demand that action; it was Dr. Brown who insisted that they take it to keep it safe and out of unauthorized hands.**
>
> **When it was returned, only one unit was supplied to Dr. Brown. In the years that followed he built other units and a network to go along with them. That tight network established, he continued his various research projects.**

Some of Brown's activities were an expression of the Caroline Group's focus on security and cryptography. Referring to Brown's second trip to Europe in 1956, Morgan wrote:

During the second trip he handled a couple of smoking bolt[121] operations for the Caroline Group, but he also turned his attention now to some forms of early computer development.

Everything was leaning toward code-breaking and the secure use of codes. Look up an operation called ATLAS[122] in the mid-to-late fifties. He was still smarting from the Pearl Harbor experience, and he kept that interest in communications – and security – for the rest of his life.

After the Pearl Harbor fiasco and the subsequent discoveries of widespread Russian infiltration into U.S. and British intelligence operations,

You couldn't trust anybody. So, Dr. Brown and his colleagues assembled their own network – Caroline to Caroline to Caroline, regardless of nationality – employing Dr. Brown's own reproductions of 'the set.'

What did that mean, "Caroline to Caroline to Caroline – *regardless of nationality*"?

Morgan explained:[123]

You may have misunderstood what happened at Pearl Harbor. It had been decided that the Navy Brass and other scientists would be shown… well, yes, it did look like a toy carnival ride.

And 'the set' was 'the set.' He hadn't really gotten much opportunity to demonstrate that. They all knew that it could communicate easily through mountains and oceans. You would think that might pique some interest.

Unfortunately, when Philby's mole was detected, Dr. Brown hit the ceiling because he recognized that the Soviet scientific establishment would actually see the potential of what had been demonstrated and that they would most likely proceed with the developments.

A contingent of the Caroline group was sent to live and work in Russia, monitoring and assisting the work that they knew would slowly start to take seed.

Meanwhile the whole Caroline Group, with Dr. Brown's development, went into near deep hibernation while he spent five years discrediting his own work and setting up a diversion for future developments. Running a laundry. Starting NICAP[124]. At the same time doing odd jobs for the facility that he was aligning himself with (as the Russian counterparts of the Caroline Group were doing).

Dr. Brown's post-Pearl Harbor diversions, the return of 'the set,' his trips to Europe, the focus on cryptography, security and early digital technologies, the scope and influence of The Caroline Group, references to its 'core' and a Russian counterpart – all of these elements flew at me until finally:

> **All this worked well. We as two groups came to oppose each other, as is only natural when you split tribes. Some of our 'taking coups and stealing pony raids' have been deadly, but at least they were confined to the US. And it was meant to be that way. Just keep the humans out of it…"**

Just keep the humans out of it? What was I supposed to do with *that*?

∗

If the return of 'the set' and the reorganization of the Caroline Group was the covert agenda for Brown's trips to Europe in 1955 and '56, then the overt reason was to conduct vacuum chamber tests of the Biefeld-Brown effect using *solid* dielectrics – what he had demonstrated to the Navy at Pearl Harbor that he subsequently derailed with the 'ion wind' decoy of *fluid* dielectrics.

Illustration from November 1956 edition Young Men *magazine. This is the same article that landed on Nick Cook's desk that sent him on his* Hunt for Zero Point.

Prior to his first trip to Europe, Brown was contacted by Jacques Cornillon, a U.S. representative for the French aeronautics company Société National de Construction Aeronautiques du Sud Ouest (S.N.C.A.S.O.). Cornillon first learned of Brown's work after stumbling across a copy of Mason Rose's *Flying Saucers* white paper at an aeronautics library in Los Angeles. Cornillon offered Brown the use of his company's facilities outside of Paris.

While in France in 1955, Brown delivered specifications for a vacuum chamber large enough to test 2-1/2-foot-diameter discs at voltages as high as 300-500kv. He promised to return the following spring to supervise the experiments.[125]

*

Some of this work garnered public notice in the mid-1950's.

The November 1956 edition of *Young Men – The Magazine for Tomorrow's Technicians and Engineers* included an article often cited in the annals of anti-gravity research. *The G-Engines Are Coming!* proclaimed the headline of an article[126] written by Michael Gladych. Citing work by "gravity-defying engineers" at such notable companies as Glenn L. Martin Aircraft, Convair, Bell Aircraft, and Lear Inc., the article promises vessels "no longer dependent on wings and rotors," like "slimmed-down versions of the old-fashioned dirigible" capable of velocities approaching the speed of light. Coast-to-coast flight times "would be cut to minutes" with "unorthodox propulsion."

A similar article appeared in the March 23, 1956, edition of *Interavia Aerospace Review.* Under the byline of 'Intel – Washington D.C.' we learn of work *Towards Flight Without Stress or Strain – or Weight.*[127] This article says "Electrogravitics research, seeking the source of gravity and its control, has reached a stage where profound implications for the entire human race begin to emerge." The article even notes that "The American scientist Townsend Brown has been working on the problems of electrogravitics for more than thirty years."

While millions were being spent for the development of jet aircraft, *Interavia* suggests a more direct approach:

> **By his present method, Man actually fights the forces that resist his efforts. In conquering gravity, he will be putting one of his most competent adversaries to work for him. Antigravity is the method of the picklock rather than a sledgehammer.**
>
> **Towards the long-term progress of civilization, a whole new concept of electrophysics is being levered out into the light of human knowledge.**

That "light of human knowledge" reached its public zenith in 1956.

After that, it all just disappeared.

76

Notes & Ideas

(1955)

In the autumn between his trips to Europe, Townsend Brown sat down at his desk and opened a black-and-burgundy, hardbound notebook with one-hundred-and fifty-two pre-numbered and college-ruled pages.

"RECORD BOOK No. 1," he wrote in blue ink in the upper left corner of the first page, and in the center of the page, dated October 1, 1955, "Notes and Ideas."

This is to be the first of a series of record books of notes and ideas, of greater or lesser importance, just as they occur to me. The pages are numbered, and the subject reference will be given in an index. Where it appears of importance, at the moment, the entries will be witnessed.

All of my life, it seems, I have jotted down notes on scraps of paper, even on paper napkins and the like, which have ultimately been lost or destroyed. In many cases, these original notes and the dates of conception have turned out to be important and the loss of the record has been a serious handicap.

In the main, the ideas recorded herein and the hypotheses developed from these ideas will relate to the subject of gravitation and the relationship between gravitation and electrodynamics. They may present from time to time certain seemingly practical applications which may be patentable. All entries are therefore dated.

(signed)
Thomas Townsend Brown
Leesburg, Va.
October 1955

A week later, on October 7, he made his first formal entry:

A Review of the Situation regarding Gravitational Isotopes.

An announcement has been made both in the newspapers and on the radio (within the last few days) that the contract for the launching gear of the proposed space satellite has been awarded the Glenn S. Martin Co and the contract for the rocket motor to General Electric.

This brings to mind the statement of M. K. Jessup in *The Case for the UFO* [128]: "If the money, thought, time and energy now being

poured uselessly into the development of rocket propulsion were invested in a basic study of gravitation, it is altogether likely that we could have effective and economical space travel, at a small fraction of the ultimate cost which we are now incurring, within one decade."

*

On February 26, 1956, Dr. Brown wrote an entry in his notebook entitled "The results of a change of inertial mass following modulated beneficiation (with low persistence)."

The next entry, April 7, 1956, is entitled "The Impulse Effect in the force developed by a simple capacitor in vacuum."

In between those two entries, he returned to Paris and conducted the first set of experiments intended to demonstrate the viability of his electrogravitic theories using solid dielectrics in a vacuum. Our knowledge of these experiments comes from two sources.

The first is *Ether Technologies*,[129] a booklet published in 1977 by a Brown colleague named Rolf Schafranke. Writing under the pseudonym of Rho Sigma. Schafranke quotes a February 1973 letter from Dr. Brown himself, reporting on the Paris tests as well as subsequent experiments later in the 1950s:

> **The experiments in vacuum were conducted at SNCASO in Paris in 1955-56, at the Bahnson Laboratories, Winston Salem, North Carolina in 1957-58, and the General Electric Space Center at King of Prussia, Pennsylvania, in 1959. Laboratory notes were made, but these notes were never published and are not available to me now .**
>
> **The results were varied, depending upon the purpose of the experiment. We were aware that the thrust on the electrode structures were caused largely by ion momentum transfer when experiments were conducted in air. Many of the tests, therefore, were directed upon the exploration of this component of the total thrust.**
>
> **In the Paris test, miniature saucer type airfoils were operated in a vacuum exceeding 10-6 mm Hg.**
>
> **Bursts of thrust (towards the positive) were observed every time there was a vacuum spark in the large bell jar. These vacuum sparks represented momentary ionization, principally of the metal ions in the electrode material. The DC potential used ranged from 70 KV to 220 KV.**
>
> **Condensers of various types, air dielectric and barium titanate were assembled on a rotary support to eliminate the electrostatic**

effect of chamber walls and observations were made of the rate of rotation.

Intense acceleration was always observed during the vacuum spark. Barium titanate dielectric always exceeded air dielectric in total thrust. The results which were most significant from the standpoint of the Biefeld-Brown effect was that the thrust continued, even when there was no vacuum spark, causing the rotor to accelerate in the negative to positive direction to the point where voltage had to be reduced or the experiment discontinued because of the danger that the rotor would fly apart .

In short, it appears that there is strong evidence that the Biefeld-Brown effect does exist in the negative to positive direction in a vacuum.

The second source is Jacques Cornillon, Dr. Brown's host in Paris. In a letter written shortly before his death in 2008 at the age of 99, Cornillon's recollections were less conclusive:

Dr. Brown came to France twice, in 1955 and 1956. The first round of testing was done in the air. This was simply a demonstration of 'electric wind.' We also observed another small force, but it was too small to measure in the air where there is ionization.

The next step was to make tests in a big vacuum chamber. Dr. Brown again sent us designs, but as this phase of the project was undertaken my company was merged into another company. The president of my company, now the president of the new merged company, Sud-Aviation, decided not to continue the experiments.

The team made some hasty tests before having the project shut down. The Final Report outlined five tests confirming that there was a definable force. At this point our team was scattered, the project shut down and we were unable to make the further tests to further refine and quantify the results.

The reports vary in their magnitude, but not in their certainty. Both affirm what young Townsend Brown observed in those Coolidge Tubes 1920s – and Paul Biefeld attested to in the affidavit he provided for the Navy in 1930.

77

Berlin

(1956)

*Townsend Brown and the man we know only as
'O'Riley' outside a bistro in Paris March 1956.*

On his fifty-first birthday – March 18, 1956 – Townsend Brown was
photographed outside Fouquet's Bistro in Paris with four unidentified sailors
and a smartly dressed civilian about a half-a-head shorter than Brown: the man
known in these pages as 'O'Riley' – who was again assigned to escort Dr. Brown
in Europe.

Morgan told me that the trips to France were financed by the Caroline Group
"in exchange for some of the other activities that had been set up, some 'smoking
bolt' operations and running a couple of German scientists to the West and out
from under Soviet control."

In a separate string of emails in 2004 and 2005, O'Riley supplied some details
about those other operations. We know from Dr. Brown's passport when he arrived
in Paris, when he went to England, and when he sailed home. But the most
intriguing stop on the itinerary may be the one that *doesn't* show up in his passport.

In 1954 – two years before Dr. Brown's visits – British and American
intelligence services began digging a quarter mile-long tunnel thirteen feet under
the streets of Berlin in what has been described as "the most audacious espionage
caper of the Cold War."[130] After excavating three-thousand tons of dirt over a

period of seven months at a cost exceeding $25-million, the tunnel gave the MI6 and the CIA an eavesdropping post almost directly under the Soviet Embassy in the eastern sector of the divided city.

For more than a year, agents in the tunnel intercepted cables between East Berlin and Moscow. They had no idea their operations were entirely compromised even before the first shovelful of dirt was dug.

The Berlin Tunnel was supervised by an MI6 officer named Peter Wright – who first crossed paths with O'Riley when Wright helped design the midget submarines that attacked the German battleship *Tirpitz* in 1942. A Caroline operative, Wright assigned O'Riley to serve as Dr. Brown's escort during their ill-fated mission in Germany in the final weeks of the war. In the early years of the Cold War, Wright was instrumental in unraveling Kim Philby's Cambridge Five spy ring. Now he reassigned O'Riley to escort Dr. Brown in 1956.

O'Riley says that Dr. Brown was never in one place for much more than 12 hours. But one of their stops was in Berlin, and much of the time there was spent underground:

> **My attention to Dr. Brown's needs in regard to the Berlin Tunnel were primarily that of a bodyguard. There were many factors at work in the area at the time. All of them were armed with sidearms and agendas. Dr. Brown was not a warlike individual. He refused to carry a handgun, even though I know he had been trained in its use. He had said that if it came down to his shooting someone to keep himself alive, he would be prepared to die first. My only thought was, "Oh, shit."**

Their time in the tunnel often reminded both Dr. Brown and O'Riley of their time on submarines:

> **We had never been on the same sub, but he had some experience with subs and I had my experience with the 'X-subs.' In that tunnel, some of the hatches were right out of sub supply. When the damned thing creaked, we would look at each other and he would smile that Mona Lisa smile of his, and I knew we were reading each other's minds.**
>
> **Dr. Brown and I didn't like the tunnel much. During the winter of 1955-56, it had snowed a good bit. The heat from the building at our end of the line would seep into the tunnel and melt the snow above. On the surface, if you looked at it just right you could see the outline of the tunnel below in the snow. They fixed that by reducing**

the temperature in the tunnel, which was damp anyway. It was all thoroughly unpleasant.

At first, the MI6 and CIA agents in the tunnel were elated with their wiretaps:

> There were reels and reels of taped conversations from the KGB, from the Soviet Embassy, from the various military bases in Russia, all being intercepted and transferred by special courier to London and Washington. I shuttled between the Berlin offices to London mainly, and then took care of special guests from visiting agencies. Dr. Brown was one of those and I was very happy to see him again.

However,

> I had an odd feeling about the traffic that was coming through. I'd been thinking that for months, but no one was really listening to me. Everyone was just rolling in the good fortune, patting themselves on the back.

> I showed one of those dispatches to Dr. Brown. He looked it over and said, "Something's not right." He had the same kind of intuitive feeling you get when you realize that someone on the other end is moderating their conversation because they know they have ears on them. We couldn't prove it though, so we just went on about our business.

In April 1956, a crew digging near the embassy in East Berlin discovered what the Soviets had known all along.

> All hell broke loose. Some of the tunnel people were given a 50-caliber machine gun to protect the radar building on our side. In the tunnel a sign was hastily erected that declared in bold type and placed beneath the borderline in the streets above, "You are now entering the American Sector."

In his 1987 memoir *Spycatcher*[131], Peter Wright wrote:

> So much raw intelligence was flowing from the East that it was literally swamping the resources available to transcribe and analyze it. MI6 had a special transcription center set up in Earl's Court, but they were still transcribing material seven years later when they discovered that George Blake[132] had betrayed the Tunnel to the Russians from the onset.

In 1961, MI6 officer George Blake was convicted of espionage and sentenced to forty-two years in the maximum security of the Wormwood Scrubs prison in west London. In 1966, he escaped from Wormwood and fled to Moscow – where he fraternized with Kim Philby and others from the Cambridge Five spy ring before his death in 2020 at the age of ninety-eight.

78

London

(1956)

Townsend and Joseph Brown on the streets of London, March 1956.

There are few photos of Townsend Brown with his adult son, Joseph.

After their time in the Berlin Tunnel, Townsend accompanied O'Riley on one his dispatch runs to London to visit with Joseph, who was stationed in the U.K. for the U.S. Air Force. Joseph had no idea of the real nature of his father's work, and the one photo taken of the two on the streets in London shows the continued estrangement between father and son.

From London, Dr. Brown and O'Riley ventured to the town of Cheltenham, in the bucolic Cotswolds a hundred miles west of London. Dr. Brown insisted on spending part of their time at the Cheltenham Festival, an equestrian event where he hoped to learn as much as possible for the benefit of his 'horse-crazy' daughter.

"Then he returned to the work at hand," O'Riley said, showing usual reluctance to tell me just what that work entailed. The only thing I knew for certain was that Cheltenham was also the location of GCHG – the Government Communications Headquarters, the U.K. equivalent of the NSA in the U.S.

With that one kernel of knowledge, I asked O'Riley if Dr. Brown was conducting some kind of work there with regard to 'the set.' All O'Riley could say was:

All I can say is that Dr. Brown developed a listening device at Cheltenham that was far superior. It caused quite a stir, especially

the way he sort of just "whipped it out there" full-grown. The British held on to it as long as they could to clean up their own backyard. Then the Americans finally made a deal with Dr. Brown to follow his ideas with submarines out of Florida.

He had not been happy with the American military up to that point. He was still very miffed over the situation stemming from the security breach at Pearl. In fact, he had his doubts about the loyalty of some very high officials. And he was absolutely right.

Sometimes it worked and sometimes it didn't but all in all I think we gained precious time by just getting the hell out there. He got very good at looking over our shoulders as we worked, sometimes not in the most comfortable of situations. But with his help we identified and shut down some direct links with Moscow. After that we started going after stuff that they had, not only shutting down their communications.

I pressed O'Riley further, wondering if he was talking about the 'smoking bolt' operations Morgan had alluded to earlier.

"I doubt it," O'Riley answered. "The object was to *not* leave a trail."

*

On March 29th, Townsend Brown arrived in Southampton. In the shops there he purchased two Hermes scarves – one decorated with horses for Linda, the other for Helen – and a purse for Josephine. Inside the purse, he hid a bottle of fine perfume and a pair of pearl earrings.

Souvenirs and gifts in hand, he boarded the French liner *Liberté* and sailed home to America.

79

NICAP
(1956)

The *Liberté* arrived at her berth in New York on March April 4, 1956. The next day, Robert Sarbacher's black Cadillac showed up at Montressor.

"As soon as he came back from that last trip to Europe," Linda recalls, "he stopped by Montressor for just a few hours with Sarbacher. He brought Helen and me each a scarf, and mother a purse. We visited for a short time. And then he left."

It was nearly a year before Linda saw her father again.

"A whole summer, fall and winter went by without his company," Linda recalled. "I had friends at school. Helen and I went on long hikes, and she hung on the fence-line to watch during my riding lessons. The Williams continued to visit. But mostly," she confessed, "I was missing Daddy."

Josephine held a day-job as a secretary and office manager in Leesburg; Helen worked for a Judge named Phillips, whose office was at the other end of the same street where Josephine worked. After school, Linda shuttled between the two offices.

When Linda asked her mother where Daddy was, what he was doing or when he would be back, Josephine's answers were vague. Occasionally a package would arrive: a box of candy canes; *The Black Stallion* and books on ancient history. Linda would squirrel away in her bedroom, pull the covers up, and read those books.

"Christmas without Daddy was awful."

*

The one thing we know Townsend Brown did during this period was form NICAP: The National Investigations Committee on Aerial Phenomena.

The record shows that "NICAP was founded on October 24, 1956, by inventor Thomas Townsend Brown. The board of governors included several prominent military men, including Donald Keyhoe, Maj USMC (Ret.), and former chief of the Navy's guided missile program Rear Admiral Delmer S. Fahrney USN (Ret.)."

NICAP if often cited as the forerunner of all private-citizen study of the airborne and unexplained – the point of origin for 'UFOlogists' who want to know if 'flying saucers' are 'real' – where they come from and what accounts for their remarkable flight patterns.

While Dr. Brown's interest in the field may have been genuine, I infer from my correspondence with Morgan that NICAP was an echo of the wounded prairie chicken. Its formation associated Dr. Brown with the fringe element of UFO conspiracy theories. The inclusion of high-profile names like Keyhoe and Fahrney added a layer of government involvement to the suspicions of a deep and deliberate cover-up.

To recall the origins of NICAP, Linda Brown pecked away at a childhood memory of a farm in Maryland, the home of a 67-year-old widow, Mrs. Walton Colcord John. Known to her friends as Clara, Mrs. John indulged an abiding interest in the unusual and esoteric, subjects that today might be considered 'New Age.' Clara occasionally compiled her ruminations – which often covered the most recent UFO sightings – in a mimeographed newsletter called *The Little Listening Post*.

In addition to her newsletter, Clara hosted some like-minded friends for an informal Flying Saucer Discussion Group. For one such gathering she invited as guest speaker a man from Leesburg, Virginia who was known to have some knowledge on the subject. Townsend Brown brought his daughter, who mostly remembers that Mrs. John "had white ponies in a nearby field."

In Clara's group, Townsend sensed one last bread crumb he could leave in his trail of distraction. He was the first to propose that the group formally organize itself.

The problem was, what would they call it? Somehow, the 'Flying Saucer Discussion Group' did not set quite the tone of dignity the group hoped to achieve. Between his trips to Europe, Linda and her parents were sitting around their breakfast table "talking about forming a group to investigate saucer sightings. He had everything ready to go, except a proper name." Since the organization's charter was going to be filed in Washington, "having the right name meant everything."

"We were sitting around the table, tossing names back and forth, pushing letters around. Helen Towt was good at all of those official-sounding names. She was the one who suggested that this new organization should be referred to as a 'committee.' She said that was a word that always got people in Washington to sit up and take notice."

Townsend wanted to use a word like "International" in the name, to reflect the global scope of the subject. But he didn't want to use the phrase 'flying saucers' because they weren't all 'saucer' shaped.

"They are just mysteries in the air," Helen said.

"Yes," Townsend said, "aerial phenomena."

Helen picked up on that phrase. "That's great," she said, "the Committee on Aerial Phenomena."

Eventually 'National' and 'Investigations' were added, and the 'National Investigations Committee on Aerial Phenomena' – NICAP – was duly christened and chartered. Townsend Brown was named the first Chairman of the Board of Directors; the rest of the board was comprised of scientists, clergy, businessmen, and both active and retired military officers. And, according to NICAP's own history,[133] there were also at least two directors with prior connections to the CIA: Nicolas de Rochefort and Bernard J. Carvalho.

From the beginning, there was a tug-of-war over the leadership and direction of NICAP.

Donald Keyhoe was one member of the board with his own agenda. A retired Marine major, Keyhoe achieved some notoriety as an author of pulp fiction and air-adventure novels. Keyhoe took a keen interest in the subject of UFOs after Kenneth Arnold's 1947 sighting added the expression 'flying saucers' to the lexicon. And like many others, Keyhoe was not satisfied with any of the official explanations.

In 1949, the men's magazine *True* commissioned Keyhoe to conduct his own investigation. Keyhoe made many of the same observations that intrigued Townsend Brown, like the observed objects' velocity and flight patterns. But as an author of science fiction, Keyhoe was less restrained than Dr. Brown about arriving at dramatic, even inflammatory conclusions.

In January 1950, *True* published Keyhoe's *The Flying Saucers Are Real.* The article focused on a paradox: on the one hand public officials – including his personal contacts among the military – insisted there was no substance to the countless reported sightings; on the other hand, he was denied access to classified accounts. The contradiction led Keyhoe to insist not only that the flying saucers were extraterrestrial, but also that the governments of the world were actively conspiring to suppress the truth.

Keyhoe's *True* article caused such a sensation that he expanded it into a book[134] published later that year, "the first in-depth, authoritative look at the flying saucer phenomenon." Keyhoe argued that the Air Force knew flying saucers originated outside our solar system, that their occupants had no hostile intent, and that it was no coincidence the sightings increased after the first nuclear bombs were detonated. With these novel themes, *The Flying Saucers Are Real* sold more than a half million copies and is still regarded as the earliest classic in the field.

When Townsend Brown invited Keyhoe to join the board of the newly formed NICAP, he anticipated that Keyhoe would arrive with his own agenda. Keyhoe needed a vehicle from which he could launch his own campaign for congressional hearings and disclosure of the secrets he was certain the Air Force was hiding. The nascent NICAP proved to be the perfect instrument through which to pursue these designs – and the organization's Founder was perfectly willing to hand him the reins.

In early 1957 – within months of NICAP's incorporation – the Board ousted its founding Chairman, asserting that Townsend Brown had proven himself "so financially inept that the board asked him to step down." Later that year Keyhoe was named to lead the organization.

*

Looking back on his NICAP experience from the vantage point of 20 year later, Townsend Brown told a journalist:

NICAP was an effort on my part to obtain worldwide surveillance for the purpose of observing UFO behavioral characteristics. I had hoped to get some hint as to their method of propulsion. I recognized that there was no explanation in contemporary physics. If there were an explanation, it might have come from a more advanced civilization.

After twenty years, I am a little disappointed. No solid technical evidence has been obtained. I am completely at a loss to understand the reasons. It is entirely possible that the human race has not progressed far enough to understand or to be able to use this information .

80

Tunnel Diode

(1957)

*Linda, Josephine and the omnipresent short wave'
radio on a beach in Florida ca. 1957.*

There is nothing about NICAP in any of Dr. Brown's notebooks. Nor are they much help in determining his actual whereabouts through the balance of 1956 and most of 1957 – the period when he was entirely absent from his family in Virginia.

In February 1957, Dr. Brown was still time stamping his notebook entries with "Leesburg, Va." But according to an email from O'Riley in the fall of 2007, "that particular dateline is an intentional misdirection. He hesitated. Wrote it under some duress. He said eventually, 'It's where my heart is, it's the truth,' and carefully penned 'Leesburg.'"

When the dateline finally does change, it reads "Umatilla, Florida – November 16, 1957".

Umatilla is 40 miles northwest of Orlando, near the center of the Florida peninsula. According to Morgan[135]:

> **You will note that after the Paris trips Dr. Brown almost immediately moved to Florida and began working on the tunnel diode development. (Remember, we are using that phrase but TTB's "tunnel diode" is amazingly different than the one that is mentioned in open sources.)**

Later, Morgan added:[136]

When Dr. Brown headed for Umatilla, he actually was working for a section of General Electric, developing that special diode program for the Navy. You are not going to find much written about that. Suffice it to say that as far as the world was concerned...well, they just don't have any idea what he was really doing.

The phrase 'tunnel diode' does not appear in any of Townsend Brown's notebooks or patents, but Morgan was referring to an invention that came out of Japan just a few months before Brown moved to Umatilla.

A tunnel diode is a transistor-like device that utilizes 'quantum tunneling' – the ability of an electron to jump from one place to another without actually transiting the space in between. But, as Morgan pointed out, Dr. Brown's version of the tunnel diode was "amazingly different" – and one of his most significant inventions.

Subsequent email exchanges with Morgan left the impression that Townsend Brown's version of the tunnel diode was already at work in submarines and would eventually find new use in a technology that did not even exist before 1957: satellites.

*

The Space Race began in earnest when the Soviet Union launched Sputnik on October 4, 1957 – a month before Townsend Brown changed the dateline in his notebook entries to Umatilla.

In May of 2004, I received a phone call from Morgan's syrupy-voiced colleague in Texas, who directed my attention to pages 364 and 365 in *Body of Secrets*, James Bamford's expansive history of the National Security Agency. Those pages describe the earliest research into satellite reconnaissance in the late 1950s. Bamford starts with Reid D. Mayo, an NRL scientist, who was...

> **...stranded with his family at a rest stop in Pennsylvania during a snowstorm in early 1958, Mayo began to work out the details with a pencil on the back of a stained placemat. "I did some range calculations to see if we could intercept the signal from orbital altitude, and the calculations showed that clearly you could, up to something over six hundred miles."**
>
> **Mayo had earlier completed another eavesdropping project: "The submarine service had us installing a small spiral antenna inside the glass of the periscope and affixed to that spiral antenna was a small diode detector. It allowed the submarine skipper to have an electromagnetic ear as well as an eyeball above the surface. And it**

worked so well that we thought that there might be some benefit to raising the periscope just a bit – maybe even to orbital altitude.

By the end of 1958, the project that Mayo is describing was codenamed "Tattletale." The intent, as Reid Mayo conveys through Bamford, was "to build a satellite capable of detailing the exact locations and technical parameters of every Soviet air defense radar system."

Townsend Brown's mis-named 'tunnel diode' was the critical component that made that "electromagnetic ear" equally effective beneath the surface of the ocean or from hundreds of miles out in space.

*

As Townsend was datelining his notebook entries with "Leesburg, Va.," in the first months of 1957, he was making plans to bring Josephine and Linda down to Florida.

"Actually," Linda recalled, "I think that Daddy missed us just as much as we missed him."

In a letter dated February 27, 1958, Townsend wrote:

> **I feel very much better down here – that terrible feeling of tension and urgency is gone. I have decided that I really feel more at ease here than in Hawaii or even Laguna. Umatilla reminds me of Lihue in many respects.**
>
> **But it is lonely, rattling around in this house by myself, trying to get my meals, etc. And it is so very quiet. I really will be glad when the hi-fi gets here. There is a good place for it in the big living room.**

By the middle of March, Josephine had packed the little green teapot and boxed up the contents of Townsend's Dupont Circle apartment. He also wanted to round up files that had been left behind in California, some of which were from his time in Hawaii. The house he had secured for them "has a large living room and ample space to sort everything out and get these things in order."

Linda remembers a small trailer arriving at Montressor that contained all the boxes from Dupont Circle. After the trailer was hitched behind a 1953 Chevrolet coupe, Josephine, Linda, and Helen watched Montressor disappear in the rear-view mirror. They stopped for lunch at a drug store in Leesburg, after which, "Helen went one way, and mother and I went the other."[137]

"When we arrived, it was just so wonderful," Linda recalled. Their new home was a modern, ranch-style house in the center of town. "It was gorgeous, and more beautiful than any place I had known before, with about fifty orange trees in the back. Dad unloaded his oriental rugs with great joy, set up his hi-fi and put on records. The Broadway musical *Kismet* was his favorite and the house filled with music. On Sundays, he listened to the Mormon Tabernacle Choir, for the organ as much as for the vocals.

"The place just smelled so wonderful because of the orange blossoms. There is nothing quite like central Florida in the early spring. Mom and Dad set up their home office and Dad was either home all day while I was at school or at work, but he was always home for dinner. It was a special time having Daddy there in the evenings, the house filled with music."

Townsend split his time between the Winterhaven projects and classified intelligence activities. At home, he and Josephine worked side-by-side in the large space they'd set up as their office. "Two big desks," Linda recalls, "his and hers, in front of the big sliding glass doors that opened out to the orange grove."

"Music from his hi-fi system always filled the room. They set their own schedule, and paused at four in the afternoon for tea, out on the patio, in the sun. They really enjoyed each other's company."

On weekends, road trips took the family swimming, canoeing and sunbathing in places like Alexander Springs, Silver Springs and St. Augustine.

Linda recalls another constant companion on these weekend jaunts: an RCA 'Stratoworld' shortwave radio that accompanied Townsend Brown wherever and whenever he traveled. Linda recalls the unit appearing right after her father's first trip to Europe in the winter of 1956.

"Everywhere we went, that shortwave went with us. He put it in the back seat wrapped in a canvas blanket. It was *always* with him, even if we went canoeing. I never really questioned it. It was sort of a standard thing to get our sunbathing area set up, the canvas down, and then our towels, and always the radio sitting up in a corner. He used it mainly for the music.... or, at least, so I thought."

The family's idyll in Florida was typically brief.

"By the end of that summer," Linda said, "Dad left for North Carolina."

81

First, We Build a Fire

(1957)

Agnew Bahnson

There was nothing Agnew Bahnson enjoyed more than showing off the rolling green North Carolina countryside from the cockpit of his twin-engined Beechcraft. One afternoon in the early spring of 1958, his co-pilot was Townsend Brown, whom had recruited to help revolutionize the entire field of aeronautics.

Brown started consulting with Bahnson in the fall 1957, supervising experiments in electrodynamics and gravitation at Bahnson's privately funded laboratory near Winston-Salem. The arrangement started out as temporary; Josephine and Linda stayed in Florida through the winter. Now the work was going better than expected, and Bahnson wanted Brown to settle in for a more permanent residence and bring his family up to join him.

Through the cockpit windshield, Townsend spotted a small lake, its clear depths reflecting the blue sky rather than the browned muddy run off. He motioned to Bahnson. As the plane banked into a turn, he saw a stream running along the edge of a meadow and nestled amongst the pines, a small log cabin at the end of a quiet road. Bahnson got a fix on the location. After landing, Agnew and Townsend made some inquiries and discovered – as was often the case when Townsend or Josephine set their sights on a particular domicile – that the place was for sale.

In a letter to Josephine and Linda, "Dad announced that he'd bought the property – fifteen undeveloped acres in the foothills of North Carolina, the cabin built of 'logs huge and hand-hewn.' His letters were positively glowing." Townsend sent Linda a map he drew of the property, a memento she still treasures.

In early April Josephine and Linda headed north from Florida. After picking up Townsend in Winston-Salem, the reunited trio was surprised to discover three feet of freshly fallen snow along their way into the foothills.

"It took us a long time to get down the dirt road through the drifts," Linda recalled. "Then it took Mom and Dad a while to get the cabin door open because of the snow that had piled up against it. And we were hardly dressed for this kind of weather."

While rummaging around in the trunk for footwear to replace the sandals she'd worn from Florida, her parents finally got through the front door of the cabin, and Linda heard her mother shout, "Oh, my!"

"Couldn't be good," Linda thought, "but I had no idea…."

Inside the cabin, they discovered that much of the cement chinking between the roughly formed logs lay crumbled on the floor. Panes of window glass were broken out, snow had drifted into the interior, and a cold wind was whistling through their new home. Linda watched in silence as Josephine navigated among the piles of snow toward a space that might be a kitchen.

"Suddenly, Mother let out a loud and defiant, "Oh, NO!" at the sight of piles of dirty, spoiled-food-encrusted dishes she found frozen solid into the sink.

There was an old, dusty bed in the living room but little else. There was a table and four chairs in the kitchen. Linda found another mattress in an upstairs loft.

For a few minutes they all sat in silence on the bed in the living room. They were cold and tired, it was getting dark, and through the broken windows they could see it was starting to snow again.

Suddenly Townsend sprung to his feet. "First, we have to build a fire!"

"From that moment on," Linda recalled, "every experience we had in that log cabin was joyful. It was as if someone had turned the switch on!"

There was plenty of dry firewood and kindling stacked on the porch. Josephine got the fire crackling while Townsend and Linda swept away the snow and patched the window. They beat as much dust as they could out of the mattresses, boiled snow for water, prepared a hot meal from Townsend's supply of canned goods, and were soon snuggled into their new adventure.

Over the next few weeks, the snow melted, ducks appeared on the lake, jonquils bloomed in the meadow, and Josephine's porcelain teapot shined from a perch upon the mantle.

*

Ten years younger than Townsend Brown, Agnew Bahnson Jr. was also a child of affluence and privilege. His father had built a fortune with Bahnson Industries, designing and installing custom air-conditioning systems for the region's prosperous textile factories. Agnew Jr. spent part of his teens hitch-hiking across the country and worked for a while as a merchant seaman. He spent some time in Europe and climbed the Matterhorn twice. He was nineteen years old when he graduated Phi Beta Kappa from the University of North Carolina in 1935. After a year studying engineering and industrial management at Harvard, he went to work in the machine shop of his father's company. By the age of thirty-two, he was president of the company.

With the company's resources at his command, Bahnson built a laboratory where he could investigate everything from nuclear physics to gravitation. In 1956 he conducted a symposium on gravity research for the American Astronomical Society in New York; in 1957 he sponsored a follow up International Congress on Gravitation, bringing more than fifty world-renown physicists to the University of North Carolina. At one of these events Bahnson learned of the ground-breaking work in an unfamiliar field called "electrogravitics" – and set about looking for Townsend Brown.

"They searched for him," Linda Brown said, "until Daddy found them."

At Bahnson's lab, Brown intended to continue the work that was interrupted after his departure from France in 1956 to the point of filing patents. Some experiments were conducted with solid aluminum disks; others utilized 'canopy' models that resembled a silk-and-aluminum-foil umbrella, with electrodes running down the curved ribs. 16mm film footage from the lab shows variations with two and three concentric canopies. Weights were added to a rod suspended vertically through the canopies, which provided a means for measuring the experiments' progress.

*Inspecting one of the solid aluminum 'ballistic electrode'
discs used in experiments at the Bahnson labs ca. 1957*

Another segment of the film footage shows a visit from two highly accredited professors from UNC, physicists Bryce DeWitt and his wife, Cecile DeWitt-Morette. Townsend described their visit to Josephine:

> **On Monday we had a meeting here with Dr. and Mrs. Bryce DeWitt. We had been working day and night, Saturdays and Sundays, for the past two weeks preparing for it. I had worked until 3 a.m. the night before, so I was afraid that I might not be awake when they got there. But everything went along all right and I believe the meeting served the purpose – although, like all of the other meetings of that type in the past, the ice and reserve was almost impossible to break through. Frankly, I got the distinct impression that neither one of them really grasped what it was all about.**

> **Agnew is quite enthusiastic and spends more time in the lab than in his own office. He has just finished a letter of five pages to the DeWitts and the people at Princeton and the patent attorney, outlining his ideas as to how to proceed from this point.**

After the DeWitt's visit, Agnew Bahnson expressed some frustration with the Dewitt's rigors of orthodoxy in his personal notes:

Until the DeWitt's visit, we were working exclusively with condensers of a conventional type to prove the basic effect.[138] I realized that even if it were proven to *our* satisfaction there would be little interest in high scientific circles that it was new and useable because it would probably depend on the acceptance of an ether theory – which would call for a 180° turn from presently accepted concepts. It is easier to say, "We can't explain it from known knowledge, but we are sure some 'specialist' could," and therefore discount its importance. So I decided to strive for an irrefutable demonstration of value.[139] This we would like to do before disturbing the scientists or the governments of the world[140].

One goal of the experiments was '100% counterbary' – the ability of a canopy to lift a load equal to 100% of its own weight. Bahnson's notes record steady progress toward that goal until[141]:

This evening we got 100% counterbary at 210kv with 35" stitched bamboo canopy and the 18" half ball of aluminum foil spaced 13½" below with no foil on the bottom and the supporting guts cut out. Rig weighed 98 grams.

The lab journal entry is co-signed[142] by Agnew, Townsend, J. Frank King and Beth Ball. The 16mm film shows the team toasting with champagne in laboratory beakers.

*

All the propulsion experiments Brown conducted in the 1950s – whether they were electrokinetic (fluid dielectric) or electrogravitic (solid dielectric) – required a tethered power source. Even the "toy carnival ride" demonstrated at Pearl Harbor involved discs rotating around a pylon wired to a high-voltage power supply.

For any kind of air-or-space-craft – winged or circular – to fly untethered, it would have to carry its own source of high voltages. Conventional flying machines carry their own fuel source – a tank of refined petroleum. But for a vehicle to be electrically propelled, it would have to carry its own generator, and in the mid-20th century generators were neither sufficiently small or weight-efficient to fit aboard any of Townsend Brown's experimental flying discs.

His remedy was another invention that surfaced during his time in North Carolina, a device he called the 'flame jet generator.'

The flame jet generator is an extension of the 'complete system[143]' that Seaman Townsend Brown articulated for the Naval Research Labs. The first component of that system was a motor; the second component was a pump, and the third component was an electrical generator. As Brown wrote to the NRL in 1932:

When the electromagnetic device is held stationery and conductive fluid forced past it, usable electric current is generated.

That is precisely how the flame jet generator operates: An electrified needle charged to fifty thousand volts is inserted into the exhaust flow of a jet engine. The needle imparts a negative charge to the exhaust molecules; those charged molecules are then forced through a stack of concentric, nozzle-like rings, producing a higher voltage on each successively larger nozzle. By the time the charged gas reached the last nozzle, Brown estimated that the output could reach fifteen-*million* volts.

In a jet plane, the flame jet generator could increase both thrust and fuel efficiency. Townsend Brown's patent #3,022,430 also describes how the flame jet generator could also revolutionize electricity generation on the ground.

Most of the electricity in the world is generated through a heat exchange process that would make Rube Goldberg[144] proud: Fossil fuel is burned to generate heat, the heat boils water, the boiling water produces steam, the steam turns a turbine, and the turbine turns the armature in a generator to produce electricity. Townsend Brown's flame jet generator takes all the extra steps out of the equation: fuel is burned, and from the hot exhaust electricity is generated.

Without all that heavy hardware – boilers, heat exchangers, turbines and generators – Brown and Bahnson envisioned a source of high voltage compact enough to put on an airplane – or a flying saucer.

There is little evidence that much progress was made on the flame jet generator while Brown was in North Carolina. There is evidence however that the U.S. military got wind of it,[145] and were not about to let it go.

Even the flame jet generator needed an external energy source in the form of a fossil-fueled jet engine. Townsend would still have to find another, even *more* powerful source if a vessel that could 'just sail away' was ever going to be entirely self-contained.

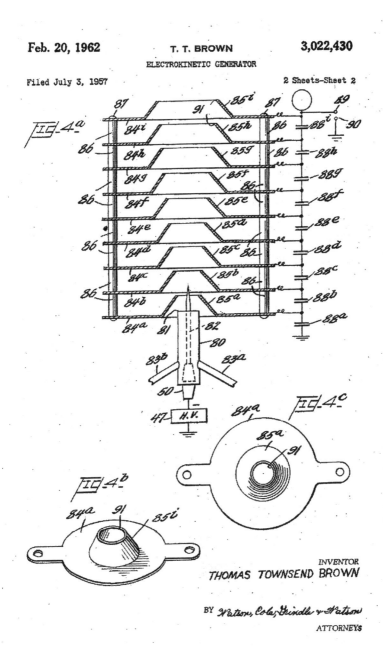

Patent for the Flame Jet Generator

82

Something Happened
(1958)

Linda Brown putting 'Beauty' through her paces.

Linda Brown remembers the spring and summer of 1958 as the happiest time of her childhood. The cabin they lived in – and owned! – sat amid 15 lush green acres. "It was mainly woods, a stream fed into a wonderful little lake with a spillway on the other side. Beyond the spillway was a trail that went into the mountain laurel and pines. I walked and walked, missing Helen more than just a little bit."

Linda enrolled in the elementary school in nearby Walkertown and was surprised at how easy it was to make friends. When a group of kids came over to check out the new kid, a boy walked right up to Linda, stuck out his hand and said "Hi!" with an accent that sounded to Linda like something "straight out of *Andy Griffith*."

"My name is Tommy Carmichael," the boy said. "Welcome to Walkertown! Do you play softball?"

"No, I've never really learned."

Tommy laughed. "Well come on then! We'll teach ya!"

About a week after the school year ended, Linda had another dream. There were no flying saucers or chestnut-bearded spacemen in this one.

"I had been dreaming about having my own horse forever," Linda said. "Just a week or so before school let out, Daddy told me that, since we had the land, and if I promised to be totally responsible for it, he would buy me a horse. You can imagine how excited I was!"

For the next week or so, Townsend and Linda drove around to farms in their rural community, but with each prospect, "Dad kept saying, 'No, that's not the right one…. No, not the right one.'"

And then one night, "a totally black horse with a long mane and tail" came to Linda in a dream. "It was saddled but had no rider. It was a mare, tossing her head and running alongside a white fence. I distinctly remembered the saddle blanket which had big white, red and black stripes."

When she shared the vision with her father, he said, "Sweetie, I think there's a reason why the horse in your dream was riderless. That horse is looking for you."

Horse and rider found each other the next day – at Tommy Carmichael's family's farm.

"Tommy walked the mare toward us. She was so black that you couldn't even really see her at first but as soon as I saw that striped blanket, I grabbed Dad's arm. I was thunderstruck."

Townsend turned to Mr. Carmichael and said "We'll take the horse. And we want that saddle and blanket, too."

Almost immediately, Linda started calling the mare Beauty, a nod to Anna Sewell's classic horse-and-girl novel, *Black Beauty*.

To celebrate the occasion, Townsend took Linda to a local restaurant. Linda chattered on about what great care she was going to take of her new treasure. Then Townsend presented her with another. Out of his pocket he pulled a tiny box. Inside was a silver ring with a dazzling blue lapis-lazuli stone.

"This will help you remember this very special moment," he said.

Linda put that ring on her finger in June of 1958 and wore it every day of her life – until New Year's Day 1966 when she gave it to Morgan and received a subway token in return.

*

Of the nearly 1,200 email messages I received from Morgan, none was more perplexing than this one in April 2004:

While in Florida in 1957 Dr. Brown continued to refine and develop that network of 'sets' and the organization that went with them.

That year, Agnew Bahnson contacted Dr. Brown and set up further work on the propulsion system, which is a direction that Dr. Brown had decided he needed to pursue, Actually, he was becoming interested in developing further what he called then the Flame Jet Generator.

However, in August of 1958 something major happened which changed his course suddenly and drew him almost immediately into the organization that I now call home. As in my situation, this move was encouraged by old ties put together initially by the Caroline Group. Again, details will slowly follow...

...if at all.

I was left entirely to my own devices to discern Morgan's meaning, what "major" thing happened in 1958, what organization Dr. Brown was drawn into – which Morgan calls "home." Sifting through some other messages, I came up with this answer:

On August 23, Mao Tse-tung ordered the bombardment of the Matsu Islands, triggering the Second Taiwan Strait Crisis. These tiny islands, less than ten miles from the Chinese mainland, were among the last strongholds of Chiang Kai-shek's vanquished Nationalists, who used them to stage raids on the Communist controlled mainland. Mao – who believed that half of the population of China could survive a nuclear war – was determined to set his version of Communist ideology apart from the Soviet Union. China was still six years from acquiring its own nuclear weapons, but that did not deter him from poking the Eisenhower administration with his determination to liberate the last Nationalist strongholds, including Taiwan.

Determined to support what was left of Chiang Kai-shek's government in exile, Eisenhower dispatched a naval force to the area, where they started running into communication problems. In *Body of Secrets*, James Bamford writes[146] that Eisenhower was frustrated that...

...it took an average of 8 hours and 35 minutes for a message containing critical intelligence to reach the White House. President Eisenhower demanded that the time be reduced to minutes. At a National Security Council meeting on August 27, 1958, attended by Eisenhower, CIA director Allen Dulles agreed that there was little purpose in developing critical intelligence overseas unless we had the communication means to insure its rapid transmission to Washington.

Later that month Louis Tordella was appointed Deputy Directory of the NSA – the post that holds the most authority[147] over the Agency's actual operations.

Tordella arrived with an extensive resume in electrical engineering and cryptanalysis. He moved quickly to accelerate the development of supercomputers and fortify the alliance between the intelligence community and electronics industry that Eisenhower would challenge three years later as "the military industrial complex."

Less than a month in his new position, Tordella went to the Oval Office with a plan. According to Bamford: [148]

> **Tordella proposed a system known as CRITICOMM. After Tordella outlined the costs and benefits, Eisenhower turned to the Deputy Secretary of Defense and said, "Do it." Within six months NSA was able to reduce transmission time from more than 8 hours to 52 minutes. In another six months the agency was able to have a CRITIC, or critical intelligence message, on Eisenhower's desk within a brief thirteen minutes, regardless of where it had originated. Eventually, the time shrunk to between three and five minutes.**

When I read that passage in Bamford's book, I knew instantly where I had seen it before. In one of his first letters[149] to me in the spring of 2004, Morgan wrote:

> **Before Brown's input, it took nearly eight hours to get a message flash (CRITIC, the highest priority) from somewhere . . . say . . . Moscow. By August 1958 the time had been cut to fifty-two minutes and now it's down to . . . well, the human is the slowest thing in the process.**

If the human was "the slowest thing in the process," then I understood Morgan's was telling me that the 'the set' had found its first *very unofficial* role in a National Security and Intelligence setting.

And, yeah, that would qualify as "something major" happening.

83

Strange Things

(1958)

For Nikola Tesla, just another day at the office - reading a book under a canopy of artificial lightning at his Colorado Springs facility ca. 1900.

Agnew Bahnson's personal notes from the fall of 1958 reflect the frustration and discouragement he'd commented on prior to Brown's arrival. In a lengthy entry dated October 28, Bahnson sums it all up:

> **Electrodynamics appears to be an interesting frontier of both applied and pure research. Electricity, which is essential to modern society, is poorly understood from a basic standpoint of what the field forces constitute or what they may imply.**

He observes that part of the difficulty stems from the scale of their experiments – the limited size of the bell jars at their disposal and the proximity of the bell jar walls to the high-voltage apparatus within. Then he notes the ambivalence of the scientific community to his experiments:

> **Our research has approached electrodynamics on a macroscopic level. Much of the last year has been devoted to the objections of the classical viewpoint toward observed phenomena. The very premise that a simple condenser of a certain geometrical configuration will show not only an attraction of one plate to another but also a movement through space of the entire assembly has not only been doubted, but has been written off in terms of ion wind effects.**

One of the major objections raised was the macroscopic effects observed. But one should recognize that we are working on a macroscopic level of 200kv with relatively confined quarters. The comment has also been voiced that strange things happen at high voltage and particularly in high vacuum. This hardly appears to be a defensible excuse for the modern scientist to ignore the phenomenon.

A truly new and practical propulsive means is one of the high priority goals of both military and civilian science. Our experiments indicated a propulsive means, generally unexpected, both in air and in vacuum.

It appears a paradox that the modern scientist is intrigued by the microscopic evidence in an unfamiliar field but will quickly discount the macroscopic phenomenon, even though no conclusive explanation is forthcoming.

With a well-equipped laboratory to investigate these phenomena, it appears appropriate for qualified scientists to not only appraise the macroscopic results but to also see the more subtle microscopic experiments which have not been conclusively explained. The search should not be abandoned.

The problem becomes: can the investigation of these strange things be fruitful?

That 'strange things happen at high voltage' *cannot be overstated*. Bahnson was writing about phenomena that occur in the kilovolt range. Townsend Brown was even more interested in the strange things that happen in the multi-*mega*volt range.

The question Bahnson poses in conclusion is precisely the question that followed Townsend Brown through the entirety of his life.

*

On October 30, 1958, Bahnson describes a visit to the lab by Dr. Jonas Whitten and Dr. Daniel Kahn, both representing the Glenn L. Martin Company. The third item in the agenda is a presentation on the subject of "Electrohydrodyamics by T.T.B."

That is the last time Brown is mentioned in Bahnson's notebooks.

The Brown family's North Carolina adventure lasted less than seven months, from the middle of April until the end of October 1958.

What Linda Brown remembers most about leaving Walkertown is her own tears.

"It was the most wonderful home I had ever had. We had ducks that would walk up to the cabin from the water's edge and Dad would feed them. And Beauty knew that the sight of Dad was always good for an apple or two."

When the only home her family ever owned was sold, the new owner said to Josephine, "I can't go fishing until you folks leave. She's got all the fish named!"

Dr. Brown was still in North Carolina on September 29th when he posted an entry in his notebook entitled "Theory of pressure confinement." Echoing the sentiments expressed in's notes, he writes:

In plotting the lines of force in various electrode configurations, it becomes apparent that some rather surprising results could be produced which, at first glance, would seem to be in direct violation of the basic electrostatic laws.

A couple of simple diagrams showing the attraction and repulsion of electrical charges, and then

In the case of a simple saucer, it is advantageous to ground the cathode, allowing the anode canopy to carry a high charge relative to ground. The situation would then be as follows:

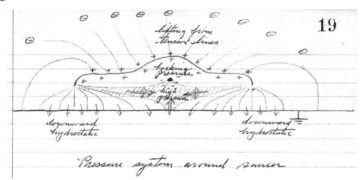

After completing this entry in Volume #2 of the notebooks he had been keeping for more than three years, Townsend Brown closed the cover.

The next time he opened Volume #2 was on October 23, 1967, when he wrote on page 21:

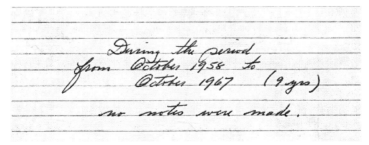

84

Strike Another Match

(1966)

Over the summer of 1966, working conditions steadily deteriorated in Building #4 at the Decker Industries compound. On good days, progress on the electrokinetic loudspeaker proceeded apace. On bad days the team had to contend with Ron Moyer – the president of the firm and Martin Decker's surrogate on-site – who never let an opportunity to assert his authority pass unbidden.

In late August, Mr. Moyer posted a list of some twenty employees he felt were hostile to his leadership. On pain of termination, those individuals were instructed to sign new contracts stipulating their compliance. Puscheck and Spirito were at the top of Mr. Moyer's list.

"The man has flipped his wig," Townsend Brown said to Linda – a sarcastic reference to Moyer's ill-fitting toupee.

"He can rot," Spirito said.

Since there was less for her to do, Linda only went to the lab when her father pulled together a full day's work. "I'm glad I didn't sign up for another full-time stint, because my name would have been at the top of Moyer's list, too."

Townsend spent more time working from the den of the Philadelphia apartment as suspicion mounted that Decker Industries was in some dire financial straits.

Tula was still living with the Browns and encouraging Linda to have as much summer fun as they possibly could. They spent time with friends Tula made, but Linda "always felt like the third wheel in most situations. I was just not interested in getting fixed up in any way."

Around Labor Day, when Tula was called back to Ohio for a family emergency, her parting words to Linda were, "This won't all be gone by the time I get back, will it?"

Linda tried to laugh the question off, but there was no denying the desperation when Decker fell behind on payroll. Townsend speculated openly that it wouldn't be long before 'other forces' would close in on Decker 'like wolves.'

A few days after Labor Day, Townsend answered the phone on his office desk. After listening for a few moments, he slammed the handset down.

"Fuck!"

"That got my attention," Linda said, "That was the first really strong swear word I had ever heard him say. Then he threw his glasses down – that was a sure sign he was really pissed – and stormed out of the office. Mr. Spirito stayed for a few seconds, and then quietly excused himself and left the office, too."

The last time Dr. Brown had blown a gasket like that was when he learned of the security breach at Pearl Harbor. Morgan told me:

> **The phone call was to inform Dr. Brown that Nassau had discovered that Decker had developed side associations which could quickly turn into security problems for the operation. Dr. Brown's viewpoint was to maintain the situation through to the end of the testing and he strenuously objected to the action taken. The idea was to close down as quickly as possible. And yes, I believe his word was "fuck."**

Recalling that both Morgan and O'Riley had steered my attention toward the submarine *Cutlass* that was anchored in Philadelphia the same time as Dr. Brown, I tried to glean further insight into what other "testing" he was told to conclude. Typically, such queries went unanswered.

But "after that," Linda said, "everything around us changed."

Townsend didn't want to abandon the work. He kept going to the lab on weekends, often staying overnight. October 1, with his pay two months in arrears, he went to Decker's office. Decker brushed him off with a wave of his hand and "Goodbye!" Townsend turned on his heel and walked out.

Closing her journal for the month of September 1966, Linda wrote:

> **I figure that Dad will tell me more about what is going on as he can, but there is definitely something afoot.**
>
> **I am happy that the past few months are behind me. They have been wonderful – and terrible! I don't want to relive any of it. OK, that's not entirely true. I still relive the parts that have some real meaning to me, like the feel of Morgan's breath on the nape of my neck. But he is not here now, is not going to be, and that's just the way that it's going to be.**

Recalling a line from a Bob Dylan tune[150], she added: *Strike another match, go start anew...*

∗

The match was struck on October 5, when Townsend flew to San Francisco.

While he was there Martin Decker's attorney spoke to Josephine, asking her to convey an offer: Decker was willing to sell his entire interest in the fan/loudspeaker project for $600,000. Josephine declined the request, saying "it's insulting."

A state of flux prevailed over the next several months, with Townsend mostly absent and funds running short. Her days as a white-coated lab-hand behind her, Linda found seasonal work in the women's' clothing section of Strawbridge & Clothier, an upscale department store in downtown Philadelphia, the paychecks barely enough to keep food on the table. The prospect of heading west was appealing.

"What do I have here, actually?" she wondered in her journal:

> **I doubt I will ever see Morgan again. Maybe I really do have to strike out fresh. Tula has made the comment that she would move to California with us if we would have her. She wouldn't stay in Philadelphia without us, and she definitely does not want to go back to Ohio to settle down. Perhaps this is all meant; the only spark of excitement I feel is when we start talking about the warmth and sunshine of California. California Dreamin'...**

The uncertainty took a toll on Josephine, too. In November, Linda wrote:

> **Daddy called tonight to tell us to hang on. Things in California are going well but nothing is solid yet. Mother sat on the edge of the bed after his call and started to cry, which broke my heart. It should not be like this, I thought! She does not deserve this! I sat beside her and we held on to each other. She looked very tired tonight. Tired isn't really the appropriate word. "Worn" is better. Worn, and perhaps suddenly older.**

Townsend returned to Philadelphia to spend Christmas with the family and stayed through the first week of January.

> **Christmas wasn't much. We got a poor excuse for a tree and barely decorated it, just put it up in the alcove by the bay window in the apartment and said "There. It's Christmas."**

Tula returned to Philadelphia, and Townsend stayed through the first week of January, 1967. The entire time, The Mamas And The Papas *California Dreamin'* was playing in the background.

The evening of Saturday, January 7th, a variety of scenarios were put on the table. As the family-plus-one sat around the kitchen table, Tula volunteered to go to the train station and get some schedules and rate cards. Everybody was astounded when, out of the blue,

> **Daddy threw a whole packet on the table. Train schedules and prices. Tula's jaw dropped when those schedules came out of his pocket and landed on the table in front of her. We all got a good laugh at her reaction.**

Loading everybody and everything on a train was one option. There was even some discussion of taking a boat through the Panama Canal and it wouldn't have surprised me if Daddy had the schedules for that, too. But neither of those scenarios addressed what would happen to the Cadillac.

The travel discussion was interrupted by the telephone. Out on the coast, Townsend had re-teamed with Beau Kitselman and Bradford Shank, who had run into difficulties building their own model of the fan/loudspeaker to demonstrate for potential investors and needed him to come to the rescue.

Townsend flew out to the coast the next day.

On January 18, he called from California.

"Sweetie," Townsend said, "I've been listening to *Kismet* tonight..."

Linda recognized that immediately as family code for "Listen up, I'm about to say something really important"– and that other ears might be on the line.

"Are you ready for the trip?" Townsend asked.

"I hope so."

"I have been thinking," Townsend said – another form of family code – "that we need to pack *everything in the study.…*"

Linda could tell from her father's measured tone that he was talking about his office at the Decker facility. "That was the only place he ever referred to as his 'study.' The room at the house was always 'the den.'

Townsend continued, "I know that some of those things are too heavy for you to move yourself. So I was thinking that you could ask Morgan and his friend to help you. They are strong enough to get the job done."

Linda thought her heart "was going to thunder out of my body," at the mention of his name, but her father was talking about Morgan and Carlos like they were Mayflower moving men helping her smuggle stuff out of the Decker compound.

"Oh," Townsend went on, "and while you're at it, try to find that lucky peacock feather for me, will you? I don't want to leave it behind." Linda knew exactly what "lucky peacock feather" meant, too.

"I don't know, Daddy. Morgan may not want to help me. We've had a fight."

"Don't worry, Sweetie. The fellow loves you. He will be there when you need him."

85

Operation Peacock

(1966)

Townsend's final instruction to the girls was "be prepared to leave – without notice."

Suspecting that Martin Decker's operations might be under surveillance, they were careful over the next few days not to do anything to arouse suspicion. Linda got the oil changed in the Cadillac but held off on getting new tires, certain that "would be a real giveaway." Fortunately, Tula's father was coming to Philadelphia with a pickup truck to take some of her stuff back to Ohio, so Josephine and Linda stashed some of their stuff with Tula's, to retrieve when they went through Ohio to pick up Tula for the remainder of the trip to California.

Then they waited.

On a cold January night a few days after the *Kismet* phone call, Josephine prepared a pork roast for dinner, declaring it would be the last full meal she was going to cook before they started in on whatever canned goods were left in the pantry and cupboards.

Around ten o'clock, the doorbell rang. Linda pressed the button on the intercom. "Who's there?"

"Morgan."

"It was seriously cold," Linda recalled, "and I ran out to meet him with no jacket or shoes on!" Morgan opened his heavy canvas coat and wrapped Linda against him. "I couldn't have gotten any closer without being inside him. We stayed in the cold courtyard as long as possible so we wouldn't have to share each other with Mom or Tula. But eventually the cold crept in. My feet went numb."

Once inside, Morgan wolfed down a serving of pot roast and a mug of strong coffee before addressing the task at hand. Turning a hard look toward Tula he said, "We have something to do tonight. It's a bit dangerous. I think that you can do it, and you would be good at it, but someone else can do it if you don't want to."

Tula didn't hesitate. "I'm in."

Morgan grabbed a piece of paper and drew a map: the entrance to the Decker compound, the access road, the gatehouse at the top of the hill. He told Tula, "your job will be to bat your eyelashes. The car you'll be driving will be running like shit. You're going to park it at the bottom of the hill, and then walk up to the guard shack. Ask the guard to come down the hill to look at the car, then ask him to call a tow truck."

Shaking herself away from the sight of Morgan in black jeans and turtleneck, Linda asked, "What do I get to do?"

"Just get your darkest jeans on," Morgan answered, "and a black sweater. I'll tell you more later."

A short while later, the newly minted secret agent and his deputized Mod Squad headed into the cold night and piled into a late model sedan with out-of-state plates. Thirty minutes later they parked a few hundred yards from the entrance to the Decker compound. As Morgan got out, he instructed Tula to slide behind the wheel. Then he opened the hood, performed some mischief on the engine, and told Tula, "It's going to run like crap, but you only need to get as far as the bottom of the road. If it quits before you get there, just coast the rest of the way."

As the sedan sputtered out of sight, Morgan and Linda scurried up the slope. At the top of the hill, another figure stepped out of the shadows: Carlos, Morgan's former roommate in New York and now his partner-in-spy-training at Camp Peary.

The trio waited outside the wall of the compound while Tula coasted the disabled sedan to the bottom of the hill. At the gatehouse, she put all of her Southern Seminary charm to work on the guard.

"Oh, *suh*," Tula pleaded, "my car is broken and it's so late. Would you please see if you can see what's wrong? It just started acting so strange and I know I'm not out of gas. I'm from Georgia and I just don't know a soul around here and it's so dark."

The guard accompanied Tula down the hill to have a look – neglecting to notice that the license plates on the car were actually from Alabama.

With the guard diverted, Morgan and Carlos poised to get Linda over the wall. She hesitated at the thought of the high-voltage line she knew ran along the top of the wall, her thoughts filling with "visions of flashing lights and armed guards."

Morgan explained that they had placed an insulated pad over the wall, "so that the wall would think it was still operational" when in fact it wasn't.

"Trust me," Morgan said, "and try not to be scared. Fear causes hesitation – and hesitation causes your worst fears to come true. I'll go first. Carlos will give you a leg up; just hit the pad and throw yourself over. I'll catch you. But once you're on the other side, move quickly. Carlos will be right behind you and you don't want him to land on you!"

Morgan scaled the wall; Carlos squatted, cupped his hands for Linda's foot, and boosted her over. Morgan caught her on the other side. Moments later Carlos was beside them. They ducked across the open space to Building #4. The door was locked, but Morgan opened it "as if he had the key." Once inside, Morgan and Linda headed down a flight of stairs to the basement. Carlos peeled off in a different direction and Linda lost sight of him.

Dr. Brown kept his notebooks and files in a safe, but Linda knew the combination. Using Morgan's standard-spy-issue, pencil-beam flashlight, she found a stack of black, hard-bound notebooks on the middle shelf alongside a larger loose-leaf binder, which turned out to be Dr. Brown's 1942 treatise on the *Structure of Space*. She grabbed all the notebooks and several files. The whole operation was over in less than a minute. Linda handed everything to Morgan.

Morgan carefully placed *six* notebooks into a black canvas satchel.

Dr. Brown had written on page 21 of his *second* notebook that "no notes were taken" between October 1959 and October 1967. But in January 1967, there were *six* notebooks – when there should have been only two.

*

Morgan secured the black satchel and headed up the stairs with Linda. From a window, they could see Tula and the security guard at the gate waiting for the tow truck. When Carlos appeared, Linda remembered the one other thing they were supposed to retrieve.

"Oh! I almost forgot! Where's that damn bird?"

Carlos lifted a bundle he had tucked under his arm. "It's right here," he said. "He's a little pissed off right now, but he's gonna like his new home."

Right on cue, a tow truck arrived. The guard escorted Tula back down the hill, leaving the gatehouse empty. Morgan grabbed Linda's arm and they hugged the outer wall of the building until they got to the gate. Then Morgan just opened the gate and the three young commandos walked out of the Decker compound. As they disappeared into the shadows, they could hear Tula, still sweet-talking the guard.

"Thank you so much, you have been *such a gentleman!*"

Once the crippled sedan was hooked to the tow truck, Tula climbed into the cab with the driver. The tow truck disappeared into the night and the guard returned to the gatehouse.

A few moments later, three shadowy figures emerged from the woods. One was carrying a black canvas satchel. Another had an angry peacock under his arm, "all trussed up like a Christmas turkey." They found their way to a van that

Carlos had parked a little further down the road and drove a few miles to an empty parking lot. There, according to Linda, "lo and behold, that sedan was parked." There was no sign of the tow truck, which had already taken Tula home. And the sedan was now sporting California tags.

After putting their haul in the van, Morgan and Linda got in the sedan and waved goodbye to Carlos.

"See you in California," Carlos said.

"We started driving back toward Philadelphia," Linda said. "Now the car was running great, but I was feeling lost."

"We'll see each other soon," Morgan promised as he let her out of the car. "Who knows? Maybe we'll meet up at Golden Gate Park one of these days."

"He was just so sure of himself, and I knew nothing," Linda remembered. "I didn't even know what part of California we were headed for, or when we would be leaving. I knew nothing and he wasn't saying a whole lot. I think Morgan just wanted to get me home safely and be gone."

The next morning, Tula loaded her stuff along with Linda and Josephine's luggage into her father's pickup truck and headed for Ohio. All the Brown's had left to carry was pared down to a large beach-bag. They had left the Cadillac out of the garage so that Linda and Josephine could go for spontaneous drives – downtown for lunch at Wanamaker's to visit a museum, or a leisurely cruise along the Main Line so that a longer trip – to, say, California – might go unnoticed.

Shortly after Tula's departure, Josephine answered a call from California. She hung up and said, "We are leaving. Now." They tossed the beach bag in the back seat and headed west out of the city.

*

Four decades later, the man I came to know as Morgan had risen to the highest echelons of the United States' intelligence and security hierarchy, overseeing affairs both classified and truly 'secret.' But he would always look back fondly on the events of that cold night in January 1966.

"After being vetted in Nassau and dealing with O'Riley," Morgan wrote, "I hit The Farm in the summer of '66, Super Bad Ass. I thought I could keep up with any of them and outstripped most. I was so full of myself. But I never would have guessed that my first assignment would be heisting a peacock."

86

Into The Sunset

(1966)

The first stop after leaving Philadelphia was Zanesville, to visit with Josephine's family.

"One gab session with Aunt Sally was enough to set my teeth on edge," Linda said. She quickly boarded a Greyhound to make the 120-mile trip to Kent, to decompress with Tula.

A few days later Josephine called Linda, who expected to hear the departure date for the next leg of their trip west. Instead, through tearful sobs she heard, "The group in Los Angeles has defaulted." Townsend had found a house in San Francisco, but everything was still in flux. Linda decided she had to get back to Zanesville as quickly as she could.

At two o'clock that afternoon, Josephine answered the phone to hear Linda ask, "Mom, would you do something for me?"

"Of course, dear," Josephine said. "Anything."

"Would you come and pick me up? I'm at the Zanesville bus station."

"Oh, Baby, thank you! I'll be right there."

That evening, Josephine confided that her time in Zanesville had not been very pleasant. "The rumor mill in Zanesville had decided that Mother was down on her luck," Linda recalled, "so of course, no one had time for her."

"Momma," Linda said, "I got in the car to go to California. If we are going to be broke, then let's be broke in California!"

Josephine looked out the window – and burst out laughing.

The next morning, the Cadillac resumed its journey westward. They stopped first in Kent to gather up Tula and stuff they'd shipped off in her father's truck. The first thing Josephine put in the trunk was the leather hatbox containing her little green teapot.

✳

It is fitting that Linda and Josephine are driving west – into the sunset. By the time the Cadillac left Zanesville for the last time[151], the patterns that define Townsend Brown's life and legacy were well established. Combing through the source material unveils many more anecdotes but, really, nothing new.

Particularly after Pearl Harbor, Townsend Brown lived his life on at least two levels: On the surface, he continued to develop 'the fan' for commercial exploitation, when that work was really intended to provide cover for the same technology being quietly put to use in classified – and *secret* – applications.

Throughout the remaining years of his life, while he appeared on the surface to be striving to create the cover of earned income from his ideas, he knew full well that the Caroline Group always had his back.

As Morgan explained:[152]

> **Now that you have a glimpse into how much of a smokescreen Dr. Brown was pumping out, you can understand. It might have looked to others that he was "financially challenged" (Linda's phrase – she prefers it to "broke") but he was *exactly* where he wanted to be all the time, living exactly in the manner he wanted to live – and Josephine went along for almost every step.**
>
> **Think back to Ashlawn. Josephine overrode his "hide in the shadows." Ashlawn was his concession to her and to Linda and look how they lived while they were there. Hardly poor. I can remember being mightily impressed – and I had grown up in that area, where such things are expected. Dr. Brown went to some effort to make sure that Linda was able to present the kind of social front that he believed she and Josephine were entitled to for at least those last couple of high school years. As soon as Linda shipped out to Southern Seminary, poof! The Ashlawn lifestyle went right out of the window.**
>
> **George[153] never understood why Dr. Brown ended his life as poorly as he seemed to end it – living in a crowded little Quonset hut, with his family: his wife, his daughter, his son-in-law and grandchild all right there. He could have been anywhere.**
>
> **He seemingly died "broke." But he was never "broke." And he died with the people he loved.**

*

Once the threesome reached San Francisco, Linda was surprised when they met up with Charles Miller who she'd last heard from when he closed up Ashlawn. Recalling that Morgan said that he and Carlos were headed west with the peacock and notebooks they'd heisted from Decker, Linda wondered if Morgan was also in the area.

In San Francisco, Townsend secured two rooms at the El Rancho Motel near Fisherman's wharf, paying the rent with a black American Express card.

The location of the motel made it easy for Linda and Tula to explore the city by cable car. They found the Wharf, the Aquatic Park, and the curious community flourishing around the intersection of Haight and Ashbury streets in the idyllic period the world would eventually know as 'The Summer of Love.'

"We met hippies," Linda recalled, "and even ran into some kids that Tula knew from Kent. The Haight-Ashbury scene was all flowers and music. I took to wearing boot-high moccasins, and wore my hair down. I would have had to smoke pot to be any more of a hippie myself, which, oddly, I never did. Mostly, I was looking for Morgan – which Tula thought was just about the most ridiculous thing imaginable."

They were all still living out of suitcases and motels – all paid for with that American Express card – when they headed south to Encino, where Townsend reconnoitered with Brad Shank and Beau Kitselman. "Encino was the pits," Linda said, but their motel had a pool and the beaches of Santa Monica and Malibu were only a day trip away.

Six weeks of the nomadic lifestyle was enough for Tula. Linda concurred: "We had just enough money to pay for our rooms and food and no idea where we would settle. Being on the road was pretty tough when you factor in all of the unanswered questions."

All the time that Linda and her family wandered up and down the coast, Linda believed, was a quest to complete the commercial development of the fan. With no reason to think otherwise, she posted a journal entry that spring:

I have become strangely single-minded about the project. I have found myself saying that I don't care where we live or how we live. I just want this fan on the market. We can do what we want afterwards. My God, we have nearly starved for this thing on and off for how many years? Daddy has poured his life's blood into it. Mother has grown old with it, and I have grown up with it. Nothing is more important.

After dropping Tula off at LAX for a flight back to Ohio, "Dad said that we were going to spend some time in the desert near Palm Springs."

87

I Want A Home

(1967)

Townsend and Josephine in Santa Monica, California ca. 1967

Townsend Brown was in his early 60s, the age when most men of his generation anticipated their retirement. But he was still driven to deliver one of his inventions to the public marketplace. To that end, he drove with Linda to Palm Springs to meet with an industrialist named Floyd Odlum.

Twelve years older than Brown, Odlum's career placed him at the center of the defense industry. He started out as an attorney in the 1920s, speculating his way to a considerable fortune in electrical utilities and cashing out before the market crashed in 1929. He started reinvesting in the early 1930s, becoming one or the richest men in America with stakes in businesses as diverse as RKO Studios, Convair Aircraft and Northeast Airlines. In the 1950s, while the Pentagon was still preoccupied with heavy bombers, Odlum salvaged the U.S. ICBM program by funding the Atlas missile project out of his own pocket.

Odlum was the financier, but his wife was the star: the pioneering aviatrix Jackie Cochran. At her husband's suggestion, Jackie started flying in the 1930s to expand her small cosmetics business, finding instead a whole new calling. In 1941 she was the first woman to fly a military aircraft across the Atlantic; in Britain she ferried planes from factories to airfields. When the U.S. entered the war, Cochran trained women to fly transport missions, freeing men to fly in combat.

In 1943 she commanded the Women's Air Force Service Pilots auxiliary of the U.S. Army Air Force – the 'WASPS' – eventually rising to the rank of Colonel in the Air Force Reserve. While her friend Amelia Earhart flew for distance, Jackie Cochran flew for speed: She set more than sixty domestic air-speed records and nine international speed, distance and altitude records.

Of their numerous residences, the couple's favorite was the Odlum-Cochran Ranch near Indio, California, at the edge of the Salton Sea, where they often entertained movie stars, corporate executives, generals and politicians.

On April 15, 1967, The Odlum's hosted an elegant luncheon to introduce the Browns to their influential friends. As she and her father drove into the ranch, it was obvious to Linda that Floyd Odlum could finance the fan project from his pocket change.

At a circular table for ten, Townsend and Josephine sat with Floyd and Jackie; across the table Linda found herself seated between two of the world's most famous airmen. On her left sat General Curtis LeMay[154] – the Air Force veteran who organized the bombing of Japan during World War II; to her right was Colonel Chuck Yeager – the first man to break the sound barrier in 1947.

After lunch, Townsend introduced these pillars of arms and industry to his ground-breaking technology with a table-top model of the Fan. Some of the luminaries and their well-coiffed wives treated the event like a magician[155] was conducting some after-dinner parlor tricks. One wife mumbled as Linda set up the demo, "My, he even brings his pretty assistant along."

Others walked around the unit, peering between its baffles, seeing no moving parts and trying to discern why a breeze was coming through it. General LeMay "hung around in the background, acting like he knew all about what made it work and saying he had known about this development for a long time."

Jackie Cochran boomed, "Well, Curt, you really understand how this works? I am so relieved to hear that! Why don't you explain it to us all so that we can spare Dr. Brown the effort?"

LeMay just laughed and chomped his cigar.

*

Before he would commit, Floyd Odlum wanted Townsend to demonstrate the fan to one more luminary who had been unable to attend the luncheon. Two weeks later, Townsend, Josephine and Linda piled back into the Cadillac headed back to the Bay area to meet with physicist Dr. Edward Teller – the self-anointed 'father of the hydrogen bomb' – at his home in Berkeley.

Linda recalls Dr. Teller as an intimidating presence. "But his wife was nice," she recalls, "and offered me tea. We sat over by the windows of the study as Daddy showed Dr. Teller the Fan."

Dr. Teller, like so many others before him, walked around the fan and inspected it from all angles. He peered into the empty space between its plates and wires. He paused to feel the warm air blowing gently on his disbelieving face. Then he looked up and said with some annoyance, "Show me a picture." Townsend sketched out a schematic and put a sheet of paper in front of him.

The famous physicist with a Ph.D. from the University of Leipzig, a pioneer of quantum mechanics and a peer of Heisenberg, Bohr, and Fermi, studied a sketch that was handed to him by a freshman drop-out from the Cal Tech and said, "I don't understand what makes it work."

Mrs. Teller turned to Linda and whispered over their teacups, "You don't know how nice it is to hear that."

*

After befuddling Edward Teller, Brown negotiated with Floyd Odlum about which of Odlum's many companies would be the best fit for Townsend Brown to develop the Fan. When they settled on a Santa Monica company called Guidance Technologies, Mr. Odlum handed Townsend a $4,000 check as a "good faith" deposit, and Townsend decided it was time to head south.

"We were still living out of suitcases," Linda recalled. The wandering life was taking a toll on Josephine, who had experienced some light-headedness caused by high blood pressure. "After one dizzy spell," Linda said, "a doctor asked if she had any reason to be upset about anything. She just smiled at him and got a prescription for some medication."

Townsend wanted to take a zig-zag route down the coast to sight-see along the way, but that idea did not sit well with Josephine, who broke down into tears. "I want a *home*," she sobbed, "I have had *enough*."

They drove the direct route down Highway 101 and arrived mid-June in Santa Monica, driving up and down the wide boulevards before finally stopping at the Embassy Apartments on Third Street, just a few blocks from the beach. The place had "a certain amount of 'olde worlde' charm. A Spanish flair, tile roof, massive walls with arches, decorative ironwork at the windows, but Mother and I were lukewarm on it. Both of us thought of earthquakes and wondered how the walls would stand."

Linda waited in the car while her parents went inside. A few minutes later, Josephine came bounding back to the car. "Come see our new home!"

Inside, Townsend was negotiating with the landlady for an apartment on the second floor. "It was really lovely, full of expensive tile and beautiful brass fittings." The apartment had one large bedroom and a sunken living room with high ceilings, and French doors that opened onto a balcony that was engulfed by an enormous magnolia tree. They also looked at an efficiency apartment on the same floor with a window that looked out toward the pretty wishing well and gardens.

Back in the larger apartment, Linda noticed that "Mother was standing in the middle of the living room just taking it all in." After a few minutes, Josephine turned to Townsend and said "this is it." Townsend turned to the landlady and said, "We'll take this one – and the little one down the hall."

Josephine unpacked her teapot, and Linda bought herself a houseplant. For the first time in all the years she'd been living with her parents, Linda Brown had a place of her own.

88

Burning Daylight

(1967)

Guidance Technologies, Inc. was a small electronics company that assembled missile guidance systems in a grey cinder-block building near the Santa Monica municipal airport. By the end of June, Townsend was anxious to resume the work that had been suspended for the better part of a year and started setting up shop at GTI – even as negotiations between Odlum, other GTI shareholders and 'Nassau' dragged on.

On June 28th, Dr. Brown signed a preliminary contract. "It means we will be working without real funds for the next two weeks," Linda wrote. "Daddy was pressured … and is pissed."

That evening, Townsend drove Floyd Odlum to Odlum's bungalow at the Beverly Hills Hotel. "Daddy wasn't going to ask him for any money, but as he left the car, Odlum handed Daddy $1,000 and said, 'Maybe this will buy some groceries!'"

A final contract was signed on Thursday August 3; on Friday final arrangements were made and on Monday they started building a new Fan. Linda expected the work to go quickly, since so much of the work was ground they had previously covered. Within a couple of days, she wrote, "Daddy already has the wiring set up and I have nearly finished the frame. We figure we'll be finished in one week flat."

Come lunch each day, Linda and her father would "go next door to this little sandwich shop and listen in on the gossip about this secret project over in the far corner of the building." Suspicions were further aroused when people like General LeMay and aviator/industrialist Bill Lear[156] started showing up to visit the new operation.

Some days, Linda was busy. Some days there was nothing to do but write in her journals. Too often, her thoughts would turn to Morgan, to what might have been, and the remote possibility of what might still be. Now that she was settled, Morgan could find her if he wanted to. And she still had the subway token "good for one fare" if she ever needed him.

Progress at GTI slowed down in September and Linda began to express frustration with the whole enterprise. After one arduous ten-day stretch, she decided to take a personal day, "to do exciting stuff like laundry. I headed to the library, figuring I could at least learn something." After an afternoon with a physics book, she walked home with "my toes dragging. I wasn't tired, just… low."

When she got back to the Embassy, her father greeted her with his "I've got a plan!" look on his face.

"How about San Francisco for the weekend?"

They flew to San Francisco – Linda's first flight on a jet – and after settling into a hotel ran out to grab the bars of a cable car for a late dinner at a German pub. "We thoroughly enjoyed ourselves," Linda noted, "even though we were probably the only totally sober people in the whole place."

Saturday morning, they went shopping. Townsend indulged in a couple of pairs of dress slacks and a leather, western-cut jacket, then insisted on buying Linda a knit sweater-coat, despite her protests that she "didn't really need anything." They found a scarf for Josephine, and a leather purse. "It all went on Dad's American Express card." Linda expressed some concern over the steadily increasing balance, but her father just "smiled and insisted that it was his treat and nowhere near" what he felt she really deserved.

Back at the hotel Townsend informed Linda that he needed to "meet some people" – an expression so familiar that she was certain that was the real reason he had come to San Francisco. He told her they'd meet up again at six o'clock and "We'll go somewhere nice for dinner."

Linda "headed straight for Haight Ashbury. She was "enjoying the scenery," but also admitted to herself that she was "searching through the faces in the crowd for Morgan."

Townsend made reservations at their favorite Chinese restaurant. After being seated, Townsend informed Linda that he had rented a station wagon so that they could retrieve things from storage in San Francisco and drive back to Santa Monica. If they left "at noon, sharp" they could have a fairly leisurely drive down the coast.

After they had ordered, Townsend repeated himself. "Remember, Sweetie," he said, "we are leaving at noon… sharp." Then he excused himself from the table, and Linda figured he was heading for the restroom.

After a few moments, Linda felt the presence of somebody standing next to her.

"Your Dad said he will meet us at noon," Morgan said, "if that's what you want to do."

*

Linda woke before dawn the next morning, surprised that Morgan was not still beside her. She wrapped herself in a towel and wandered about the apartment, "like a cat, investigating." She figured all the clothes in Morgan's closet would fit in a single bag. There were no pictures on the walls and little in the refrigerator. No desk, just a big leather chair, a lamp, and a scattered pile of books – none of which she had taken time to notice the night before.

When Morgan returned, he explained simply: "I run every morning," Morgan gesturing toward the shower. Linda dropped her towel and followed his lead.

As the morning sun burned the fog off the bay, Linda and Morgan slept again in each other's arms. "I remember one of his arms under my pillow, the other laid protectively across my middle. I studied his face – his cheek bones and the bridge of his nose, his lips, the little scar on his upper lip. I felt more at home than I had ever felt in my life. Right there, at that moment, I was totally secure."

Still, there was the matter of the clock. "Remember, Sweetie," her father said before leaving the table, "we leave at noon, sharp."

After a late breakfast, Linda noticed two motorcycle helmets in a corner.

"You still ride? You have your bike here?"

"I've got a deal with my higher-ups," he said. "Since my job involves a certain amount of danger on their behalf, they've let me carve out a bit of personal danger for my own enjoyment. So, uh, yeah... I've got a Harley downstairs. The second helmet is for you."

They climbed onto the Harley. Morgan kicked the starter pedal. The Harley's big motor rumbled to life. Linda put her arms around Morgan and they "roared off toward the Haight, burning daylight" – a phrase Morgan used whenever he wanted to move along to the next thing. They stopped for hot chocolate, cruised past hippies on Strawberry Hill spreading blankets and playing guitars and flutes, and picked up the unmistakable scent of early morning pot. Linda clung tightly to Morgan, feeling the rhythm of his breath, the growl of the engine and the hum of a road that she wished could go on forever.

*

At noon, the Harley glided up to the Hotel. Townsend was waiting beside a white Chevrolet station wagon that was loaded with the stuff that Charles Miller had transported from Ashlawn to San Francisco two years earlier.

"Dad got in and started the engine," while Linda stood on the passenger side with Morgan. "We looked at each other for the longest time, his eyes full of something so tender that I cannot even describe it."

Morgan broke the silence: "I am going this way," he said, pointing down the street, "and you are going that way," he gestured toward the idling car.

"I took the opportunity then to be the one who kissed Morgan," she said. "I wanted him to remember. Then I got in the car and closed the door, and we drove away."

*

Morgan recalled the moment Linda closed the Chevy door.

That was another moment that might have been a turning point, where I was given the opportunity to change my future. Linda's too. But I chose this path.

Sometimes when you do that, other possibilities are also set aside. I didn't know what the deal was entirely, either. This system opens possibilities and then sits back and watches to see what choices you make.

Dr. Brown put us together. He gave us a chance to either come together or say goodbye.

After that Dr. Brown never again put us in a situation where we could be together. He put two roads in front of me. I chose one, and he closed the door on the other.

89

Get A Life

(1967)

When she stepped into her apartment at the Embassy, Linda discovered that the little houseplant she'd bought when she first moved in was "deader than a doornail," which she read as "what my future was going to be unless I did something about it." She admits to packing her bag at one point. "I was just going to break all the rules and go up to San Francisco and just *make* things work with Morgan. But of course, I never did that. I figured if he had wanted me in his life, he would never have let me get into that station wagon."

In the back of her mind was the admonishment from Tula, who wrote from Ohio, "You are a fool Brown. Get over him. He's long gone."

Townsend could see that Linda was spiraling into "a bit of depression." His solution was to send Tula a plane ticket along with the promise of a job at GTI. Before Tula arrived, Dr. Brown took Linda shopping and used his American Express card to buy her a stylish, console-model record player. "It was a beautiful thing," Linda said, "with a marble top – the first real piece of furniture that I ever owned."

The next day, while Linda was waiting for the console to be delivered, her father came down the hall to her efficiency and said, "I want to show you something." He led her upstairs to a larger apartment that overlooked the rear courtyard. As she walked in, she was surprised to see her shiny new stereo installed in the living room.

"You deserve it, Sweetie," Townsend said, handing Linda the keys to the apartment that she and Tula would share through the fall and into the following winter.

*

At GTI, Linda's work once again revolved around building a prototype of the fan that could be mass-produced. She helped build a unit much smaller than what they'd developed in Philadelphia that was nicknamed 'Tiger' – only an inch thick and a foot high, but powerful enough to produce "a real blast of air. We were trying to make the design easier to manufacture, but that was supposed to be the job of a project manager that we waited for."

When an engineer named Tom Wirt arrived to spearhead the project, "the first thing that he did was reach for a tool on the other side of the grid I was working on – and put his hand right through the fine wires I had just strung. He was mortified. And I was just, well, resigned – and quietly pissed. Not because of what had happened, but because we had waited so long for a man who turned out to be, as Dad said under his breath, like a 'bull in a China shop.'"

Through the summer and into the fall, Linda built prototypes, took notes, wrote letters, worked on patent drafts, and reminded her father to eat "before he became light-headed from hunger."

"Dad set me up in a corner with instructions to blend in – but keep notes. Mother had taught me how to keep up with the conversation, so I'd be in my corner, looking at papers and typing but actually being a court reporter while everybody thought I was just transcribing stuff."

Looking back with the benefit of forty-plus years of hindsight. Linda wondered if all the work on the fan was an elaborate smokescreen.

A steady flow of interested and interesting individuals streamed through the lab at GTI.

"Bill Lear spent almost every day at the shop in November, even going to lunch with us across the street. There were many meetings between he and Dad and some others." General LeMay was also a frequent visitor, reminding anyone who would listen that he understood perfectly how the Fan worked. His contribution to the effort consisted of blowing smoke from his inch-thick cigars into the one side of the panel and watching it come out the other side clean and pure.

"All of these threads are disconnected," Linda reflected. "Odlum had placed us there with GTI to develop the Fan but nothing was ever accomplished. Was there something else going on that I didn't know about?"

In her archives, Linda found fragments of a report her father left behind suggesting the steady march of good intentions accompanied by only nominal results: in September, the work focused on "making demonstrations, contacting a commercial product designer, obtaining design drawings and mock-ups and building some small experimental models." In October, the Product Engineer was finally on board, leaving Dr. Brown free to concentrate on advanced design and patents. By November, another series of demonstrations were conducted for "Beckman, RAND, Lear, Airesearch, Bergen & Company, and GTI stockholders."

The last demonstration was in November for the RAND Corporation.

RAND was (and still is) the prototypical think tank – essentially, the 'brains' of the military-industrial complex that examined new technologies before turning them over to the 'muscle' Boeing, Lockheed, Northrop or Grumman – companies that turned new ideas into hardware that could fly, float, shoot and drop. The company also maintained consulting contracts with the intelligence side of the national security apparatus, evaluating and recommending technologies for the country's growing alphabet soup of agencies like the CIA, the NSA, and the NRO.[157]

RAND's offices were not far from the GTI plant in Santa Monica. Dr. Brown went ahead in the Cadillac; Linda and Tom Wirt followed in a van carrying the demo unit. As they arrived at the "drab looking complex," Tom told Linda, "there is an elevator inside that goes *down* at least 23 floors." Inside, armed, military police guarded unmarked doors. Tom started humming the theme from a popular TV show – *Mission, Impossible.*

Linda expected that the RAND people would respond like all the others: "Most people look absolutely stunned when Dad turns on the power. The red ribbon leaps up into action, with nothing else moving. And, of course, these men will know already that the Fan is a space propulsion device in disguise."

Townsend put on his "usual song and dance" routine, demonstrating the unit as both a fan and a loudspeaker. The Fan showed off its magical ability to move air without any moving parts and produce remarkable audio fidelity without magnets or pulsating cones. It worked just as it had for Morgan at Ashlawn, just as it had for all the finely dressed ladies and gentlemen at the Cochran-Odlum Ranch, and just as it had for Dr. Edward Teller at his home in Berkeley.

But something was different about this audience. The RAND people "were ominously quiet. There were no puzzled looks, none of the usual, furtive walk-arounds. No questions. No comments. Like they already knew all about it."

When the meeting ended, Dr. Brown asked Linda and Tom to pack the unit back into the van and take it back to GTI.

When he got back to the Embassy that night, Dr. Brown had surprising news.

"It's over, Sweetie," Dr. Brown said. "The project is closing down. It's time now for you to get on with a life of your own."

*

"Something serious happened that day," Linda wrote to me. "I have always known that but couldn't imagine what it was. I still don't, really. But I am beginning to get a whiff of something…"

Not surprisingly, Morgan offered some insight:[158]

In April of '67, Linda was out riding with Chuck Yeager's son while her father was floating around in Odlum's swimming pool, bobbing about and figuring out how the next few months were going to play out. In September, some important paperwork was handed over by the people who were safeguarding it – me and Charles Miller, actually. Then there was the meeting at RAND. Odlum by then had

acquired a sizable interest in Northrop. Northrop had already been informed, and the project's 'black' application was handed over.

The "important paperwork" that Morgan says "was handed over" was some of the material that had been spirited away under cover of darkness from the Decker compound along with a trussed-up peacock. That material had been stored under the watchful eye of both Morgan and Charles in San Francisco until it was transported to Santa Monica in a Chevy station wagon. Under the smokescreen of the GTI operation, it was developed and then assigned by RAND to the Northrop Corporation – a die that was cast well before the final demonstration.

In January 1968 – just a few months after Townsend Brown told his daughter their project was over – Northrop announced that they were researching the effects of applying an electrical charge to the wings of an airframe. From The January 22, 1968, edition of *Aviation Week:*

Northrop Studying Sonic Boom Remedy

Hawthorne, Calif. – Use of electrical forces to condition the air flowing around an aircraft at supersonic speeds may lower drag, reduce heating and soften sonic boom, Northrop Corp., said here last week.

Although practical application of the technique is quite far in the future, Northrop said its findings show enough promise to justify government funding of more intensive research. NASA is reportedly interested in the method.

Air molecules ahead of the aircraft would be ionized through a corona. The nose of the aircraft would be charged to the same negative potential, forming an electrostatic force field which would tend to repel or alter the course of the molecules as the aircraft approached.

The 'breakthrough' that Northrop reported in 1968 came more than forty years after Townsend Brown first observed the propulsive effect of highly charged capacitors in his basement in Zanesville, Ohio.

*

At Thanksgiving 1967, Tula and Linda were preparing dinner in their apartment at the Embassy when there came a knocking at their door. Upon opening they found two good looking young men, George and Lee, new tenants at the Embassy who had recently arrived from the east coast. They had a few LPs, but no record player, and asked if the girls might have a portable they could borrow.

Linda and Tula looked at each other, then at the handsome men standing in their doorway, and hatched a different plan.

"We're going upstairs for dinner," Tula said, "Why don't you guys come back later for some desert, and we'll all listen to your records together on our nice new console stereo?"

A few hours later, George and Lee returned to the apartment. When desert was served, Linda seated herself next to George.

Four decades later, she was still at his side.

90

Avalon

(1985)

Townsend and Josephine in Avalon on Catalina Island ca. 1978

GTI filed for bankruptcy at the end of 1967.

The court instructed the remaining corporate shell to keep paying Townsend a consulting fee of $1,500 a month. Linda said, "That GTI check was the main staple for Mom and Dad, along with their Social Security checks during their later years. Somehow Odlum forced GTI into a long-term contract that did not require Dad to put in any actual time. That money came in every month for a very long time."

Between 1968 and 1985, Josephine's teapot found at least a dozen more residences: Pacific Palisades; Rancho Mirage; San Francisco and Atherton, California; Catalina Island; Chapel Hill, North Carolina; Tampa, Florida; Catalina, again; Melbourne, Florida; San Diego, California; and finally, again, to Catalina.

As Linda said, "Daddy never visited anywhere, he just moved there."

Townsend began to experience difficulty breathing in the early 1960s – during that period when "no notes were taken." The problems with his lungs stemmed from his decades of exposure to the ozone output of the Fan and the lingering aftereffects from the injuries he sustained in Germany during World War II.

"Daddy has been very ill lately," Linda noted in her journal on November 12, 1968. "At first he began spitting up small amounts of blood. Now he is hemorrhaging. Tomorrow he is being admitted to UCLA Hospital. Yesterday he was very frightened. He was positive that if he went into the hospital he would never come home again. He was frightened, shaking, depressed. Tonight, he is much calmer. His courage has returned full strength."

In April 1971 Townsend and Josephine were in southern California to deal with some of the GTI bankruptcy proceedings. At one point Townsend turned to Josephine and said, "Let's go over to Santa Catalina and see what that's like."

Josephine was not in the same adventurous mood. "You are not getting me on another island, Mister, without a round-trip ticket!"

Townsend responded with two round-trip tickets for the seaplane to Avalon Harbor.

"They flew over on a Thursday afternoon," Linda said, "and in twenty-four hours he convinced Mom that this was a neat place and they needed to move there." By Friday they had leased a beautiful house on the hillside overlooking Avalon and an office space downtown. Then he secured another property in one of the canyons a mile from the center of town that included a small office building and an abandoned aviary that had once been called Bird Park.

The following week, the family packed a U-Haul and put it on the barge to Catalina.

Shortly after they'd settled on the island, Townsend's lungs acted up again. He was flown to Palo Alto and admitted to the Stanford University Medical Center. Linda and her now-husband George[159] were living in Santa Monica when Josephine called: an operation was scheduled to remove her father's damaged lung. "I won't let them take both of them," he'd quipped.

Linda and George drove up. Charles Miller drove down from San Francisco. "Daddy was in Intensive Care. We were only allowed four fifteen-minute visits each day. The rest of the time our main purpose was to keep mother laughing."

When Townsend's condition was stable enough for travel, Charles drove him and Josephine back to southern California. Charles accompanied them to Catalina and stayed for the rest of the summer, doing whatever heavy lifting was required.

Josephine found it easy to form a new circle of friends. In Avalon, the gingerbread town at the heart of island life, mail was delivered only as far as the post office, so that became the island's social nucleus. "You saw everybody," Linda said, "exchanged greetings, got caught up, made new friends." Josephine lined up bridge games and joined a Women's club. Townsend sunned on his private deck. When he felt strong enough, he worked at his office at the Bird Park. He presented something of a mysterious character, pleasant and congenial when required but not really saying much about his work or why they'd moved to the island.

"I would have loved to have heard some of the gossip," Linda said.

When his health returned, Dr. Brown embarked on a new line of experiments to tap into the natural electrical potential of common rocks, a pursuit that he called "petrovoltaics." He already knew that if high-enough voltage could be pumped into a solid-dielectric capacitor, it would produce a counter-gravitational force; petrovoltaics was a logical reciprocal to that idea: the assumption that the force of gravity would produce a voltage, however minimal, in solid materials. He tested the theory by attaching electrodes to a variety of common rocks he picked up all over the island.

He articulated his idea for a "gravitational power source" in a proposal he named for the ancient Persian gate of Persepolis: "Project Xerxes."

Josephine liked the way Xerxes sounded when it was spelled backwards.

*

The interest in "electricity from rocks" led – finally! – to the commercialization of Townsend Brown's Fan – known to the world now as The Sharper Image Ionic Breeze Air Purifier.

In 1975 Townsend spoke about ion effects at conference sponsored by the Stanford Research Institute in Palo Alto – northern California's equivalent of the RAND Corporation. After the conference, he was approached by an inventor named Jim Lee, who shared Townsend's interest in ionic wind effects.

I spoke to Mr. Lee in December 2005:

> **I had a company in Concord, California called Zatek industries. I was interested in Brown's ion wind technology and was trying to make something of it.**
>
> **Townsend Brown was having a lot of financial problems. He had assigned his patents – which is a very bad thing to do – instead of just licensing them. People took a bunch of his patents and paid him a little money up front, then didn't pay him anymore. He ended up losing all his patents. That left the poor old guy in really bad shape. His health was failing and he had no money.**
>
> **We put him on as a consultant. He was working on his petrovoltaics, so we set him up in a corner and provided him**

with material and time and money and he played with that for six months or a year, and he was available to consult with us on the ion wind technologies.

Mr. Lee said it took nearly ten years to iron out the bugs in the original electrokinetics patents, finally producing a device that reduced the ozone output and the power consumption. In 1988 Zatek obtained a patent which it then licensed to the Sharper Image Corporation, which sold countless millions of its Ionic Breeze Air Purifiers through its catalog, retail stores and TV infomercials. Sharper Image promoted the product as something they developed in their own laboratories. The seminal inventor was given no credit. His heirs earned no royalties.

The Quonset hut on Catalina Island where Townsend Brown lived in 1985 (photo ca. 2003).

And Project Xerxes? Jim Lee relates a familiar pattern:

He'd applied for some grants. He wrote up a report, went to Washington and consulted with a consortium of scientists in Florida. But when he got back, the project was completely killed. He just closed up shop and said, "We can't do this anymore."

It was all very sudden and mysterious. Like he'd touched on some arena that he shouldn't have been playing with. That was the end of it. He left, and went back into retirement, and I never talked to him again.

*

In his final years, Townsend returned to the phenomenon he first observed in the 1920s: fluctuations in the Biefeld-Brown effect caused by what he called Sidereal Radiation. He established monitoring stations at locations around the world, including Hawaii and Mexico. Despite his age and declining health, Linda says he was traveling "all over the map. His first stay on Catalina was the longest we lived anywhere, and he was spending six months at a time either in Hawaii or the Yucatan."

When his health began to falter in the summer of 1985, Townsend and Josephine moved into the Quonset hut that Linda shared with George and their twelve-year-old daughter Jennifer near Pebbly Beach, halfway up one of Catalina's many fragrant, eucalyptus-lined canyons.

"As little as our place was, we had plenty of room. Having Mom and Dad at the house was an enormous help to us with Jennifer. Mother still had her friends for bridge, and Dad had a secluded place in the back where he could sunbathe."

Townsend picked out a plot in the Avalon Cemetery, in a quiet corner beside a concrete bench "so visitors would be comfortable."

He organized his papers, including the notebooks that Morgan and Linda had retrieved in 1967 from the Decker lab.

Then he called a cab to take him to the Catalina airstrip[160]. Linda tried to stop him. "Don't worry, Sweetie," he said. "Everything is going to be all right."

As soon as he returned home to Catalina, he started unplugging the sidereal radiation recorders, and he stopped eating.

"Mother set his meals at a beautifully appointed table," Linda wrote, "with flowers and her silver. But Dad didn't care anymore. He would trundle out of the bedroom wrapped in this wonderful silk robe that she had bought during their time in San Francisco, but his heart wasn't there, not even in her good company. He would visit for a short time and then go back to the room to finish up on whatever he was doing or take a nap."

October 27, 1985:

Daddy died tonight. Quietly, in his own room. He just slipped away from us.

I had walked in to check on him before I went to bring George home. George and I talked about how weak he was, about having to hospitalize him. I said, "Daddy will be miserable. If he wakes in the middle of the night at the hospital, he will think he is alone. George said, "We'll see how he's doing tomorrow."

Mom and I went in to check on him. He was asleep on one hand, with the other laid out on the pillow. Mom had pulled the blankets up around his shoulders, but he was already gone. She just wasn't willing to accept it.

I did the same thing. I pulled the blankets up. I knew then that he was not breathing. I couldn't find his pulse.

George walked into the quiet room, and I said, "Sweetheart, I think Daddy's gone," and his response was, "I think you are right, Babe, I think you are right."

Mother was sitting on the couch when we came out of the bedroom. She searched our faces, looking for the message that she knew would come: "Momma, he's gone."

*

Thomas Townsend Brown was laid to rest at the Avalon Cemetery on Catalina Island, in the shade of the eucalyptus trees.

George and Linda selected a simple gunmetal-grey casket. "Very Navy," Linda said. Josephine dressed her husband of almost six decades in an Aloha shirt and brown slacks, as if she was seeing him off on another of his many trips.

Linda told me, "He would often say, before a departure, 'I go to prepare a place.' This time he wasn't coming home or getting ready to bring us with him. I watched Mother, who had been packing for him most of his life, dress him for burial. It broke my heart."

The day of the funeral, many of the good people of the island walked up the long hill from the village to pay their respects to the friendly, learned man they often saw passing time on the beach or chatting with the harbormaster. The townspeople knew little of the man they had come to bury; most came to offer comfort to Josephine, or to express their condolences to Linda and her husband George, the tireless mechanic who kept so much of the island's machinery running. Linda was "touched to tears" by the number of people who came to her father's memorial service.

Linda's older brother Joseph flew in to pay his respects. While father and son never fully reconciled, Joseph had a family of his own now, and was making a good life for himself as a teacher and athletic coach in Oregon. "Daddy was very proud of Joseph," Linda said.

As Linda stood graveside and read the eulogy she had prepared, she looked up and saw a familiar figure standing near the gate of the cemetery. In the tradition of his profession, Morgan had come to honor his fallen comrade 'from the wings.'

Linda's eyes dropped back to the paper in front of her, quoting from something she had found among her father's papers the night before:

There is little feeling of personal achievement in science. Research is like groping one's way through a forest. The further one goes into the darkness, the more are the unknowns, and the more insecure one feels he has become.

Sometimes I remind myself of a fish, loose from the hook and flopping about on the pier. I just keep flopping, in the hope that sooner or later I'll flop into the water.

Other times, human beings are like worms crawling. It doesn't matter which way we wriggle, so long as we keep on wriggling. Somehow, we are shown the way, by forces far more powerful than we are aware, that seem to work, inexorably, irresistibly, upon our lives, and guide us.

Linda looked up. Morgan was gone.

*One of the last photos of Townsend and Josephine
together on Catalina ca. 1984.*

Epilogue:
Timing
(2023)

> Deep in the human unconscious is a pervasive need for a logical universe that makes sense. But the real universe is always one step beyond logic.
>
> *From The Sayings of Muad'Dib by the Princess Irulan*
>
> *(Frank Herbert - Dune)*

A week after the funeral, on a sunny day without a breath of wind, Linda walked up the hill to the Avalon cemetery. She stood by the graveside bench and marveled at her father's thoughtfulness in choosing a plot with a comfortable seat. Crying softly, she sat down and immersed herself in memories.

After a few minutes, she dared to speak aloud.

"Are you alright?"

A gentle breeze rose up the canyon into the eucalyptus trees.

*

Writing about Townsend Brown is like describing wind. We can't see it; we only see the movement of leaves and branches as the wind blows through them.

From the outset, I thought of Townsend's story as a jigsaw puzzle with no photo on the box. Find the edge pieces. Form a frame. See if you can fill it in with clues. I would not argue with any reader who concludes the puzzle remains incomplete.

Did Townsend Brown really discover the practical link between electricity and gravity that Einstein postulated in his Unified Field Theory? Is it truly possible that mankind will one day sail away from Earth as easily as Townsend pushed his sailboat away from the dock on Buckeye Lake?

Through the decade after I sidelined this project, these broad themes nagged at me. With all I learned from this investigation, I kept returning to Dr. Brown's description of rocketry as a 'brute and awkward force," and his inference that humans are trying to get off the planet with the same force that cavemen used to barbecue their wildebeests.[161] I suspect that truly advanced civilizations are zooming around the cosmos while we've just figured out that burning carbonized remains of dead dinosaurs can get us all the way to the grocery store.

Science advances in awkward leaps forward and back. In one millennium, the Earth is flat. In the next millennium men are walking on the Moon. I never lost the conviction that this story is part of that trajectory.

*

Two years after Morgan appeared at the periphery of Townsend Brown's funeral, he faked his own death in a motorcycle accident in Tennessee. By then Linda, George, Jennifer and Josephine were living near the town of Banning in the southern California Desert. Not long after they moved there from Catalina, Josephine was diagnosed with lung cancer. The prognosis was terminal.

While she was in the hospital, Josephine had a visitor.

"I knew you'd come, Son."

Morgan didn't tell me a lot about that visit, and Linda knew nothing about it. Morgan told me he and Josephine talked about some of Townsend's secret work – like the flame jet generator that disappeared when he stopped writing in his notebooks in 1958, and what ultimately became of his demonstration for the RAND Corporation in 1967.

"Bombers," Josephine said. "They made bombers, didn't they?"

"I couldn't answer," Morgan told me, "but, then, I really didn't have to."

Josephine succumbed to lung cancer in the spring of 1988.

It was not until March of 1992 that *Aviation Week* broke the story that the B-2 Stealth Bomber uses an electrokinetic effect in its wings. An adaptation of the flame jet generator produces a negatively charged cloud of ions in the exhaust, and applies a positive charge to the leading edge of its wings. The result is a classic Biefeld-Brown Effect: the B-2 surfs its own electrostatic wave, the negative cloud "chasing" the positive wing, reducing fuel consumption and helping to keep the bomber aloft at high altitudes where thin air reduces the wings' conventional lift.

The B-2 was built by the merged company Northrop Grumman. Northrop was a company owned by Floyd Odlum.

*

Before I was lured into this rabbit hole, I was familiar with dosimeter badges like those worn on white lab coats at the Decker compound. Such dosimeters showed up in the final chapters of my first book. *The Boy Who Invented Television* ends with the only published account of the work that Philo T. Farnsworth did in the field of nuclear fusion.

If it can ever be perfected, controlled fusion offers the promise of a clean, safe, virtually unlimited source of industrial energy. Science has been trying to harness that "star in a jar" for more than seventy years. The kernel of knowledge that would solve the riddle remains elusively out of reach, tempting skeptics to insist that "fusion is the energy of the future and always will be."

The 'flying saucers' that Townsend Brown demonstrated had to be tethered to an external power source. If they were to become actual flying machines, a power source must be found that's capable of producing extremely high voltages, and it must fit into a device small and light enough to be placed onboard an air-or-spacecraft. The flame jet generator may have been one way to approach that dilemma. Another solution may have come to Townsend's attention in the 1960s: a soccer-ball-sized fusion energy device – the Farnsworth Fusor.

When Linda Brown and I opened the Rubbermaid tubs of documents that she brought to our first meeting in Las Vegas, we found among her father's papers a page from one of Philo Farnsworth's fusion patents.

When I asked Morgan about it, I got one of the few direct answers[162] to a direct question that he ever gave me:

> **OK, fasten your seat belt. This is uncharted territory. You deserve an answer to that question, and I would not have dropped the bait out there about the radiation at Decker if I didn't intend to answer you.**
>
> **Yes, there was fusion work being carried on at the Decker Labs.**
>
> **Dr. Brown intended you to find this or he would not have left that fusor patent in his file. And now you know why you were the one chosen for this book.**
>
> **I don't know how you are going to write about this. We are getting to the core of some very secret stuff. I do not use the word "classified" for reasons I believe you understand now.**
>
> **I'll leave it at that for when you feel up to it. We have to feel our way through this, Paul. I am sure that we are doing the right thing and that we are in the right place.**
>
> **Beyond that, this is as big a mystery to me as it is to you. I suggest we just take things slowly and methodically and give the "inspiration" a chance to guide our paths.**

*

I returned to this project after a decade-plus hiatus because I could not stop wondering: If such things as gravity control and fusion energy are indeed possible, why are they not at our disposal today? If these secrets are being kept out of the reach of humans, then by whom – or what – and why?

Which returns me to The Kernel of Curiosity in every piece of this jigsaw puzzle, the question I've been asking since I received Morgan's very first letter in 2004, is: What *is* 'the Caroline Group'?

Morgan made frequent allusions to "the core" or "the spine" of the Caroline Group, all sufficiently vague that I could not tell if he was referring to personnel deeply entrenched in the national security apparatus, or something extraterrestrial or interdimensional.

For example, this comment:[163]

The Caroline Group is worldwide in its scope. The fabric of its membership is made up of folks who speak universal languages, not just the spoken tongue. Math. Music. The Arts. *The message of the core group can more easily be discovered in those other forms* , and communication comes easier to the humans who seem to have a more creative nature.

Might that include a biography of an 'obscure 20th century scientist?'

In subsequent messages, Morgan alluded to the conversations he had at Ashlawn, when Dr. Brown said that time travel "...is possible, in your lifetime." In March 2005, Morgan confided:

The technology is a time machine. A way of reaching forward, and back; of traveling between dimensions that are available to us. Now you can see that *it is also beyond our capabilities spiritually* .

How to change that? Get people to sit around a campfire and tell stories of wondrous things and brave individuals, and eventually they come to accept that vision as a possibility. Come to see that possibility in themselves and take ownership of it.

Or make a movie with a Möbius-loop title like *Back To The Future,* and in the final scene show a mad scientist named 'Doc Brown' (?!?) coming back *from* the future, pour beer and banana peels into his 'Mr. Fusion' Home Energy Reactor, pull his goggles over his eyes and say "Where we're going, we don't need roads.[164]"

*

Though Morgan and I exchanged nearly two thousand email messages, I never met him face to face[165]. I often wondered how long my most valuable source was going to last. When I lightly prodded him about the prospect that he might disappear again, he replied, "Paul, you have to realize: given the nature of my profession, I have already outlived my life expectancy."

Then he reminded me of my father's Boy Scout pin, that I had sent him in exchange for the 'thump stick' when Linda visited in the spring of 2004.

> I keep your Dad's pin under my collar. Should it ever find its way back to you, I want you to know that it arrives with my blessing and continued support for your future. I also want you to know that I want you to keep my thump stick as a remembrance of me and that I leave it with you knowing that it will teach you as it has me. Poised on your wall it will probably prove to be an even more formidable weapon than it was in my hands.

For much of the time that we corresponded, I suspected that Morgan was in action in one of the post-9/11 theaters of war, Iraq or Afghanistan. In spring 2005, I learned that he was recuperating from a knee injury; his team was still in the field, and he wrote of longing to be back at their side.

June 27, 2005, as Linda and I were about to leave our homes to meet in Philadelphia, I received message #1,189, Morgan's last email. The subject header is "Timing."

> You know, there is a lot to be said for timing. A time to live, a time to die.
>
> I sit here, trying to preserve myself. I don't exactly know what for. Two more pilots died a few minutes ago. And three of my own men a little earlier. My good boys, and I am not there.
>
> This won't do.
>
> So yes, I am going fishing.
>
> And yes, this trip for you and Linda will be very important.
>
> Go with all the love that is in my heart.
>
> Morgan

After I got that message, Linda and I met as planned in Philadelphia.

At the end of a long day sniffing out the trail of Townsend Brown, I was putting my feet up in my hotel room when a knock came at my door. I expected Linda, since we planned to order pizza and compare notes. I opened the door, and there was a large young man in cotton shorts and a gigantic tee shirt. He must have been six-four and nearly three hundred pounds.

I don't remember what he said. I just remember he was holding his arm out slightly, his hand at first clenched in a fat fist. My eyes traced down his arm. His hand opened. There in his large palm was my father's Boy Scout pin.

Over the next week, O'Riley directed me to press accounts of an incident in Afghanistan: a Chinook helicopter had crashed (or was shot down) in the mountains near Pakistan on June 28, 2005 – the day after I got Morgan's last email. The Pentagon reported that sixteen servicemen – eight Navy SEALs and eight other soldiers – were killed in the crash in the deadliest single attack on American forces in Afghanistan.

O'Riley let me know that there were not sixteen, but actually seventeen souls on that helicopter.

*

Early in our correspondence, Morgan promised me that one day, when this book is finished and published, we'll all meet on a private island in the Caribbean to celebrate our collaboration.

"If all else fails," he wrote, "we will take over an entire island. I'll trade your Dad's pin back for the thump stick. And we will have a bonfire on the beach and party, big time. No need for reservations. Accommodations are wonderful and security is never a worry. Yes, looking forward to that, BIG TIME."

I still have the thump stick. It rests on a wall, above the desk where I type these final words – not far from my father's pin.

If any of the stories that I have tried to tell in these pages are true, then I have every reason to believe that party on the beach is still going to happen.

Morgan will be there with Linda, and we will warm ourselves by a bonfire on a secluded beach and listen for the sound of time.

*

The Flammarion Engraving[166]

*

**The Universe is not only stranger than we imagine,
It is stranger than we *can* imagine.**

– Arthur C. Clarke

Acknowledgements

Writing in the winter of 2023, it is a little strange to look back at all who have come and gone over the two decades since this project started in 2003. After two decades in the making, that this has always been a "multigenerational" undertaking has never been more apparent.

First and foremost, I must acknowledge Townsend Brown's daughter Linda.

When I first approached Linda Brown with the idea of collaborating on her father's biography, she expressed deep reservations. Over the course of several months of 'snail mail' correspondence, we found enough common ground that Linda overcame that resistance. The project that went off a cliff in 2009 is not what she signed up for. It is easy to see now how that experience was just one more 'bitter pill' atop a stack of challenging recollections.

Linda and I were in daily contact for the better part of six years. A substantial portion of the material in these pages was derived from her personal journals. Given the lack of substantive information from other sources, this book probably would not exist were it not for the reflections of a devoted daughter who had the presence of mind to maintain a voluminous record of her travels.

She had every right to be shocked and angry when I abruptly pulled the plug in January 2009. In retrospect, the reservations she expressed before we started opening those Rubbermaid tubs seem entirely justified.

While my own actions seemed necessary at the time, I still owe Linda an 'amends' (that's '12-step' jargon) for the abrupt manner of the disruption. I can only hope the rendering of this edition is a step in that direction.

Similarly, while the story remains full of mysteries, there would be no story to tell at all were it not for my equally voluminous correspondence with my covert pen pals, 'Morgan' and 'O'Riley.'

Looking back to the very beginning, I guess I should start by acknowledging 'Janoshek.' I'm just not sure if I should be thanking him or cursing him for the otherwise anonymous email that opened the rabbit hole in the summer of 2002.

Were it not for Mike Williams' persistence over a period of several years, this completed (?) volume would not exist. I can recall the first time I tried to tell Mike what I was working on, when he and Kathy were living in New York City in 2005 or 2006. It all seemed crazy and confusing at the time, but Mike saw enough in the material to take a more than passing interest. He voluntarily took my initial 'kitchen sink' manuscript and whittled it down to something digestible.

Looking back to what I now think of as 'The Before Times' – 2003-2008 – there were several people who played an active role exploring the rabbit hole, mostly through contributions to the online forum at ttbrown.com/forum. Only some of these people used their real names – or, rather, what sound like real names – and others used only online handles: Mikado, Trickfox, Jim Zimmer, Mark Culpepper, Nate Cull, Radomir, Kevin.b, Langley, and Victoria Steele among many others.

Thanks also to: Lace Lynch, my steady and reliable Zanesville correspondent; Ryan Wood – who showed me how to navigate the labyrinthine corridors of the National Archives in College Park, Maryland; Jan Lundquist, who helped me shop the initial draft to agents and has long maintained her own personal interest in Townsend Brown's odyssey; and Mike Lovett and Craig Havighurst and other good friends who have listened to me wax on about these mysteries for years.

Those mysteries persist: Did Townsend Brown discover the key to a parallel universe? Or is the speculation that swirls around such possibilities the result of a deliberate a misinformation campaign designed to conceal other - possibly more prosaic but no less important - aspects of Brown's life and work? Is the secret in what he discovered, or more a function of his clandestine work in the realm of espionage and counterintelligence?

The answers to these questions have yet to emerge in a verifiable form. The best we can do for now is to assemble what we do know about Townsend Brown's life and send it into the void, letting it resonate with 'the sounds of time.'

A 'multigenerational' undertaking, they told me from the start. What does that even mean? Only that the process of human wits growing sharper is a protracted proposition.

Thirteen years. That's just how long it took my wits to get sharp enough to tell *a* story, if not *the* story.

There is no telling how long it will take the rest of mankind to catch on.

Paul Schatzkin

February 11, 2023

Endnotes

1 'Epic Fail' (January 2009) ttbrown.com/epic-fail

2 Chapter 74 - *Winterhaven*; footnotes

3 The Internet Wayback Machine has archived pages from the site starting in 1997.

4 There is a tendency in some circles to dismiss Farnsworth's contribution, but in1927 his Image Dissector camera tube was a breakthrough of epic proportions, one that made everything that came before it obsolete and everything that came after it possible.

5 Radical Software Vol. II #3, The VideoCity Edition, Summer 1973; edited by Phil Gietzen

6 WaterstarProject.com: Point of Origin, Santa Cruz 1973

7 That website, soteria.com, is no longer online.

8 National Investigations Committee on Aerial Phenomena - Chapter 80: *NICAP*

9 Meadowcraft, Enid Lamonte; *The Story of Thomas Alva Edison*;

10 Everson, George; *The Story of Television*

11 Schatzkin, Paul; *The Boy Who Invented Television*;

12 Sir Isaac Newton, *Principia Mathematica*

13 The photoelectric effect that Einstein articulated in 1905 is the first essential principal that led to television in the decades that followed.

14 A. L. Kistelman, *Hello, Stupid*;

15 The Michelson-Morley Experiments are explored in more detail in Chapter 50: *Structure of Space*

16 Robert A. Millikan,

17 Millikan's Oil Drop Experiment

18 IBID *Hello Stupid*

19 Townsend Brown Autobiography (from Family Archives)

20 Charles Augustin de Coulomb

21 Chapter 80: *NICAP*

22 Burridge, Gaston; *Townsend Brown and His Anti-Gravity Disc*

23 Chapter 24: *Opportunities for Technicians and Scientists*

24 More on the Naval records in 'Notes from the Rabbit Hole' - Chapter 35: *Never Heard of the Guy*

25 *Radical Software* Vol. II #3, The Video City Edition

26 Max Crosley, *The Electro Magnetic Spectrum Blues*

27 Philo T. Farnsworth died in March 1971 at the age of 64.

28 "Gravitator" is sometimes shortened to "Gravitor"

29 The theory that large objects bend the space around them was proven by the Eddington Expedition to observe a solar eclipse in 1919.

30 All the correspondence referenced in this chapter was found in the Brown family archives.

31 … for which the recording industry awards – the Grammies – are named; imagine what the award would be called if had been named after the Phonograph.

32 Johnson, Fenimore; *His Masters Voice Was Eldridge R. Johnson*

33 Dr. Bartsch's staff included: Dr. C.W. Price, a zoologist from the U.S. Dept. of Agriculture; his assistant Charles Weber, from the Smithsonian; G.R. Goergens, a photographer from the Dept. of Agriculture; Elie Cheverlange, an artist from the Smithsonian, and John W. Mills, the 'dredging master,' from the Carnegie Institution of Washington; and Anthony Wilding, from the Smithsonian, who served as the Expedition's recording secretary.

34 Johnson's son Fenimore, as well as two personal friends: Dr. George Darby, a dentist from Merion Park Pennsylvania and Walter J. Kennedy, from Camden New Jersey, an engineer who maintained son Fen's yacht, the *Elsie Fenimore*.

35 Linked bibliography at https://ttbrown.com/biblio

36 There will be more on these sources in Part II - Black.

37 Stephenson, William S.; *A Man Called Intrepid* (autobiography)

38 Morgan > PWS 040618

39 Navy records indicate that Townsend Brown was first recommended for promotion to Lieutenant, Jr. Grade on January 12, 1933; the promotion to that rank was finalized on April 18, 1933. During the voyage of the *Caroline*, Brown would have been a "Seaman 1c" on his way to being a "Lieutenant (jg)." Since Mr. Johnson was writing about the voyage many years after its completion, it is understandable that he is referring to Brown as "Lt." Where Johnson is referring to Brown, he has been quoted directly. For simplicity's sake, 'Lt.' is used in the chapter and for the remainder of his Naval career.

40 ibid

41 Morgan > PWS - snail mail March 2004

42 As this aspect or the story unfolded, I was instructed to track down a book called *The Secret Team* by L. Fletcher Prouty, a retired Air Force colonel who worked as a consultant with the Central Intelligence Agency during the

1950's and 60's.

First published in 1973 and updated in 1990, *The Secret Team* is focused on the shape of the world after the Second World War II. In the preface to the 1990 edition, Prouty writes:

It is time to face the fact that true national sovereignty no longer exists. We live in world of big business, big lawyers, big bankers, and even bigger moneymen and big politics. It is the world of 'The Secret Team.'

Prouty then explains how such interests navigate safely within the veiled layered veils of a robust, national security establishment, actually using the apparatus of the state to wrap a cloak of invisibility around what is essentially a stateless operation. These teams, according to Prouty, have this power precisely because…

… they have the ability to take advantage of the most modern communications systems in the world, of global transportation systems, of quantities of weapons of all kinds…. They can use the finest intelligence systems in the world, and most importantly they are able to operate under the canopy of an ever-present "enemy" called "Communism."

Fletcher Prouty died in 2001. Were he alive today, we could easily see him update this paragraph for the first decades of the 21st century by substituting the word "terrorism" for "communism."

The power of the Team derives from its vast intra-governmental undercover infrastructure and its direct relationship with great private industries, mutual funds, and investment houses, universities, and the news media, including foreign and domestic publishing houses.

Prouty is writing in the 1970s, but he could just as well have been writing about William Stephenson and Eldridge Johnson forty years earlier.

43   (n) or (nmi) was military shorthand for "no middle initial"

44   (approximately $13 million in 2022 dollars).

45   Linda Brown knew nothing of her parents' divorce until Lace Lynch – a genealogist and historian who tirelessly sifts through the records at the Zanesville public library – discovered the divorce decree among court records in April 2006. For all the years that she had spent sharing confidences with her mother, Josephine never said anything about having been divorced in 1937. Never having known that her parents had once been divorced, Linda never had the opportunity to ask them, "why?"

46   "Sidereal Time" is defined as "Time based on the rotation of the earth with reference to the background of stars."

47   Attested by Dr. Abbot (Smithsonian Inst.), Dr. Fleming and Gish (Carnegie Inst.), Dr. Miller (Case) and Dr. Maris (Navy),

48 What remains unsaid here is the inference that Brown's obsessive pursuit of 'Sidereal Radiation' was borne of the nagging suspicion that he was not detecting an inanimate form of physical radiation, but that within the radiation there persisted some form of…. intelligence. There is scant documentation on this subject, so the topic has been side-stepped from the primary narrative and pinned here as a footnote.

49 quoted from Brown's Naval records

50 Entire text online: *A Sailor's Life*

51 Hyde, H. Montgomery; *The Quiet Canadian: The Secret Service Story of Sir William Stephenson*

52 Over the decades to follow, Vega was transformed into the famous Lockheed "Skunkworks" facility that spearheaded the most advanced aviation research of the twentieth century.

53 Wouk, Herman; *Don't Stop The Carnival* (novel)

54 Chapter 54 - *Good For One Fare*

55 Buffett, Jimmy *Don't Stop The Carnival*

56 Buffett, Jimmy; *Only Time Will* Tell

57 Buffett, Jimmy; *Desdemona's Building A Rocket Ship*

58 Robert Woodward was one of the Washington Post journalists who, along with Carl Bernstein, cracked the Watergate investigations during the 1972 presidential election, resulting in Richard Nixon's resignation in 1974.)

59 Morgan > PWS 050301

60 Hardcopy letter, undated

61 Of all the gin joints in all the towns… it seems an odd coincidence that the Brown's found a bungalow on "Wonderland")

62 When she disappeared somewhere in the Pacific in 1937, Amelia Earhart was flying a much larger, new Lockheed Electra

63 Brown never warmed to / had any affinity for the expression "anti-gravity" - to him it was always a matter or 'stress in dielectrics' - which produced synthetic gravitational fields. It was not so much as negating gravity as product an equal or greater opposing force the activation of dielectrics.

64 Luminiferous aether or ether ("luminiferous", meaning "light-bearing") was the postulated medium for the propagation of light. It was invoked to explain the ability of the apparently wave-based light to propagate through empty space (a vacuum), something that waves should not be able to do. The assumption of a

spatial plenum of luminiferous aether, rather than a spatial vacuum, provided the theoretical medium that was required by wave theories of light. (Wikipedia)

65　The word has numerous spellings. Where it appears in the literature as 'Aether' I use that spelling; otherwise, I use the more contemporary spelling, 'ether'.

66　'Quantum Communications" might be an equally viable expression, seeing as how what we're talking about is 'tugging on the quantum continuum.'

67　Einstein/Szillard Letter August 2, 1938

68　Farrell, Joseph P.; *Reich of the Black Sun*

69　Greene, Brian; *The Elegant Universe: Superstrings, Hidden Dimensions, and the Quest for the Ultimate Theory*

70　Greene, Brian; *The Fabric of the Cosmos: Space, Time, and the Texture of Reality*

71　Pru Clearwater *The Infinite Field* (find her on Spotify)

72　Cook, Nick; *The Hunt for Zero Point* (Amazon) p. 194

73　Any resemblance btw 'Morgan' and 'Marckus' is *purely* coincidental. Right? Right. Glad we could get that sorted out.

74　Smokey Stover Archive: www.smokey-stover.com. Cartoon used with permission.

75　And, yes, David Grohl has said that the name of the band was taken from the name of the UFOs

76　This might be a good time to just remember that the there is a direct connection between Neil Armstrong's "One giant leap" and German rocket science in the person of a certain Werner Von Braun.

77　Roberts, Andy; *Foo Fighters: The Story So Far* (Project 1947)

78　Bamford, James *Body of Secrets*

79　The 2008 draft of this manuscript included a reference to classified material that was scheduled for release in the year 2012. That new information has been obtained and found to have little bearing on the Townsend Brown story. According to James Bamford, TICOM was "the last great secret of the Second World War." According to those who have inspected the material released in 2012, the only secret amounted to why it had all been kept secret for 70 years.

80　Of the six-thousand-some Halifax bombers that saw service during World War II, only three remain intact today. One of them, the NA337, was recovered from the frigid waters of Norway's Lake Mjosa fifty years after it crash-landed there in April of 1945 and was fully restored in the 1990's. According to Morgan, the NA337 is the same plane that delivered Townsend Brown behind enemy lines in Germany in the closing weeks of World War II.

81 I enjoy the irony that Spaulding Gray is most renowned for an epic novel he called "Monster In A Box" - which is how I felt about this project a lot of the time.

82 For the uninitiated, Ian Fleming wrote the novels that created the character known as James Bond, aka 007.

83 Quotes from O'Riley from email correspondence with him after being introduced by Morgan.

84 Operation Carpetbagger was a World War II operation to provide aerial supply of weapons and other matériel to resistance fighters in France, Italy and the Low Countries by the U.S. Army Air Forces that began on 4 January 1944. (Wikipedia)

85 Dorril, Stephen; *MI6*

86 Major General Dwight D. Eisenhower, Supreme Commander of Allied Forces in Europe 1942-1945

87 Campaigne was a rarity among military officers – a Ph.D in mathematics. Before the war began, he had proposed a novel encryption device to the Navy. The Navy rejected his design but offered him a correspondence course in military cryptanalysis. When he passed, the Navy offered him a commission – which arrived just two days before the Japanese attacked Pearl Harbor.

88 As mentioned in Chapter 36: *Back to Ohio*

89 The name 'Robert Sarbacher' will be familiar to anybody who has studied UFO conspiracy theories from the 1950s.

90 Like so many of the characters who populate the life of Townsend Brown, Martin Decker is pretty much a mystery, too. He was a well-respected member of the "Main Line" Philadelphia society in the early 1960s; But Google the keywords "martin decker philadelphia" and you will discover that the entire world wide web is virtual void of any reference to the man.

91 Lermontov, Mikhail; *A Hero of Our Time* (1840) is an example of the superfluous man novel, noted for its compelling Byronic hero (or antihero) Pechorin and for the beautiful descriptions of the Caucasus. There are several English translations, including one by Vladimir Nabokov and Dmitri Nabokov in 1958. (Wikipedia)

92 Much like I had known Pem Farnsworth for 15 years before she was willing to share the story of the night that she and Phil returned to the fusor lab, the night he said, "that's all I need to see."

93 Brotherton, John; *A First Full of Kings*

94 Morgan's account of his illness and recovery resonated with me on a number of levels. First, of course, there was his profound account of his vision and of

recognizing the presence in his life of something from "another dimension." But there was another element, something much deeper and more personal. I have family history with the illness that had inflicted Morgan: My father died of multiple myeloma. Harvey Schatzkin was all of 37 years old when he died in 1958. Morgan would have been roughly the same age when he recovered.

95   Hawaii became the 50th state in 1959

96   In Marxist philosophy, the dictatorship of the proletariat is a condition in which the proletariat holds state power. The dictatorship of the proletariat is the intermediate stage between a capitalist economy and a communist economy, whereby the post-revolutionary state seizes the means of production, compels the implementation of direct elections on behalf of and within the confines of the ruling proletarian state party, and instituting elected delegates into representative workers' councils that nationalize ownership of the means of production from private to collective ownership. (Wikipedia)

97   The Dept of Defense superseded the venerable Dept of War, one of the four oldest departments in Federal Government. When George Washington formed the first cabinet in 1789, there were only four posts: Secretary of State (Thomas Jefferson), Secretary of the Treasury (Alexander Hamilton), Secretary of the Dept of War (Henry Knox) and the Attorney General (Edmund Randolph). In 2023, there are 15 'cabinet level' positions in the Executive Branch.

98   *Garden Island* August 3, 1948

99   The disposal of records is handled pursuant to Title 44, United States Code, Section 3301 and Title 36, Code of Federal Regulations, Chapter 12, Sub-chapter B, Part 1228, issued by the National Archives and Records Administration (NARA). ...

100 Klaus Emil Julius Fuchs (29 December 1911 – 28 January 1988) was a German theoretical physicist and atomic spy who supplied information from the American, British and Canadian Manhattan Project to the Soviet Union during and shortly after World War II. While at the Los Alamos National Laboratory, Fuchs was responsible for many significant theoretical calculations relating to the first nuclear weapons and, later, early models of the hydrogen bomb. After his conviction in 1950, he served nine years in prison in the United Kingdom, then migrated to East Germany where he resumed his career as a physicist and scientific leader. (Wikipedia)

101 The Cambridge Five was a ring of spies in the United Kingdom that passed information to the Soviet Union during World War II and was active from the 1930s until at least into the early 1950s. None of the known members were ever prosecuted for spying. The number and membership of the ring emerged slowly

from the 1950s onwards. The general public first became aware of the conspiracy after the sudden flight of Donald Maclean and Guy Burgess to the Soviet Union in 1951. Suspicion immediately fell on Harold "Kim" Philby who eventually fled to the Soviet Union in 1963. (Wikipedia)

102   Given its highly classified nature, the precise date of this demonstration is unknown.

103   Chapter 21 - *How I Control Gravitation*

104   chapter 26 - *A Complete System*

105   This is a reference to 'The Philadelphia Experiment,' an alleged account of experiments on a Naval vessel that has often been associated with Townsend Brown. The event itself has never been proven beyond the realm of conspiracy theories, let alone any evidence of Brown's involvement. The first draft of this manuscript included some reference to 'TPX' which has been excised and revised / posted among the online Appendices (ttbrown.com/apxs/)

106   This chapter recreates a conversation many years after it happened. The dialog is mostly fabricated, but the gist of the conversation described here is based on Tula's rather vivid recollection of that evening with Townsend Brown, and has passed muster with Linda Brown, who was also present.

107   Charles Francis Brush (March 17, 1849 – June 15, 1929) was an American engineer, inventor, entrepreneur, and philanthropist. (Wikipedia)

108   *The Kinetic Theory of Gravitation* begins with the statement: "Gravitation is due to intrinsic energy of the Ether" – in 1914, almost 30 years after Michelson and Morley gained fame for their inability to detect any such thing.

109   Morgan informed me that 'Woody' was a link to the Caroline Network: "He handled the banking when it was necessary."

110   So much for the confidentiality of "Copy No. 21," which [redacted] apparently handed directly over to the special agents of the FBI. It would sure be helpful to know to whom this letter, and this Registered copy #21, of the *Project Winterhaven* proposal was addressed. But, since the FBI has destroyed these files, we will probably never know.

111   Heinrich Hertz proved the existence electromagnetic waves between 1886 and 1889, laying the foundation for all the radio and television communications of the 20th century over frequencies that bear his name, i.e., 'kilohertz."

112   Back to *Structure of Space* (Chapter 50): a gravitational signal is continuous because we are tugging on the quantum void, not sending waves through it.

113   When Andrew Bolland was assembling his website, Linda Brown provided him with her file of *Winterhaven*, which was Registered Copy #36. After Andrew

posted that on his website, he provided photocopies to Tom Valone, William Moore, and others. When Valone supplied a copy of his copy to Nick Cook, Valone said something about the 'Freedom of Information Act,' but FOIA had nothing to do with it.

114   *ibid* Page 31

115   Josephine's parents, the Beales, were still living at the Georgetown address after moving there during the war, when Josephine was divorced from Townsend and working directly for William Stephenson.

116   Jacques Bergier: maybe born Yakov Mikhailovich Berger (8 August] 1912 – 23 November 1978) was a chemical engineer, member of the French-resistance, spy, journalist and writer. He co-wrote the best-seller The Morning of the Magicians with Louis Pauwels as a work of "fantastic realism" (a term coined by the authors). (Wikipedia)

117   Alan Turing's 'bombe' was an electro-mechanical device used by British cryptologists to help decipher German Enigma-machine-encrypted secret messages during World War II. The US Navy and US Army later produced their own machines to the same functional specification, albeit engineered differently both from each other and from Polish and British bombes. (Wikipedia)

118   This is the same 'Russian Bank' that cigar-puffing gentlemen played at the Graycliffe Hotel in the Bahamas back in Chapter 38 - *Parallel Lives*

119   Albert Einstein died April 18, 1955, at age 76 in Princeton, New Jersey.

120   Morgan > Paul 4/18/2004

121   Agency slang for an operation so swift and thorough that there was "nothing left behind but smoking bolts on the floor."

122   The Atlas Computer was one of the world's first supercomputers, in use from 1962 (when it was claimed to be the most powerful computer in the world) to 1972. (Wikipedia)

123   Morgan > Paul 9/3/2004

124   National Investigations Committee on Aerial Phenomena - Chapter 80, *NICAP*

125   Just prior to his passing in 2008 at age 99, Cornillon released a report on the Biefeld-Brown Effect experiments conducted in Paris under the name of 'The Montgolfier Project' (the Montgolfier Brothers flew the first lighter-than-air balloons in France in the 18th century). Despite reports to the contrary, the results clear: "The Final Report for the Projet Mongolfier, April 15, 1959, outlined these five tests confirming, as in the prior tests, that there was a definable force. At this point our team was scattered, the project shut down and we were unable to make the further tests to further refine and quantify the results."

126 Gladych, Michael; *The G-Engines Are Coming* (Young Men - the Magazine for Tomorrow's Technicians and Engineers)

127 Intel, *Towards Flight Without Stress of Stain* (Interavia)

128 Jessup, Morris K.; *The Case for the UFO*

129 Rho Sigma (Rolf Schafranke), *Ether Technology: A Rational Approach to Gravity Control*

130 Operation Gold was a joint operation conducted by the American Central Intelligence Agency (CIA) and the British MI6 Secret Intelligence Service (SIS) in the 1950s to tap into landline communication of the Soviet Army headquarters in Berlin using a tunnel into the Soviet-occupied zone. The plan was activated in 1954 because of fears that the Soviets might be launching a nuclear attack at any time. Construction of the tunnel began in September 1954 and was completed in eight months. The Soviet authorities were informed about Operation Gold from the very beginning by their mole George Blake but decided not to "discover" the tunnel until 21 April 1956, in order to protect Blake from exposure. (Wikipedia)

131 Wright, Peter; *Spycatcher*

132 George Blake (11 November 1922 – 26 December 2020) was a spy with Britain's Secret Intelligence Service (MI6) and worked as a double agent for the Soviet Union. He became a communist and decided to work for the MGB while a prisoner during the Korean War. Discovered in 1961 and sentenced to 42 years in prison, he escaped from Wormwood Scrubs prison in west London in 1966 and fled to the Soviet Union. (Wikipedia)

133 Hall, Richard H.; *A Personal Perspective on the Role of NICAP*

134 Keyhoe, Donald; *The Flying Saucers Are Real*

135 Morgan > PS June 23, 2004,

136 Morgan > PS 050418

137 More about Helen Towt and Charles Miller can be found in the online appendices

138 Re-reading this passage in September 2022, I was struck with fresh insight re: what is really going on here: Brown is 'seeding the ground.' He is showing Bahnson what will work, and they are getting *deliberately minimal* results. Brown is showing Bahnson the *least* he possibly can of technologies that he *knows* work in a far more impressive manner – maybe sometime in the future, or on another planet, in another galaxy or another dimension.

139 Agnew Bahnson personal notes January 5, 1958

140 This idea of "disturbing the government" – and the impact of revolutionary technologies on 'world security' – provided the theme of a novel that Agnew

Bahnson wrote and published in 1960, *The Stars are Too High*, in which a secret, privately funded group constructs a revolutionary, saucer-shaped flying craft with gravity-defying capabilities. See footnotes and bibliography for links. Agnew Bahnson died in 1964 when the plane he was flying crashed on take-off; conspiracy theories abound, suggesting that Bahnson's death was not purely accidental, but the way his family tells the story, there is little doubts that despite Bahnson's skill and experience, his death was caused by "pilot error."

141 Bahnson lab journal January 11, 1958

142 J. Frank King was Agnew Bahnson's brother-in-law and first to tell Bahnson of Townsends Brown's work in electrogravitics. Beth Ball is unknown, presumed to be a staff member of the Bahnson facility.

143 As described in Chapter 26 - *A Complete System*

144 Do I really have to introduce Rube Goldberg?

145 The speculation that the B1 Stealth Bomber uses the flame-jet-generated electrokinetic effect to increase lift and thrust and high altitudes is articulated in *Secrets of Antigravity Propulsion* by Paul LaViolette)

146 Bamford, James; *Body of Secrets* pp 588-580

147 At NSA, the 'CEO' is typically a political appointment,; the deputy director is the hands-on manager of the Agency's actual operations, like the COO.

148 On page 585, Bamford also references "supers switching devices called tunnel diodes."

149 Morgan's first snail mail letters are undated and I did not save the postmarked envelopes, but this would have been ~March or April 2004.

150 "...and *it's all over now, Baby Blue.* (Bob Dylan

151 After that, neither Townsend Brown nor Josephine – both natives of Zanesville – ever returned to Zanesville again. And it would be nearly forty years before Linda would ever return to Zanesville, but then only to conduct some research for her father's biography.

152 Morgan > PWS 050529

153 Linda's husband

154 LeMay was also the character model for the blustery General Buck Turgidson in Stanley Kubric's cold war movie Dr. Strangelove.

155 "Any sufficiently advanced technology is indistinguishable from magic." -- Arthur C. Clarke

156 William Powell Lear (June 26, 1902 – May 14, 1978) was an American inventor and businessman. He is best known for founding Learjet, a manufacturer of

business jets. He also invented the battery eliminator for the B battery and developed the car radio and the 8-track cartridge, an audio tape system. Throughout his career of 46 years, Lear received over 140 patents. (Wikipedia)

157   NRO is the National Reconnaissance Office – the agency that manages and monitors satellite surveillance.

158   Morgan > PWS 'spring' 2005

159   Linda and George married in 1972. The marriage ended in divorce in 2017 (or 18?). Their first child Jennifer was born in April 1973, and they moved to Catalina to be close to Linda's parents. George opened a shop in Avalon and became the island's chief mechanic.

160   In the Prologue, Dr. Brown's destination is stated as "San Antonio." Did he mean Texas? There's also Cabo San Antonio in Cuba, which was one of the stops on the *S-48* submarine's voyage in 1932. (Chapter 25, *A Seagoing Sailor At Last*)

161   If you're not getting the reference, what I'm talking about here is 'fire'. Even the most advanced rockets are propelled on a pillar of fire, as evidenced by the huge balls of flame that erupt from the rocket engines before liftoff. This is precisely what Dr. Brown had in mind when spoke of rocketry as 'brute force and awkward.'

162   Morgan > PWS 040627

163   Morgan > PWS 040616

164   https://www.ttbrown.com/we-dont-need-roads/

165   For an account of one occasion when Morgan and I may have been in the same space, visit the online appendices

166   The Flammarion engraving is a wood engraving by an unknown artist, so named because its first documented appearance is in Camille Flammarion's 1888 book L'atmosphère: météorologie populaire ("The Atmosphere: Popular Meteorology"). It has been used as a metaphorical illustration of either the scientific or the mystical quests for knowledge.

Index

Keep a fire for the human race

Let your prayers go drifting into space

You never know what will be coming down

. . .

And somewhere between the time you arrive

And the time you go

May lie a reason you were alive

But you'll never know

——Jackson Browne

For A Dancer (1974)

85353748-c3e9-4774-8abf-373de79c35a2R01